FROM THE AUTHORS OF
THE UMPIRE STRIKES BACK
AND **STRIKE TWO**
AN ALL-NEW, ALL-HILARIOUS
ADDITION TO BASEBALL HISTORY ...
THE FALL OF THE ROMAN UMPIRE

"ONCE UPON A TIME I was well known. I was the famous American League umpire known for my flamboyant style. I wouldn't just call players out, I would call them outoutoutoutout!, then aim my trigger finger at them and 'shoot' them out. I talked to fans as well as players—the only thing unusual about that was that I did it during the game. I appeared on numerous television programs. I spoke at countless banquets. I did television commercials. I wrote books. And when I retired from the field I became a color commentator for NBC's Game of the Week.

"It turned out I wasn't so good at colors. I was asked to appear on fewer television shows. My commercials stopped running. As time passed, people seemed to forget about me. I learned a harsh fact about life in the world of sports: A friend is someone who can get you tickets to the *next* game. Today, occasionally, someone still recognizes me, and comes up to me and asks: 'Hey, didn't you used to be Ron Luciano?'"

Bantam Books by Ron Luciano and David Fisher

THE FALL OF THE ROMAN UMPIRE
STRIKE TWO
THE UMPIRE STRIKES BACK

THE FALL OF THE ROMAN UMPIRE

ROMAN UMPIRE

Ron Luciano
& David Fisher

BANTAM BOOKS
TORONTO · NEW YORK · LONDON · SYDNEY · AUCKLAND

THE FALL OF THE ROMAN UMPIRE
A Bantam Book
Bantam hardcover edition / June 1986
Bantam paperback edition / April 1987

Library of Congress Cataloging-in-Publication Data

Luciano, Ron.
    The fall of the Roman umpire.

    1. Luciano, Ron.   2. Baseball—United States—Umpires
—Biography.   1. Fisher, David, 1946–   . II. Title.
GV865.L8A34   1986   796.357'092'4 [B]   85-90476
ISBN 0-553-26133-9

Published simultaneously in the United States and Canada

PRINTED IN THE UNITED STATES OF AMERICA

KR   0 9 8 7 6 5 4 3 2 1

To all my relatives who still talk to me
R.L.

And to Bob Simon, who loved baseball and
who loved to laugh.
D.F.

ACKNOWLEDGMENTS

The authors are extremely grateful to Kurt Bevaqua, Jerry Reuss, Bert Blyleven, Rick Miller, Bob Shirley, Greg Pryor, Jim Wohlford, Ron Oester, Tony LaRussa, Johnny Grubb, Rick Camp, Doug Sisk, and Denny Walling, for their time and cooperation. You will be reading about them in the future.

We would also like to thank the following people for their continued cooperation and good will: Peter Guzzardi, Alison Acker, Matt Shear, Kathy Jones, and all of the rest of the extraordinary people at Bantam Books. John Boswell and Patty Brown of John Boswell Associates. Don Bacon, the great Bill Brown of the Detroit Tigers, Hank Calleo, Joanne Curtis, Bob DiNunzio, Nick DiNunzio Jr. and Sr., John Fox, Joseph Garbarino, Bill Haller, Bob Huckabone, Jay Horowitz, The Jesters, Wayne Minshew, Don Cassidy, Donald Davidson, Richard Griffin, Arthur Richman, Bob Iback, Duffy Jennings, Larry Whiteside, Paul Jensen, Bob Korch, Ann Mileo of the New York Yankees, Nina, Fonda and Mary, the Nortons, Cosmo Parisi, Richie Phillips, Bucky Picciano, Bob Porter, Rock Rivers, Dave Rossi, Joe Safety, Joan Sinclair, Tom Skibosh, Mike Swanson, Tony Termini, Vince Vetrano, Dean Vogelaar, John Young, Ira Berkow, Marie Lane, Steve Brener of the Los Angeles Dodgers, Dave Aust of the San Francisco Giants, Howard Starkman, Robert Morton, David Raymond, the Waltons and Nicky English/Bonnie Fabian.

CONTENTS

DIDN'T I USED TO
BE ME?

Fame is fleeting, and I am six-six, three hundred pounds, and couldn't catch a mounted butterfly. Once upon a time I was well known. I was the famous American League umpire known for my flamboyant style. I wouldn't just call players out, I would call them outoutoutoutout, then aim my trigger finger at them and "shoot" them out. I talked to fans as well as players—the only thing unusual about that is that I did it during the game. I was invited to appear on numerous television programs. I spoke at countless banquets. I did television commercials. I wrote books. And when I retired from the field, I became a color commentator for NBC's *Game of the Week*.

It turned out I wasn't so good at colors. I was asked to appear on fewer television shows. My commercials stopped running. As time passed, people seemed to forget about me. I learned a harsh fact about life in the world of sports: A friend is someone who can get you tickets for the *next* game. Today, occasionally, someone still recognizes me, and comes up to me and asks, "Hey, didn't you used to be Ron Luciano?"

The fact that my fame had passed me by was brought back to me recently when I called my former boss at NBC, Michael Weisman. Mike was just a bright young producer when I first began working with him, but after we'd worked togther for two seasons he was made executive sports producer for the entire network. "Hey," I said to his secretary when she answered my call, "it's Ron. Is he there?"

There was a brief, and perhaps slightly suspicious, pause. "Uh, Ron who?" she asked politely.

"Ron Luciano," I answered proudly. Must be new, I figured.

"I'll see if he's in." I knew she really meant that she would see if he was busy. She sat next to his door—if she didn't know if he was in there, she probably wasn't doing a great job. She returned in a minute. "Could you spell that name, please?"

What is this? I wondered. A test? Of course I could spell my name. "R-o-n," I said.

"Um, I'm sorry, Mr. Lanzano," she said, "I meant your last name."

So I spelled that for her. Correctly. Once again she put me on hold. I didn't mind. As head of NBC Sports, Mike Weisman has so many responsibilities, I couldn't expect him to put everything aside just to talk to the old friend who made him what he is today. Finally she got back on the phone. "Uh, Mr. Luciano," she began politely, "Mr. Weisman asked me to apologize to you for not sending the check for the auto repairs, but he'll put it in the mail today."

I laughed. Ho. That was certainly amusing. He thought I was *another* Ron Luciano. So I slowly and carefully explained that I wasn't an automobile mechanic, I was the former American League umpire, color commentator, television actor, and author.

"Oh," she said with a sigh of recognition, "*that* Ron Luciano. That's different. I'm sorry, but Mr. Weisman said he's out of the office. Can he call you back next year?"

I can take a hint. I left my phone number and hung up. I didn't have to call Mike Weisman to be reminded I wasn't famous anymore; I could call anybody.

I've done a lot of different things in my life. I just haven't done any of them very well. In fact, Failure seems to be my middle name—my parents told me it was an old Italian word. The year *after* I played football at Syracuse University the Big Orange were national champions. The Detroit Lions were a championship ball club when they drafted me. They haven't won anything since. The Buffalo Bills were the class of the American Football League when they signed me. Two years later the entire league went out of existence. I became a baseball umpire in the American League in 1968. The next time they beat the National League in an All-Star game was 1980. I became a baseball commentator on NBC. Baseball went on strike. I left NBC. It became the number one network. I opened a sporting goods store in Endicott, New York. Put an entire mall out of business. I did commercials for Gulf Oil of Canada. Gulf Oil! What could I do to a giant oil company? They sold the company and changed the name.

Putting a mall out of business is one thing, but Gulf Oil? Until then I had been very popular in Canada. I never knew why, although a Canadian friend of mine, Sean Kelly, once explained: "In Canada they think you're good-looking." But apparently even in Canada the word is getting around: Remember Ron Luciano? Don't.

For example, Toronto celebrated its 250th anniversary in 1985. In August I received a call from someone I'd met while putting Gulf Oil out of business. "Golly, Ron," he began, "it's so darn good to talk to you. Well, Ron, as you probably know, we're celebrating a mighty big anniversary in Toronto this year, and baseball is very popular here because of the Blue Jays."

I did know both of those things.

"But I'll bet you didn't know that Babe Ruth started his career in Toronto."

Babe Ruth? *The* Babe Ruth. Wait a minute. I knew that the Russians claimed to have invented the telephone and television, but Toronto claiming Babe Ruth? That was un-American.

"He did; he played some ball up here. So we've built a new park for baseball and erected a monument to Babe Ruth in it. We've decided that when we dedicate the park, we want somebody well known in baseball to unveil the statue. I mean, somebody everybody today can identify with baseball. . . ."

I began looking through my busy schedule. It looked like I was free.

". . . It's going to be a big weekend affair, some parties, a lot of food. Of course we're willing to pay some money, the mayor'll be there, the prime minister might come to the dedication."

I'd have to take my suit out of the cleaners.

". . . and right away I thought of you. See, we've been trying to get ahold of Joe DiMaggio and can't find him, and I said, 'I'll bet Ron Luciano has Joe DiMaggio's phone number. . . .'"

Joe DiMaggio? I'm bigger than Joe DiMaggio. At least four inches bigger.

". . . and gee, Ron, if you happen to be in town, stop by."

Things were different once. Once I was known to every baseball fan in the nation. I was an umpire, a man in blue, an arbitrator. I ruled the playing fields of the American League with a hot dog in one hand and a soft drink in the other. Without skilled umpires, I knew, the game could not exist. Oh, players were important, I accepted that, but there were plenty of players—too many players as far as some umpires were concerned. But there were only a select few people with the knowledge and judgment required to control a major league game. Quick: three runners on one base, the fielder tags the second first, the last runner second, the first runner last, who's safe, who's out? Without these men of consummate skill and professionalism, the game would deteriorate into a succession of fights and arguments. Umpires *are* the game of baseball, I believed. As an umpire, I was the most important person in the game.

Then I retired and became a broadcaster. It was only then that I realized it was broadcasters, not umpires, who really are the most important people in the game. The umpires went on strike, the game went on. Game? Baseball is no longer just a game, it's a business. Major league baseball remains a profitable investment for most team owners because of huge television contracts with the networks and local TV. Without those contracts the game of baseball would probably be out of business. And the broadcaster serves as the link between the fan and the game. Broadcasters create the image of the team. Vin Scully *is* the Dodgers. Mel Allen *is* the Yankees. Harry Caray *is* the Cubs, or the White Sox. Broadcasters attract the viewers that enable the networks to afford to show the games. Broadcasters, I realized, *are* the game of baseball. As a broadcaster, I was the most important person in the game.

Then NBC decided to allow me to pursue other creative endeavors, also known as being given a "negative renewal," also known as being fired. For the first time since I put on an iron mask in 1965, I was out of baseball. I was in Endicott, New York, which is *way* out of baseball. And as I sat in front of my television set watching other umpires working the games being broadcast by other broadcasters, I realized it is not the players who are the most important people in baseball, not the umpires, and not the broadcasters. It is the fans.

Without the fans major league baseball would cease to exist. Without people like me watching the game on television and buying the sponsor's products, or actually going to the ballpark and buying a ticket, there would be no grand old game. If the owners weren't making money generated by the fans, they couldn't pay the players; if the players weren't paid, they wouldn't play; if the players weren't playing, the umpires certainly couldn't umpire, and that would leave the broadcasters with nothing to talk about.

The survival of baseball as we know it depends on

the fans. Therefore, fans *are* the game of baseball. As a fan, I am the most important person in the game.

I was not a baseball fan while growing up. I was a football and lacrosse fan. All I knew about baseball was that I couldn't play it. I played football. Other kids were satisfied throwing a rubber ball against a wall; I threw myself against the wall. I didn't understand baseball—what kind of sport is it where you can't hit anybody? The first time I ever attended a major league baseball game I was the right-field umpire. I had never bought a ticket to a game. I'd never driven to a game in a traffic jam, bought armfuls of peanuts, popcorn, and nachos, spilled beer on the person sitting in front of me, rooted for the home team, got mustard all over my pants, stood up for the seventh-inning stretch and knocked over a soft drink, taken instructions from a demanding scoreboard, participated in a "wave" or booed an umpire. I'd never been a fan.

While working as an umpire, I'd learned that there are different kinds of fans. There are those people, young and old, who stand outside the park before and after every game hoping to get an autograph to keep for a lifetime—or sell to the first buyer. There are those fans who live and die for the team, who know every statistic about every game—what player hit what, when, and where, and who was the pitcher. And then there are those fans who simply enjoy the game, who don't really know every statistic, but are as happy to learn that there are young players coming up to the majors with great names like Montreal's Razor Shines and the Brewers' Billy Joe Robodoe as they are to know that of Pete Rose's first 4,192 hits, twenty-nine were off pitchers who later became dentists, nine were off pitchers who later became orthopedic surgeons, and twelve came off future convicts.

I'm that last kind of fan. I like to know about the players. The thing I miss most about being on the field is being privy to the gossip. I loved knowing which pitcher wanted to kill which manager, and I loved asking that manager if he knew which pitcher wanted to kill him. The only statistics I knew were

that four balls equaled one walk, three strikes consti-
tuted a strikeout. If I wanted to root for statistics, I'd
go watch an accountant work.

As an umpire I saw the game from the field. As a
broadcaster I saw it from the press box. But until
recently I had never seen a game from the stands. I
had often wondered what baseball looked like from
there; I knew the view had to be good because I'd had
too many fans tell me, "How could you miss that
call? I could see it from the stands and you were a lot
closer." So I decided to rediscover the game of baseball, this time as a fan. I knew the job didn't pay as
well as being an umpire or a broadcaster, but I also
knew I couldn't get fired.

The first part of the job of fan, I quickly learned,
was getting tickets to the game. There are three ways
of getting tickets to a game: You can order them in
advance, you can buy them at the ballpark, or you can
be given them. The interesting thing is that no matter
how you get the tickets, whether you buy them or
receive them, the person who hands them to you will
assure you they are the best seats available. *Available*
is always the key word.

Free tickets are the best tickets. Sitting in a ballpark
knowing the people next to you had to pay for their
tickets makes the entire experience more enjoyable.
There are a number of different ways to obtain free
tickets. You can get them from the ball players, umpires, or ball-club officials; you can get them as a gift
from someone who buys them himself or whose company has season tickets; or you can get them from an
organization that distributes them. Remember, it's not
the source that's important, it's the lack of price that
counts.

Members of participating teams and umpires are
allotted a certain number of tickets for every game.
Usually there are some players or umpires who don't
use all their tickets, so they give them or trade them
to someone who can use them. These tickets, of course,
have value. They can be traded for meals, dry cleaning, for almost anything. Someone I know, for exam-

ple, got stopped for speeding just outside New York City. After a long conversation with the officer, this person agreed to leave four tickets for the officer and his family for the next game. The officer wanted to make the deal, but was reluctant. When asked why, he admitted, "I don't know. I stopped [he named a Yankee player] right at this same spot two weeks ago—and he stiffed me!"

The ticket king among umpires is my friend, my protégé, Kenneth Kaiser. Kenny, Bill Haller, Darrell Cousins, and I worked the first game ever played in Seattle's Kingdome. Although Bill and I had been to Seattle before, it was the first trip for Kenny and Darrell. We had arrived in town late the night before and had a quick dinner. In the umpires' dressing room the next day I was making out our ticket list. "Want to leave tickets for anybody, Bill?" I asked.

Haller laughed. "Everybody I know in Seattle is right here."

"Darrell?"

He shook his head. "No."

"Kenny?"

"Twenty-one." Twenty-one tickets! The man had been in the city one night, not even a full night, just a few hours, and he had met twenty-one friends?

"Are you sure, Kenny?" I asked. "You want to leave twenty-one tickets."

Kenny thought for a moment. "No," he finally said, "better make it twenty-three."

The first time I ever bought a ticket for a major league baseball game was in August, 1985. Not that I couldn't have gotten into the ballpark for free. After all, I used to be Ron Luciano. Some of the gate attendants would still remember me, and they couldn't possibly still be angry. But I wanted to know what it felt like to be a paying fan.

Not good is what it felt like. I bought my first ticket at Baltimore's Memorial Stadium for a game between the Orioles and Kansas City Royals. There was a time I couldn't have even bought my way into that stadium—Orioles manager Earl Weaver and I had

had such a bitter feud that the American League would not assign me to his games. I had been warned by League president Lee MacPhail never to mention the word *Weaver* again. He didn't even want me to say "We—" But time passes, grudges are forgotten, memory dims heartache, bygones are gone, and so was Weaver. He had retired.

Or so I thought. Then I remembered. A few weeks before this Orioles–Royals game, Baltimore had re-hired Earl Weaver as manager. The Weaver. And as I walked up to the ticket window to pay for my first ticket, I suddenly realized I was contributing to his salary.

I stepped out of line. I couldn't do it. Pay to see Earl Weaver manage? I'd rather pay to see two aging polar bears in a zoo sitting on truck tires. I'd rather pay to see a computer poetry-writing contest.

I stopped, and reminded myself that I was a mature adult, that what had happened between us had simply been a difference of opinion between two professionals, both highly motivated, during the passion of the game. That he really wasn't cursing at me, and kicking dirt on me; he was doing it to authority, and I was wrong to take it personally. I was a fan now. I could sit back and simply enjoy the game.

And I could sit in my seat and call him anything I wanted to call him and nobody could do anything about it. I stepped right up to that window. "One right next to the Oriole dugout," I said.

But long before reaching that window, the fan usually faces the most frustrating of all problems: getting to the ballpark and parking the car. In some cities the only way to get to the ballpark by game time is to be born there. When an important game is being played in certain stadiums, you can watch the seasons change while trapped in a traffic jam.

Driving to the ballpark on a hot summer day inevitably causes one to ponder the eternal question: the air conditioning or the tow truck? Some of the most exciting moments of my life have been spent sitting in a car on the way to the stadium, watching the thrilling race between traffic flow and my temperature gauge.

It did not surprise me at all that major league baseball moved out of Washington, D.C. RFK Stadium, the home of the Washington Senators, was a nice enough ballpark, but it had a peculiar problem. You couldn't get there. No roads led to that ballpark. No matter which street or road you tried, it always dead-ended into a one-way street running the wrong way. And even when you managed to find a road that went in the correct direction at least part of the way, it always led to a traffic circle with six spurs running off it. Trying to guess the right spur was almost as much fun as watching the race between traffic flow and the temperature gauge.

Seattle's Kingdome is just the opposite. Every road in the Northwest leads there. And no matter where you are in Seattle, or in the entire state of Washington, you can see the Dome sticking out. You can be a thousand miles away from the ballpark, stop someone and ask for directions to the Kingdome, and the answer will be, "Oh, that's easy. Just go up there to the corner and make a right. Follow that road for a thousand miles. It'll be on your right after the candy store."

In fact, the only people in Seattle who can't find the Kingdome are the cab drivers. Cab drivers never know where the ballpark is. Any ballpark. Umpires generally take cabs to the games they are working. I did it for years. It took me that long to realize that "Uh, you know how to get there?" was not the name of a taxi company.

Cab drivers always seemed to recognize us. They may not have known anything about baseball, but somehow they knew we were the bad guys. Amazingly, before a game, cab drivers never knew which exit to take to the ballpark, but after the game they were always willing to tell us where to get off.

Getting there is only half the fun. Trying to find a place to park your car within one time zone of the ballpark is every bit as enjoyable as the drive itself. Some people grow up wanting to be millionaires. Others simply want to own parking lots near baseball stadiums. The signs I love are the ones that read PARKING $2. GAME DAYS $20 AND FIRSTBORN CHILD. Or PARKING $2. EVENT DAYS—IF YOU HAVE TO ASK, YOU CAN'T AFFORD IT. I always thought they should put one parking spot near a stadium in the Neiman-Marcus Christmas catalogue.

The first time I went to Baltimore I was amazed to discover that they have a large parking lot adjoining the stadium. Hey, I thought, this is pretty convenient. Just a few steps away from the park.

Then I saw their sign CARS WILL BE PARKED BUMPER-TO-BUMPER THIS DATE. That means that no space is left between cars. *Bumper-to-bumper* means one car will be touching your front bumper and another car will be touching your back bumper. It means the first person to park in that lot shouldn't plan on leaving until after the fall harvest. Can you imagine the thrill of getting to the ballpark early so you can park close to the gates, and then having to sit in your car for two hours after the game waiting for those people whose cars are kissing your bumper to realize the game is over.

One major advantage of driving to a game in Cleveland is that there is never any traffic, coming or going. At worst, you're going to be parked "bumper."

In the minor leagues some teams are actually thoughtful enough to paint a large spot right next to the ballpark and hang a large sign above it reading NO PARKING. RESERVED FOR UMPIRES.

Are you kidding me? I just made a call in the bottom of the ninth inning to cost the home team the game and now every fan in the ballpark is going to walk past my car? Umpires barely out of their training masks know that the one place you never, ever park your car is in that spot. Any car parked in a spot marked "umpires" is only one controversial call against the home team away from being turned into a fruit stand.

Once, in Syracuse, when we got to the park, we discovered someone had tried to beat the one-dollar parking fee by leaving his car in the Reserved for

Umpires spot. We didn't care, we weren't going to park there anyway. We parked nearby, then went inside and just ripped up the Syracuse Chiefs. We didn't even get the time right. I think we counted the innings wrong. It was just a terrible night—but not as terrible as it was for the person who parked in that spot.

By the time we got to the parking lot the air had been let out of the tires, some unpleasant words had been scratched into the paint, and I think someone was dumping popcorn into the gas tank. As we walked past to get to our car, I said softly to someone, "Don't forget the antenna."

"Yeah," he screamed, "we forgot the antenna."

Suppose, though, you are lucky enough to get a parking space in the lot near the ballpark. The one thing you must remember to do is write down the section and color of the area in which you parked. More friendships and marriages have been broken up by the words "Do you remember where we parked the car?" than by almost anything else. I challenge any normal human being to stand outside one of those new round ballparks like Dodger Stadium and be able to tell one area from another. Those ballparks are round, I've discovered, so when you can't remember where you left the car, it's easier to walk round and round. Experience has taught me there is only one way to find your car when parked at a round stadium: Wait until every other car in the lot has left, then hope that the car that is still there is yours.

Some ballparks, particularly those in the older major league cities like New York, Boston, and Chicago, can be reached by subway or elevated train. However, taking the subway to Yankee Stadium is one of the very few ways guaranteed to make you wish you were caught in a traffic jam.

Once a fan finally gets to within walking distance of the ballpark, he has to run the "hawker gauntlet." The only things it takes to *play* baseball are a bat, a ball, and a glove, yet within one hundred feet of Yankee Stadium a fan can buy official Yankee replica jerseys, warm-up shirts, T-shirts, sweatshirts, jump suits, muscle shirts, caps, visors, shorts, baby bibs, toddler suits, jackets, sweaters, batting gloves, bumper stickers, posters, pen bats, bat rack banks, helmets and helmet banks, decals, lamps, wristbands, dolls in uniform, sunglasses, pennants, drinking mugs, shot- and wineglasses, key rings, ashtrays, coffee cups, coasters, miniature cars, socks, buttons, cards, books and albums, autographed baseballs and autographed baseball holders (regular and deluxe models), ceramic mascots, bobbers (dolls whose heads pop up and down), inflatable bats, magnets, pencils, playing cards, puppets, pom-poms, and, for obvious reasons, a wallet and carrying bag. The Yankee logo is licensed to almost every industry you can think of, including license plate holders.

About the only thing that is missing is an official Yankee suburban home with an official Yankee mortgage.

The problem that manufacturers of some of these items and dealers face is that ball clubs are continually changing their rosters. Players may be traded or released or retire, but their bumper sticker lives forever. The only thing less useful than a Yankee bumper sticker reading "And on the seventh day God created Rick Cerone" is a Yankee bumper sticker reading "And on the seventh day God created Bucky Dent."

There are, if you are wondering, no official umpire souvenirs.

The first thing a fan encounters when finally entering a ballpark is somebody trying to sell him something. Well, there's a big surprise. In this case, what is being sold is the Official Score Book and Souvenir Program. At one time this was a slim two-to-six pager consisting of the rosters of the competing ball clubs, a few small ads, the home team's schedule, and a two-page scorecard in the middle. It cost fifteen cents, maybe a quarter. Quietly this scorecard has become a score book. A score book is really a magazine, but they can't call it a magazine because most teams already have a monthly magazine, which *is* called a magazine, although sometimes it is really a newspaper. None of these publications are to be confused with the Official Yearbook, which is also a magazine, or the Official Information Guide, which used to be called a press guide or media guide.

The Official Score Book and Souvenir Program features articles on the home team players and coaches, the schedule, statistics, photographs, a lot of big ads, and, in some editions, a one-page scorecard near the middle. It now costs at least a dollar. One of the few exceptions to this can be bought in the Chicago Cubs' Wrigley Field where the Official Scorecard costs only thirty cents. However, a pencil is an additional twenty-five.

Until I became a broadcaster I had never scored a game. I did not know that there was an entire symbolic language of scoring. One line, for example, represents a single, two lines a double, a sacrifice is "SH," although I can't find the *h* in sacrifice. A K is used to indicate a strikeout, KC a strikeout with the third strike called by the umpire, and so on. But before the first game I broadcast, my partner in the booth, the great Merle Harmon, gave me a scorecard and told me I'd have to keep track of the game so I could tell viewers what was going on. I didn't want Merle to know that I had no idea what was going on, so I nodded and said, "Yeah, right."

I kept score exactly the same way I had taken algebra in school—I looked at the paper of the person sitting next to me. Merle wrote down two parallel lines, I wrote down two parallel lines. Finally, about the fifth inning, Bump Wills came up to bat for the Texas Rangers. Merle asked, "Ronnie, what's he done his first two at bats?"

How was I supposed to know? I don't have that good a memory. Merle immediately realized I was in trouble. I think it was the dazed look in my eyes and my mouth hanging open that gave it away, so he pointed to my scorecard. I understood. "Well, Merle," I said, looking at that card, "he's having quite a day.

In the first inning he had two little lines with a blue dot over them, and then he FC'ed in the third."

Later Merle did try to teach me how to score a ball game properly. He started by explaining that for scoring purposes, each position has a number. "For example," he said, "the shortstop is number six."

I looked at the roster in front of me. "No, Merle," I gently corrected him, "the shortstop is number fifteen."

Merle laughed. "You don't understand, Ronnie," he started—he was certainly right about that—"let me start from the beginning. Players are numbered by position. The pitcher is number one."

That didn't sound right to me. "Which pitcher?"

"Every pitcher. It doesn't matter."

I knew that wasn't true. Wherever Billy Martin manages, I pointed out to Merle, he always wears number one. So how could the pitcher be number one?

"The pitcher isn't number one," Merle said.

"That's what I said," I said.

"The pitcher's position is number one."

Have you ever felt like the entire world knew something and you were absent from school the day they learned it? That's the way I felt listening to Merle.

"Let's say the batter hits a ground ball to the pitcher," he continued, "and the pitcher catches it and throws it to the first baseman. On your scorecard you write one dash three. That means the pitcher, number one, caught the ball and threw to the first baseman, number three. It's really very simple."

When someone tells me something is really very simple, the one thing I know is it isn't very simple. I would've had about as much chance deciphering Japanese war codes as I would have understanding how to score correctly. Eventually I devised my own scoring system. I called it writing very small in the tiny little box. When a player grounded out, I wrote "ground out." Trying to fit all the information was difficult; trying to read it was impossible.

All right, after either buying a scorecard or saving the money to invest in CDs, the fan then proceeds directly to his seat. Not so fast. The same person who designed the access roads to RFK Stadium apparently figured out the system used to number sections in ballparks. One of the two sections behind home plate is usually section 1. After that everything else is up for grabs. In some ballparks the sections along the first-base line are given odd numbers and the sections along the third-base line are given even numbers. In other ballparks it is the reverse. Sometimes the sections are numbered consecutively. There is a surefire method for finding the proper section: Walk at least three sections in any direction. I guarantee you, that will be the wrong direction. Then turn around and walk back the correct way.

Of course, you can find the section your seat is located in only after you've managed to figure out on which level you're sitting. It would make sense to me to have every section in the second deck numbered 2-something, in the third deck 3-something. Because it would make sense is probably the reason it is not done that way. Ballparks have a language of seating that is almost as confusing as scoring language. Where is an upper loge box seat? Is there a lower box in the upper deck? Is the outfield terrace in Comiskey Park the equivalent of lower left field in Minnesota's Metrodome? What exactly do they call each of the six different levels of seating in Houston's Astrodome? And what is a loge anyway? I think the New York Yankees have made everything about seating perfectly clear to me with this scorebook explanation: "A minimum of 3,170 seats in the last eight rows of the upper level reserved seat area from sections 19 and 20 out to sections 35 and 36 will be available for all regular season games at the general admission price. The remaining seats in the last eight rows from sections 1 and 2 to sections 17 and 18 may be sold as reserved seats when the advance demand for reserved seats warrants such a sale in order to accommodate fans' requests for reserved seating. When this advance demand does not exist, these seats will be sold at the general admission price.''

In other words, a general admission seat is only a general admission seat when it is not a reserved seat. If no one wants to buy it, it's cheaper. Language like this makes two little lines with a blue dot over them seem quite sensible.

Assuming you somehow stumble into the correct section, the real problem now begins. What comes first, row A or row AA? Is row H really in front of row BB? And what *is* a loge anyway? The seat I bought in Baltimore's Memorial Stadium was a nine-dollar lower box in section 1, row BB, box 2, seat 1. It did not come with either instructions or a map.

Actually there is a vital reason that ball clubs create this confusion. If a fan could simply walk into a ballpark and find his seat, there would be nothing for ballpark ushers to do for the money you must tip them. Now, I like ballpark ushers. When I was an umpire, I had a very good relationship with them. I think they look great in their uniforms. I know they stand there through every inning of every game, and I know they work hard. What I don't know is exactly what they do.

When I walk into the park, an usher looks at my ticket, then either says with disdain, ''Nineteen sections over,'' or leads me to my seat, then dusts it off with his oversized woolen mitten. Then I give him whatever money I've saved by not buying an Official Score Book and Program. Dusting off a seat in a ballpark is baseball's answer to putting an automobile horn on the space–ship. You walk into a ballpark, carefully avoiding puddles of beer, sidestep empty popcorn and Cracker Jack boxes, try not to get gum or mustard packets stuck to the bottom of your shoes, watching out for fans above you spilling soft drinks and beer onto your head, and the usher dusts off your seat because he doesn't want you to get dusty?

Be honest, am I the only person who finds this a little strange?

Obviously not every ballpark is dirty. Some ballparks are very clean, but only Dodger Stadium is immaculate. My mother would like the name and phone number of the stadium's cleaning lady. Even the cement floors of Dodger Stadium are waxed every day. You can literally see your reflection in those floors, although, if you looked like me, you'd probably prefer to see old hot dog wrappers.

Eventually you will reach your seat in the ballpark. And after whoever is sitting in it has moved over, you can settle down and get ready to watch major league baseball. For a man like me, there is nothing like the feel of a ballpark seat. Oh, except maybe for a vise, or the lowest fare seat on a discount airline. An interesting fact about ballpark seats is that whatever size you are, the seat automatically contracts to be one size smaller. And when you do manage to squeeze into your seat, it is always a delight to discover that the distance between your seat and the back of the seat directly in front of you is approximately one inch shorter than the room needed to stick your knees out straight in front of you.

But once you're in that seat, you are finally free to relax and look around the ballpark. I love baseball stadiums, new ones, old ones; I love the feeling of being in a ballpark before a game is about to start. Every ballpark seems to have a unique feature that sets it apart from all others; the massive triple decks and traditional façade of Yankee Stadium, Fenway Park's Green Monster, the glorious fountains of Royals Stadium and Comiskey Park's exploding scoreboard, the overhanging right-field deck in Tiger Stadium, Wrigley Field's ivy-covered brick walls, the vast sea of empty seats in Cleveland's Municipal Stadium. But as I looked around these ballparks, one thing has always bothered me—who does their interior decorating? Who picks the color schemes? Who is that person and what can we do to stop him? Has it ever occurred to anyone that the same person who decided the seats in the upper deck of Atlanta's Fulton County Stadium should be red, orange, and yellow is now working on something else?

Some stadiums are just perfect. In Wrigley Field, for example, all the seats are a beautiful ballpark green, the grass is green, the brick walls in the outfield are covered with ivy. Perfect. The seats in Milwaukee's County Stadium are red and green and silver. In Baltimore the seats in the lower deck are green and blue. Beautiful. And the seats in the upper deck are red and gold and pink. Pink. Bright pink. Now, I've heard of people feeling "in the pink," but I don't know any real baseball fan who wants to sit in the pink. Can you really imagine someone going up to the ticket window and asking for "two good seats in the pink, please?"

But even Baltimore's pink pales against the upper deck of Houston's Astrodome. The upholstered seats on that level are called "rainbow colors," and the first few rows are blue, the few rows after that are red, then orange, yellow, orange, red, and blue.

At least the grass everywhere is green, or mostly green, except for Cleveland, of course. In Cleveland they have problems growing grass, so they paint the ground green. I'm going to repeat that, because it probably came as a surprise. In Cleveland they have problems growing grass, so they paint the ground green. And when players slide or, since it is the Indians, trip or fall, they do not get grass stains on their uniforms; they get paint stains.

At least the dirt everywhere is brown. Or red. Or sort of yellow. And it's that color even when it's not real dirt, but artificial dirt, or the rubber dirt, which goes with the artificial surface in Minnesota's Metrodome.

Painting the real dirt green, as they do in Cleveland, as opposed to painting the rubber dirt brown, like in the Metrodome, is probably no more unusual than outlining the fan shape of the infield on playing fields completely covered with an artificial surface. To give infielders some perspective on where to position themselves, the grounds crew draws lines where the edges of the infield would be if there was an infield. Naturally this has given the old baseball phrase "a drawn-in infield" an entirely new meaning.

Another thing that is drawn in by groundskeepers in many major and minor league ballparks is the imaginary line. This is part of the ground rules. Some parks have areas of "dead territory" adjoining the playing field. Fielders can legally catch a ball and then run into "dead territory," but cannot go into that area and then catch a ball. These are usually places in which there is potential danger to a fielder, like water hoses lying on the ground, exposed gardening tools, or open punji-stick pits. These areas are usually indicated by an "imaginary line that is painted in." The first time I heard this phrase used was in the minor leagues. During the pregame meeting at home plate the manager of the home team was explaining the ground rules, and he pointed to a corner in left field and said, "That area right there is dead territory. The imaginary line runs from the last pole on the top of the fence to the end of the . . ."

I looked where he was pointing. A white line had been drawn on the ground from the end of the outfield wall to the end of the grandstand fence. "You mean where that white line is?" I asked.

"Yeah," he said, "that white line is the imaginary line."

In the low minor leagues you work with only one other umpire. I looked at my partner, who was listening to the manager as if he had not heard what the man had said. I'd heard of blind umpires, but this was the first time I'd worked with a deaf one. Just to be sure, I looked out again at the left-field corner. My eyes had never been great, but I could see a white line where there was supposed to be an imaginary line. "Wait a second," I interrupted, "there's a line on the ground out there, right?"

The manager looked at me as if there was something wrong with *me*. "I told you," he repeated, "that's the imaginary line. You can catch and go in, but you can't go in and catch."

I think part of my problem in those days was that I took managers seriously. I don't know why, I just assumed they knew what they were talking about. "The imaginary line," I later learned, is simply part of baseball terminology. It is as much a part of the language of baseball as the "foul pole," which, as everyone knows, is in fair territory.

The "imaginary line painted in" is usually painted in with the same lime substance used to draw the foul lines, batter's boxes, and coaches' boxes. Here is today's quickie quiz: What color is lime? Here is the answer: green. Lime is green, except on a baseball diamond. A piece of lime used to flavor a drink is green. A lime ice pop is green. A slice of key lime is green. But the lines drawn with lime on a baseball field are white. Why?

That is tomorrow's quickie quiz.

Not all foul lines are drawn in lime, however. Some are not drawn at all. Some foul lines are really fire hoses painted white. Painted with paint, as opposed to being painted with lime. In order not to have to continuously redraw the foul lines, which are in fair territory and stretch from first base and third base to the outfield fence, some grounds crews lay down flat sections of hose. These have to be repainted only every few weeks. Therefore, it is indeed possible to trip over the foul line. I have never actually seen anyone trip over a foul line, although I have seen Earl Weaver stumble over some of my funniest lines.

If a fan gets to the ballpark early enough, he or she has plenty of time before the game begins to enjoy the pregame entertainment and read the fences. Ball clubs make additional revenue by selling advertising space on the outfield walls, the façade of the decks, and the scoreboard. Every scoreboard seems to have at least one beer advertised. County Stadium in Milwaukee, America's beer capital, has an ad for a beer *and* an ad for wine coolers. The scoreboard in Cleveland's Municipal Stadium has an ad for an insurance company which, considering the quality of the Indians ball club, is probably a good idea. Radio and television stations always hang their banners, airlines often buy space, and there is a lot of food advertising on ballpark walls. Take the word of an expert, it is impossible to make a hot dog painted on an outfield fence look appetizing. But perhaps my favorite sign of all appears in Baltimore's Memorial Stadium. That's *Memorial* Stadium, named in honor of the veterans of World War II, the war against the Germans and Japanese. The largest sign in *Memorial* Stadium, bigger even than the Budweiser sign, located high atop the message board, higher than the Coke sign, in huge, bright red letters, is an ad for, naturally, Toyota.

Not all ballpark signs are advertisements. During the 1985 season, for example, the Braves hung a large sign reading WELCOME TO ATLANTA-FULTON COUNTY STADIUM. CELEBRATING OUR 20TH SEASON IN ATLANTA. Uh, I don't want to be picky, but where else would Atlanta-Fulton County Stadium be? Pittsburgh?

But without doubt the dumbest sign I've ever seen is the small neat orange-and-blue sign the Mets have hung in center field in Shea Stadium. It reads WELL WATER USED. Now, I may not be any genius, but even I know that that sign should correctly read "Good Water Used."

Pregame entertainment at a ballpark takes many forms, all of them inexpensive. Baseball videos and taped highlights and lowlights clipped together and set to music are shown at stadiums with large screens. Every type of marching band appears at ballparks during the season. Somebody's relative can always be recruited to sing the National Anthem. On Polish-American Night in Milwaukee the Brewers featured the one the only Alvin Styczynski and his accordion. But once again I must return to Shea Stadium for the finest in pregame entertainment.

For two seasons in the 1970s, while Yankee Stadium was being renovated, the Yankees played at Shea. One Fourth of July the Yankees invited a local Army Reserve unit to punctuate the pregame festivities with cannon fire. Two cannon were set up in the outfield, their barrels aimed at the ground. Apparently someone was a bit worried that these reservists might take aim at one of the low-flying planes taking off from nearby LaGuardia Airport.

A member of the Shea grounds crew tapped a reserve officer on the shoulder and politely suggested, "I think I'd aim those guns a little higher if I were you."

"They're cannon," the officer responded somewhat curtly, "and we're only firing blanks."

The groundskeeper shook his head and walked away. Walked far, far away, in fact. It seems he knew that even blanks create a powerful blast, powerful enough to ricochet off the ground directly into the fence. At the appropriate moment the two cannon were fired. And then the smoke cleared to reveal a gaping hole in part of the fence, while another part of the fence was on fire. It was the greatest pregame show in history. The United States Army had managed to set Shea Stadium on fire.

There are five things a fan can do while watching a baseball game: eat, score and cheer, try to catch foul balls, read the scoreboard, and eat.

Balls hit into the stands become the possession of whoever ends up with them. A real major league baseball, a ball actually used in a game and hit into the stands, fair or foul, is just about the only thing that a fan can get for free at a ballpark that doesn't require medical attention. To me, there is absolutely nothing to match the excitement of watching a group of fun-loving fans scrambling after a baseball hit into the stands—nothing except maybe a goal line stand in the last three seconds of a 21–20 football game. Are those people crazy? We're talking about a baseball that is worth maybe $7.50, tops. Yet otherwise perfectly normal human beings, functioning citizens, respected people in the community, will dive over chairs, hurl themselves onto a pile of bodies and fight desperately for a ball fouled off by Rance Mullineks.

While I was at Memorial Stadium, the second pitch of the game was fouled into the stands directly behind home plate. A teenaged fan leaned over the upper deck railing to try to catch it, and went flying over that railing. He did a complete cartwheel, and managed to hang on to the rail with one hand. It was incredible. It was amazing. It was also about a forty-foot drop to the deck below. After a few seconds his friends managed to pull him to safety.

Watching that, I couldn't help thinking that that young man had risked his life for a foul ball—and wondering what he would have done for a fair ball.

Occasionally fans do fall out of the stands. Once when I was working in Kansas City, a fan sitting behind home plate fell over the railing, fortunately landing on the protective netting. Like a giant foul ball, he rolled right down the net and, when he reached the end, rolled over it and onto the field, dropping about eighteen feet. As he staggered to his feet, two things immediately became apparent to me: 1) He was not hurt. 2) He had had so much to drink that he was in no condition to know he was not hurt. As soon as he stood up, he started looking around for the person who had hit him. And then it seemed to dawn on him that he was standing on a baseball field in the middle of a game, being watched by maybe 21,000 fans. He suddenly stood up very straight, or as straight as he could, tucked in his shirt, and ran back into the stands as fast as he could.

When I was an umpire, I worried more about people falling out of the stands than I do now, primarily because then I had to worry that they might fall on me.

I love watching fans stand up and catch a line drive in their bare hands. It's just great. They catch the ball, hold it up for the TV cameras, smile for their friends or children, then pass the ball around. Then comes the difficult part—they have to sit there without screaming. I've been hit with foul balls. They hurt, believe me, they hurt. There is no way a fan can catch a line drive and not feel the pain. So every time I see a fan make a bare-handed catch, I know that hours later he is going to be sitting home with his hands in a bucket of ice water, trying to keep down the swelling, while having to listen to his wife or girlfriend say over and over, "There's a reason major league players use gloves, you know."

Sometimes being a fan is a tough job.

In Baltimore, when a fan makes a great catch of a foul ball, the public address announcer suggests, "Give that fannnn a contract." But the most memorable catch of a foul ball I've ever seen was in Yankee Stadium. I was working the plate. I don't remember who the batter was, but he was a right-handed hitter and he swung very late at a breaking pitch and hit a long foul ball down the right-field line. It was well beyond first base, deep into the stands. And suddenly, seemingly out of nowhere, a man stood up, reached out with a baseball glove, and caught the ball.

It was just such a wonderful thing to see. That fan was sitting closer to the subway entrance than he was to the field. He was sitting in an area into which few foul balls are hit. And he had obviously been sitting there wearing his glove for the entire game. I remember looking at him and wondering for how many years had this fan been coming to the ballpark with his baseball glove, and how many games had he sat through wearing his glove, believing that someday a foul ball would be hit right at him and he would be ready to catch it.

And I wondered what he would have done if he had dropped it.

I thought about that for a long time after that game, about how important that baseball was to him. That baseball was his connection to the game; it had actually been used in a major league game. It reminded me how valuable a beautiful memento like that could be. So I scuffed up a few new balls on the cement floor of the umpires' room to make them look as if they had been fouled off, and put them in my pocket. You just never know when an official American League ball that had been used in an official American League game and had been fouled off by Reggie Jackson in New York, Jim Rice in Boston, George Brett in Kansas City, or Rod Carew in Minnesota will come in handy.

A group of fans who will never fall out of the stands reaching for a foul ball, or will never sting their hands catching a ball, are those people who sit in the front row of the mezzanine—or is it the loge—in the middle deck directly behind home plate at Yankee Stadium. You know what these people do? They keep long-handled butterfly nets at their sides, and when a ball is fouled back so that it rolls up the protective screen, they grab their nets and trap the ball. Oh, there are few things more exciting than the clash of butterfly nets. To me, using a net to snare a foul ball, is about as difficult as trying to convince a store owner to accept cash rather than an out-of-town check. It has all the adventure of talking a politician into taking a contribution. I feel very strongly about this—if baseballs were supposed to be caught in butterfly nets, Reggie Jackson would have been a great outfielder.

Probably the most incredible foul ball in history was planted by Los Angeles Dodgers pitcher Jerry Reuss. Reuss is another one of those people who believe April Fool's Day should be a national holiday. The man likes to have a good time. One very hot day in Los Angeles, for example, Frank Pulli was working behind the plate, and he was sweltering. A lake of sweat had dripped off his body. Reuss felt sorry for Pulli, so between innings he sent the ball boy out with a drink for him. Pulli gratefully accepted it and took a long swig—of hot coffee.

Reuss watched Pulli throw the cup on the ground, and decided he'd better do something to make amends. So he took a brand-new baseball out of the umpires' ball bag, a ball that had already been rubbed with the special mud from the Delaware River to take the sheen off its cover, and was ready to be put into the game. And on this ball he wrote, "To Frank, May God Bless You," and signed it, naturally, "Tom Lasorda." Then he dropped the ball back into the bag and waited.

He couldn't wait to see the expression on Pulli's face when Frank pulled the ball out of the ball bag he wore on his waist and started to throw it into play. Each time a ball was hit into the stands, or scuffed beyond use, or the pitcher asked for a new ball, Jerry would watch Frank Pulli reach into his bag, take out a new ball, and put it into play. Eventually, he knew, Pulli was going to react. One by one, every ball in the ball bag was put into play, and Pulli never reacted. The game ended without Pulli ever discovering that signed baseball.

But not without that baseball getting into the game. In the clubhouse afterward relief pitcher Tom Neidenfuer happened to sit next to Reuss, and said, "You know, the strangest thing happened while I was pitching in the ninth inning."

"What was that?" Reuss asked.

"Well, Pulli threw this new ball out to me and Lasorda had already written on it, something like, 'To Frank, May God Bless You.' "

"Really," Reuss said calmly, "uh, what'd you do with it?"

"Threw it," Neidenfuer told him. "You think I'm not going to use a dirty ball when I get the chance?"

"What happened to it?"

Neidenfuer shrugged. "Not much. It got fouled off."

Not much! That was only the most incredible foul ball in history is all. The ball was fouled back behind home plate, into the same section in which Jo Lasorda, Tommy's wife, was sitting. A man caught it and read the inscription. And amazingly, incredibly, somebody call *Believe It or Not*, that foul ball was caught by a fan named . . . Frank! (Well, it wouldn't have been much of a story if it had been caught by a fan named Mel, or Jack.)

As an umpire I judged a ball club by its manners on the playing field. As a broadcaster I rated clubs by their ability to be competitive on television and the difficulty I had pronouncing the names of their players. But as a fan I find the true measure of a ball club is the variety and quality of food served at the stadium.

For some people a baseball game, with its intricate strategies, provides food for thought; I'm just the opposite; a baseball game makes me think of food. I

believe part of the reason for that is that umpires are
not permitted to eat on the field. So the most I ever
had was a hot dog. But I'd be working first base and I'd
look into the stands and see fans enjoying pizza or a
hamburger or an ice cream sundae. Or I'd be behind
the plate trying to concentrate and suddenly I'd be
smacked in the nose by the soft aroma of fried onion
rings or Italian sausages and I'd want some. Not just
some, I'd want a lot. At times like that, when I was
feeling sorry for myself, I'd remind myself what my
mother had taught me—that there were hungry people in China. Then I'd think, yeah, and there are
hungry people behind first base too.

At one time the entire range of ballpark cuisine
consisted of peanuts, popcorn, and Cracker Jacks with
soda-flavored ice water. Today every team has at least
one fine restaurant in its stadium, usually reserved for
season ticket holders, as well as specialty concession
areas in the stands. Houston, for example, has a complete pizza restaurant located where you can sit and
eat and watch the game. The Mets have a delicatessen-
bar, called Casey's 37, on the main level. Or, it might
be the loge level. It is named after their first manager,
number 37, Casey Stengel. The Yankees honored Casey
with a wall plaque in their Monument Park, the Mets
named a deli after him. I like the Mets' way better.
When I go, I want food named after me too.

The type of food served at a ball game seems to
reflect the ethnic identity of the community. There is
a tremendous Scandinavian influence in the Minneap-
olis area, for example, so naturally they would serve
tortilla chips with hot tangy cheese, sauce, and jalapeño
peppers; bratwurst; chili crispto; and apple crispto at
the Metrodome. Because of the heavy German-Polish
population in the Milwaukee area, County Stadium
features corned beef, roast beef, string cheese, and
Philadelphia steak sandwiches. And in Cleveland's Municipal Stadium you can get what Indian fans need
most—Good Humor ice cream.

The White Sox make eating at Comiskey Park an
international treat. Fans can choose among German

submarine sandwiches, Mexican *el moro de letrans* (doughnuts), Italian sausages, Kosher hot dogs, and Philadelphia pretzels. Comiskey Park is also the only place where you can get both the large size elephant ears (for $1.25) as well as mini-elephant ears ($1). You can, but why you would is next week's quickie quiz.

I would think the bravest person in the entire world would have to be the first person to have eaten Bar-B-Qued pork in Atlanta Stadium. Ballpark food is known to be filling rather than good. Sort of like mortar, only not as tasty. So I couldn't understand why anyone would risk their life by eating Bar-B-Qued pork at Atlanta Stadium—until I tried the Chick-Fil-A. Get it, Chick-Fil-A, filet? I got it, and I was sorry that I did. The $2.50 Chick-Fil-A meal consists of one small piece of chicken on a stale roll, with a pickle. The pickle is the highlight. My first reaction when I opened the package was, this is all you get? Two-fifty for one piece of chicken? My reaction after I tasted the chicken was, thank God that was all I got.

After eating the Chick-Fil-A, I understood why someone would risk his life eating the Bar-B-Qued pork—if you didn't eat the pork, they threatened to make you eat the chicken.

I really don't like to criticize food, but there is a rumor in Atlanta that the health policy of a major insurance company is voided if the company can prove that the policyholder ate Chick-Fil-A.

I suppose you could say I'm one of those soft-hearted, weak-kneed types, but I believe there is no such thing as bad food. Some food might not taste as good as other food, but there isn't a food in the world that can't be helped by some lovingly prepared sauce or a combination of spices, or even a dozen packs of ballpark ketchup. That includes Atlanta's Chick-Fil-A. Some ballpark food is good. I liked the smoke links in Wrigley Field and the Incredible Edibles with mixed vegetables in Cleveland and the rum raisin Frusen Glädjé ice cream at Shea and I just loved the way they prepare the sunflower seeds in Baltimore.

So I do like some ballpark food. "Ballpark" is the

key word there. I wouldn't like a lot of this food if it were served anyplace else. For example, anyplace else in the world outside a ballpark. Therefore, I don't think I'm being unreasonable when I say flatly that the single worst advertising campaign in history is the one that attempts to sell the same brands of hot dogs sold at the ballpark for fans to make at home. A male voice chimes happily, "Get that same great taste at home that you get out at the ballpark." Why? Haven't these people ever eaten a hot dog in the ballpark? There's no excuse at home. It's not like you're serving 25,000 people. Why not try something different, like cooking them? Or why not try cooking them the very same day you intend to eat them? Or why not take them out of the water when they're hot, rather than leaving them lying there in lukewarm water for an hour? Why not eat them on rolls baked within the last decade? It seems to me, if you really wanted that "same great taste at home that you get out at the ballpark," you should move into the ballpark.

Cheering for your favorite team is another fan's job that used to be simple. "Yea!" for example, is a great cheer. So are "Hooray," "Go team," and "You can do it." Nice and simple. Direct, to the point. Supportive. Spontaneous. "Strike the bum out" and "Show us where you live" are American classics. Has there ever been a more effective cheer than "Let's go Mets!"? Or a more rhythmic cheer than the White Sox fans', "Send it flyin' to the Ryan!" meaning the Dan Ryan Expressway that runs near the park.

Not that I would know about cheers from my own baseball career. There are no umpire cheers. What would they be, "Way to call safe"? "Nice 'out' call"? The one cheer that always made me cringe when I was working a game was "We're behind you." I didn't want anybody behind me. I wanted them out in front, where I could keep an eye on them.

The only people who ever cheered for me—except for the day I left home, and that was my mother— were football fans. But the thing I could never understand was why they cheered for me when I was going out of the game. A Detroit Lions coach once explained: "That's because you did a great job." I was never really too sure about that. I always suspected it was *because* I was going out of the game. I wanted fans cheering for me when I was going into the game, but they couldn't because when I was going into the game, they were cheering for the offense, which was coming out of the game. To me cheering when a player is leaving the game is like telling a guest that you're happy he's there when he's putting on his hat and coat.

The only football cheer I really knew was "Hit Ron again, hit Ron again, harder, harder."

Name cheers have always been very popular. Every time Boog Powell or Moose Skowron or "Sweet Lou" Johnson or Lou Piniella came to bat, fans would respond with a long Booooooooggg, or Mooooooooose, or Looooooooou, and announcers would inform listeners that the fans were cheering rather than booing. I don't know about that. Boog Powell struck out 1,226 times in his big league career. Are you trying to tell me that maybe one of those times there wasn't a legitimate boooooooooo snuck in there?

First-name cheers are in vogue now. That started in New York with Reggie Jackson, who became Reggie!, accent on the second syllable. And that type of cheer spread throughout the league, used when any star with a two-syllable name came to bat in an important situation. Now, I happen to believe that the White Sox's Harold Baines is one of the great young players in baseball, but I really had a hard time convincing myself to scream, "Har-old! Har-old!" The people I feel sorry for are great players with one syllable names. What do they cheer in Boston when Jim Rice comes to bat, "Jim-mum!"? And in Kansas City, when George Brett has done what he does so well again, do they cheer, "Ge-orge!"? Either we're going to have to find new cheers for these deserving people, or they're simply going to have to change their names.

Fortunately, in this age of technology, cheering is one of the few things that fans do spontaneously. The scoreboard tells the fans when to begin a spontaneous cheer, and they do. "Cheer" the scoreboard demands, and people cheer. "Clap" the scoreboard demands, and people clap. I'm waiting for the day the scoreboard first orders "cheer," then "clap," then "crawl on your belly and squawk like a chicken."

If the scoreboard isn't begging for cheers, the public address system is leading them. It's a tight situation in a ball game. Suddenly a rhythmic hand-clapping begins. Then from somewhere comes the ominous sound of thumping drums. And then a bugle blows a crisp, clear charge! Next time you go to a ballpark, look around you. How many people do you see there with drums? Count the number of bugles you see. In this age of dehumanization it is comforting to know that a nice, loving loudspeaker system can lead the way.

Fans don't need these cues. Knowing when to cheer is not that difficult—a player on the team you're rooting for does something good, you cheer. A player on the opposition does something good, you don't cheer. That's the entire strategy of cheering.

And fans are extremely generous with cheers too. Look at the newest addition to the cheers, the "curtain call." When a player gets an important hit and ends up in the dugout, fans will cheer until that player comes out of the dugout, waves his hat in acknowledgment, and returns to the dugout. Originally players were called out for curtain calls only after performing a spectacular feat. Reggie Jackson hit three home runs in one World Series game. Len Barker pitched a perfect game. Tom Seaver won his three hundredth game. Pete Rose got his four thousandth hit. These are incredible achievements, worthy of an ovation.

But now almost every player is brought out for a curtain call. Dave Kingman catching one fly ball in a row in the outfield is not worthy of a curtain call. Billy Martin changing his lineup card is not worthy of a curtain call. A fan managing to get back to his seat with six containers of beer without spilling a drop is not worthy of a curtain call. Well, maybe Dave King-man catching a fly ball . . .

Which brings us to the newest cheer of all—the wave. I have ridden a wave, and survived to tell about it. Recently I saw a sign in St. Louis's Busch Stadium that read REAL FANS DON'T MAKE WAVES. I don't know if that's true. I think fans should participate in the game as much as possible as long as they don't interfere with play. If making waves makes people happy, they should go boil an ocean.

If you've never participated in a ballpark "wave," it's not very difficult. Here, for the first time in print, are the instructions for properly participating in a "wave." But before I explain, my attorney has asked me to include the following disclaimer: I am in no way endorsing the wave. Participation is at your own risk. I cannot be held personally responsible for any injuries incurred while participating in a "wave." Just as you would before beginning any strenuous activity, consult your local physician for a complete checkup. Anyone with a family history of blood pressure, frequent heart attacks, or the pain of psoriasis should have a doctor's permission before attempting to participate in a "wave." There.

Properly participating in a "wave" is not complicated, IF YOU FOLLOW INSTRUCTIONS. First, as the "wave" approaches you, stand up quickly. Then, sit down quickly. Timing is extremely important, you MUST NOT stand until the people near you begin sitting down. Entire "waves" have been ruined by poor timing.

It is not as difficult as it sounds. Most people should be able to master it with just a little practice. Naturally, as with any new physical activity, you'll be using some muscles you haven't used in a while, so you may experience some soreness after your first few "waves." This is normal, but if that soreness persists, see a doctor immediately.

Once you've mastered the basic "wave" skills, there are all sorts of refinements. You can, for example, throw both arms straight into the air as high as you can when you stand up, then bring them down quickly, usually before sitting down again. And Californians have introduced their own variation. In a California "wave," you don't stand up; you casually raise one arm into the air, then, whenever you feel like it, lower it.

The best "wave" I ever saw was shown on television during a Seattle Mariner game. Two lone Mariner fans were sitting all by themselves, making their own "wave." One of them would stand up quickly, then sit down. Then the second one would get up, then sit down. Then the first one would stand up, then sit down. . . . Maybe it was more of a ripple.

I believe I was a good umpire. I know I was a talkative broadcaster. But I don't think I'm a very good fan. I drive my car to the ballpark and try to sneak it into the press parking lot. I try to get my tickets free, I eat as much as I can, I don't keep score, I don't cheer, I run away from foul balls, and I never read all the signs in the outfield. And as for participating in the "wave"? My feeling is that if the object of the "wave" is simply to sit down as quickly as you can, why get up in the first place?

Of course, I have enjoyed the pleasures of being a fan for the first time. Sitting in a beautiful ballpark on a balmy summer night watching a great ball game. Quietly discussing baseball with people who just happen to be sitting near me. Being able to eat as much of anything I want. Not having people yelling at me. Being able to yell at the umpires. But more than anything else, the thing that made me happiest was the discovery I made that very first night in Baltimore's Memorial Stadium.

From my seat in the stands, Earl Weaver looked even shorter than he does on the playing field.

CAPTAIN DYNAMITE AND OTHER EXPLOSIONS

I've spent a considerable portion of my life in sports stadiums—as a football player, a minor and major league umpire, a broadcaster, and as a fan. I've played in Syracuse University's Archibald Stadium, the oldest all-cement ballpark in the country, and I opened the brand-new Oakland-Alameda County Stadium. I've worked in Cleveland's 74,208-seat Municipal Stadium and in minor league parks so small they had rats the size of cockroaches. So I know stadiums inside and outside and even, like Montreal's Olympic Stadium, inside out.

Stadiums are baseball's most valuable asset. If there were no stadiums, fans would not have to buy tickets to get into the games. A few of those stadiums, however, left something to be desired. Take walls, for instance.

One of the places I worked as a minor league umpire was Pittsfield, Massachusetts. Most baseball parks in the northern hemisphere are designed so that home plate is to the south and center field is to the north. Most, not all. Municipal Stadium is not. And

Pittsfield's stadium is not. The only time that causes a problem is at sunset when, in Pittsfield, the sun sets directly in the batter's eyes. This makes it very difficult to see, and seeing is an important part of hitting. As an umpire I really didn't mind that I couldn't see the pitch as long as I knew the batter couldn't see it either. The pitch would come in, maybe the catcher would catch it, maybe not. Who knew? Maybe the pitcher didn't even throw it. None of us at the plate could see. But when I heard it hit the catcher's mitt, I made a call. "Ball!" "Strike!" Who was going to argue? If a batter asked if I was sure about it, that confirmed my call—then I knew he didn't know where it was either.

What they eventually had to do in Pittsfield was suspend the game every night from just before until just after sunset. But that was the kind of problem we expected to encounter in the minor leagues. Every minor league player and umpire secretly believed that major league organizations intentionally kept their minor league ballparks shabby and poorly lit because they wanted their players desperate to get out of the minors.

It worked. Everybody was desperate to get out of the minors. We all worked as hard as possible to get to the big leagues, where ballparks were spacious and well-lit, and there were only soft rocks on the infields and most outfields were covered with lush green grass. We knew that the sun never set in a major league batter's eyes.

And, as I discovered, we were right. Major league ballparks are the centers of civic pride, often the showpiece of the city. For that reason city governments spend tens of millions of dollars to hire the greatest architects, the finest builders and landscapers and experts in sightlines and acoustics and interior design and food services and other related fields. Every blueprint is examined over and over for the slightest problem, every nut and bolt is tested and retested for microscopic flaws, every slab of cement and every seat is inspected for defects. And the result is that the errors made in building minor league parks are never repeated in major league stadiums.

Oh, there have been a few minor problems that have come up. They forgot to include an officials' dressing room in the Oakland Coliseum, for example. And there were no public water fountains in Dodger Stadium when it first opened. And somebody miscalculated the cost of renovating Yankee Stadium by $75 million.

I can certainly understand that. Every time I'm doing something around my house I always spend more than I expect to too. I mean, a hundred, two hundred, seventy-five million, what's the difference?

I suppose there are a few other small, bothersome mistakes that have cropped up in major league stadiums from time to time. But how could anyone have anticipated when they built the Astrodome, the first indoor stadium, that grass would not grow under a dome, necessitating the invention of artificial turf and changing the game of baseball forever. I mean, I can understand that too. Personally I can't even grow grass in front of my house, and that lawn is outdoors!

If they had wanted weeds, though, I probably could have helped them.

Obviously that kind of wrinkle is unique. But under ordinary circumstances, every conceivable problem that can be anticipated is examined from every angle to ensure that when a new ballpark is built it is . . . Well, there is Candlestick Park, home of the San Francisco Giants.

When the city of San Francisco decided to build a new ballpark, they spent hundreds of days searching for the perfect site. Finally they found it on a magnificent bluff overlooking San Francisco Bay. It was near a freeway, the land was vacant so no one had to be evicted and, even luckier, the contractor hired to build the stadium happened to *own* the land.

It was almost perfect. Unfortunately they had spent hundreds of days looking, and no nights. Because about four o'clock every afternoon the wind shifts and blows off the Pacific Ocean through a gap in the hills, making it very cold and very foggy on that bluff. In the fifth inning of a night game the fog sweeps over the ballpark, and a whirlwind of peanut shells and hot dog wrappers swirls around the stadium. And it gets very, very cold.

It is, however, a wonderful ballpark for the San Francisco 49ers to play football in. Of course, the 49ers play during the day.

But, hey, I have no right to complain. Endicott, New York, is in the snowbelt. From November to March the temperature rarely gets above freezing. It's so cold all the time that people walk around saying in frozen breaths, "It could be worse. We could be watching a night game in Candlestick Park."

Other than those examples, there isn't a ballpark in the big leagues that isn't ... well, they do have *that* problem with Olympic Stadium in Montreal. I think they call it sinking. "The Big O," as it is known, was constructed for the 1976 Olympics. Many sports fans are not aware of this, but Olympic Stadium is the most unusual indoor stadium in existence. What makes it unusual is that it is outdoors.

A huge tower next to the stadium has been under construction since 1975. A retractable roof, sort of like a giant umbrella, was to have been suspended from this tower. In pleasant weather the roof would be retracted into the tower, in inclement weather it would be opened to cover the stadium. People who like the tower believe it looks like a cement version of the Eiffel Tower. People who don't like it claim it resembles an unusually large celery stalk.

The roof umbrella was constructed while the tower was being built. The tower went higher and higher, and then it went lower and lower. It is a law of physics that what goes up must come down; the designer of the tower just didn't expect it to happen so quickly. Apparently the bedrock below the tower was not strong enough to support its weight. Construction on the tower stopped. Fortunately the roof umbrella was completed and is safely in storage at a cost of only $1.3 million a year.

Everyone I know who owns a house can sympathize with the city of Montreal. Who doesn't have a problem with his roof from time to time. A few shingles blow off, it leaks, the gutters get stopped up, the roof umbrella has to be kept in storage for $1.3 million a year.

Actually in baseball economics that is not a lot of money. Any player who could cover as much ground as that roof would be paid a lot more than that.

Other than that, though, the Big O is a perfect ballpark. Other than that and the fact that the two sides don't exactly come together. As it turns out, the Big O isn't. I can understand that too. Try drawing a circle freehand on a piece of paper. See how difficult it is to make the two ends meet to complete the circle. And that's only on a piece of paper. If you think that's hard, try doing it with tons of steel and concrete. I think they should be happy they even came close. So what if the park doesn't quite come together in center field. What's a gap of a foot or two? At least the sun doesn't set in the batter's eyes like it does in Pittsfield. And Pittsfield doesn't even have a roof umbrella they can keep in storage for $1.3 million a year!

All right, mistakes *have* been made in the construction of stadiums. But what do you expect when you're spending only forty or fifty million dollars? Perfection? The important thing is to learn from those mistakes and not repeat them. For example, the city of San Francisco will never build another ballpark on that bluff.

When the Twin Cities of Minneapolis-St. Paul decided to build a domed stadium to replace aging outdoor Metropolitan Stadium, they thoroughly investigated every other recently built ballpark. They were determined that the Hubert H. Humphrey Metrodome, the newest major league stadium, would not have any of the problems other recently built parks had faced. And so, thanks to careful planning, every problem with the Metrodome is original!

Few cities need an indoor stadium more than Minneapolis-St. Paul. They have only two seasons

there, winter and July. And July is too hot. They also
have mosquitos as big as shortstops, which often made
it difficult for players to concentrate. I always liked
old Metropolitan Stadium, maybe because I liked the
Twins players and fans. There was just one thing I
could never figure out: If the Mets played in Shea
Stadium, why did the Twins play at the Met?

After investigating all other domed stadiums, the
Twin Cities decided they weren't going to put a dome
up; they were going to put it down. The Metrodome
was blasted into granite forty-two feet below street
level. The roof was to be supported by air pressure
rather than a steel framework. One of the main advan-
tages of building below ground, the architect insisted,
was that the bedrock would provide a natural cooling
system. No matter how many people were inside the
dome, air-conditioning would not be required. So no
air-conditioning ducts were installed. The Metrodome
opened in 1982. The air-conditioning system was installed in 1983.

Casey Stengel once complimented St. Louis's new
Busch Stadium, an outdoor ballpark, by noting, "It
holds the heat very well." At that time it was about
110 degrees on the field. But no ballpark ever held
heat as well as the Metrodome. If there was no one
inside the Dome, it was comfortable for everyone there.
But crowds generate body heat, which had no place to
dissipate, making it oppressively hot and humid. Fans
there didn't need the "wave" to cool them off, they
were too busy fanning themselves.

When the $300,000 air-conditioning system was
installed, it evidently created a wind current. Balls hit
into the cool airstream just took off, turning the
Metrodome into the "homerdome."

"The same architect also decided to install an
unusually thick artificial surface," Tom Mee, Twins
director of public relations, explains. "Every other
ballpark carpet has a total thickness of 1¼ inches. He
wanted to put a ½-inch nap on top of a 1¼-inch pad.
'We've really researched this,' he told us, 'and this
conformation will give us the truest possible bounce.'

"Now, this man has an architectural degree and I don't, but that didn't seem right to me. I thought a carpet that thick would be like a trampoline, that baseballs would bounce off it as if they were hitting stretched rubber. But he assured me I was wrong and the carpet went in that way.

"It took exactly one fly ball for us to find out that I was one hundred percent right and he was one hundred percent wrong. That surface has given entirely new meaning to the old phrase 'That's the way the ball bounces.' The Viking football players love it, however. They should; they bounce right off it."

That surface also happens to be exceptionally safe for fans in the upper deck. If they fall out of the stands, they have a good chance of bouncing right back up to their seats.

Besides those two mistakes, though, they made only one or two. For example, they forgot to put plumbing in the visiting clubhouse laundry room—which is okay if you intend to do a lot of dry cleaning—and in the photographers' darkroom. And someone neglected to order ticket booths or turnstiles. But ticket booths and turnstiles are not really needed—unless you intend to stay in business.

Portable ticket booths and used turnstiles were ordered in time to be ready the day the Dome opened. The portable ticket booths were fine, except that they had no cash drawers. Since the only thing ticket booths are used for is to collect money for tickets, this was considered a problem. The used turnstiles were fine, though; although they did give an improper count of the number of people passing through them. The only thing, of course, a turnstile does is record the number of people passing through it.

The Metrodome is beautiful and, even with its problems, it is operating at a profit. My sporting goods store had no problems, and I went out of business. You figure it out. But there is one thing about the "homerdome," and every other indoor stadium, that fascinates me: Why do they have enclosed boxes for football games in an indoor stadium? Why sit inside when you're already sitting inside? Do people want to stay out of the air-conditioning?

And there is one other, minor thing about the "homerdome." I mean, I really feel silly even mentioning it, but on occasion the pressurized roof has collapsed.

I've seen many unusual things inside baseball stadiums besides Earl Weaver. I've seen two men occupying one base, one man cutting across the infield to return to first base, and a manager pick up a base and run away with it. I've seen dirt painted green and called grass. I've seen a rope hung from the upper deck to serve as a foul line. I've seen checked-swing singles, bunt doubles, ground-ball triples, and obviously foul balls sail inside a rope foul line that is blowing in the wind for a home run. I've seen cow-milking contests, the world's largest submarine sandwich, and Karl Wallenda walk a highwire in a rainstorm. I've seen Minnesota's Twinkie the Loon, the Toronto Blue Jay's mascot, B. J. Birdy, the Baltimore Oriole Bird, and the Detroit Tiger, Mark "the Bird" Fidrych, and I've actually seen the Cleveland Duck. I've seen a man dress up as a chicken and become famous. But the most incredible thing I've ever seen inside a ballpark was Judge Roy Hoffheinz's apartment.

The judge was a Texas millionaire. He was the motivating force, and owner, of the first indoor stadium, the Astrodome. And when he built it, he put in a few simple rooms for himself, thus making the Astrodome the world's largest apartment. There are some people who have children playing baseball in their front yard, but the judge was the only person in history to have two major league teams and 45,000 guests in his playroom.

This apartment was something else. Precisely *what* else is the question. It consisted of two floors of living space located behind the right-field wall, and was decorated in what probably can be called "Old West bordello." The bedroom and dining room were upstairs, the barber shop, miniature bowling alley, putting green, shooting gallery complete with life-size cowboy robots sitting around the campfire, the carousel, and the tipsy bar were downstairs. The walls were covered with flocked red wallpaper and oil paintings of reclining nudes.

The tipsy bar was the highlight of the apartment. I think that probably tells you a lot. The entire barroom is tilted. Unfortunately it is tilted in many different directions. The floor slants up, the bar slants down. The mirror goes up, the light fixtures go down. The door is askew. The ceiling goes a number of different ways. The barstools are not only tilted, one of them slowly sinks whenever someone sits on it. There is a diamond-shaped glassless window overlooking the playing field. Tilted. Let me put it this way: This is the first bar I've ever been in in which, after you've had too much to drink, the room looks level.

I think the best thing that might be said about living in this apartment is that it guarantees you'll get the same great taste at home that you get out at the ballpark.

Once a stadium is built, the object is to attract as many paying fans as possible inside it. Baseball is a sport about as much as my sporting goods store was a business. There was a time when baseball was the only game in town, but that time was a long time ago. Professional baseball, meaning games that people have to pay to see, now competes with other sports and recreational activities, as well as with other forms of entertainment, for the attention of the fan. So to help attract paying customers, baseball has started offering a wide array of promotions. Both major and minor league teams have premium giveaway days, special events, contests, games, and live entertainment.

Baseball's major promotion used to be Ladies' Day, days on which women were admitted to the park at half price. That was really creative thinking. Then some baseball executive realized that if a team gave something away that cost less than the price of the ticket, but would attract more than the normal crowd to the game, that team would end up making money.

Bat Days, on which Little League bats were given to fans twelve years old and younger, and Ball Days, were the first major giveaway days.

Sponsors quickly became involved, and plain Bat Day became Some Bank's Name Bat Day. That "Some Bank" paid a percentage of the price of the premiums for the publicity. Baseball executives realized almost immediately that they could make more by *not* paying for the premiums that brought fans into the ballpark than they could by paying for them. And the more things they didn't have to pay for, the more fans they could attract. Thus, U.S. Army Beach Towel Night, Rustoleum Wristwatch Day, Purina Picnic Bag Night, and United Airlines Winter Scarf Night were born.

In 1985 a fan could go out to the game and receive a bat, a ball, a glove, a team jersey, T-shirt, jacket, cap, floppy hat, fisherman's hat, nonprotecting batting helmet, sports socks, beach sandals, a beach towel, winter scarf, sunglasses, a sun visor, a pack of baseball cards, a wristwatch, a calendar, a cooler, thermos, team photo coffee mug, a poncho, an umbrella, a backpack, shaving kit, a briefcase (fans over fourteen), key chain, transistor radio, three-ring binder, necklace, team poster, personal growth chart, a camera with which to take pictures on team Photo Day, a kazoo, a whistle, a cushion to sit on while watching the game, and a tote bag to bring the loot home in. Among other things.

Most clubs prefer to offer premiums that either come in adjustable sizes, like a plastic batting helmet with an adjustable headband, or things that aren't worn. There always seems to be one 6'5" twelve-year-old in every ballpark crowd. As major league promotion directors say, an extra large T-shirt might not be large enough, but one size bat fits all.

I will never forget the first time I worked on Bat Day at Yankee Stadium. The ballpark was absolutely filled. Fifty-five thousand people. Forty thousand of them had to be kids. On my list of favorite things, kids rank just below malaria. Kids with baseball bats are way below that. The moment I walked out onto

the field I heard IT! Thump! Thump! Thump! Only
then did the realization strike me—what kind of sadistic person would give baseball bats to 40,000 kids
in a ballpark with wood and metal seats, *before the
game*? The answer was an obvious one. Someone who
did not have to be on the field surrounded by them.
Throughout the entire game all I heard was THUMP!
THUMP! THUMP! Throughout the entire night all I
heard in my head was THUMP! THUMP! THUMP! It
was one of the worst days of my life—and remember, I
was a bad football player. About the only thing I could
think of that could possibly have been worse than
that day would have to be Alarm Whistle Night.

Contests are also popular ballpark promotions.
Minor league clubs in particular are always having
lucky-seat drawings or specially marked program
giveaways, usually for prizes like dinner for two at a
local diner or a fill-up at a local gas station. Some big
league teams have similar contests, but their prizes
are, naturally, big league. One evening when I was in
Atlanta, for example, the Braves picked one lucky fan
out of the 22,000 in the stadium and awarded him his
very own *personalized ball-point pen*! I wonder how
that fan managed to contain his excitement. Another
lucky fan that night received two—count 'em, two—
chicken picnic dinners! Of course, later they did give
away a Caribbean cruise.

When the Cleveland Indians' marketing director,
Tom Pulchinski, was with the Indians' Waterloo, Iowa,
team in the Class A Midwest League, he ran a bingo
game almost every night. "Whenever there wasn't bingo
at the local church, we'd draw very well," he remembers. "All the women came out to the park. We'd sell
cards for three games for a dollar. At the end of every
inning we'd announce, 'No runs, no hits, no errors,
nobody left on base and the first letter on the green
card is B-6.' We had one man calling numbers and a
second man leaning his head out the press box window screaming, 'Anybody got bingo?' If no one responded, we'd go right ahead and play the next inning.

"Those people took their bingo seriously down

there too. They'd get up and go to the concession
stand during the game just to make sure they'd be
back in time for the bingo between innings. About the
most exciting thing that ever happened was when
somebody called 'Bingo!' and didn't really have it."

Among other promotions Pulchinski ran in Waterloo were a Singing Dog Contest, in which dog owners tried to harmonize with their pets, and the I'll-bet-
you-can't-draw-1,500-fans-without-a-promotion-night
promotion.

They didn't.

Used Car Night has been a popular minor league
promotion that the Texas Rangers' marketing director,
Larry Schmittou, brought with him to the big leagues.
"We give away one car an inning," he explained.
"They're worth between eight hundred and one thousand dollars each. I wouldn't exactly call them clunk-
ers. Well, yes, I would. We guarantee that each car
will make it out of the parking lot, but that is all we
guarantee. We also tell our fans that some of these
cars come with the original tire air."

Schmittou has staged some of baseball's most original promotions in Arlington, Texas, among them Las
Vegas Night and the Cash Scramble. On Las Vegas
Night a drawing is held at the top of the second
inning for a trip to Las Vegas, including three days and
two nights in a hotel and five hundred dollars for
spending money.

The only catch is that the winner must leave for
Las Vegas at the bottom of the second inning.

Fans actually bring their luggage to the ballpark.
At the end of the second inning a limousine drives
onto the field to take the winner to the airport. The
losers have to stay for the rest of the game.

The minors need promotions more than the major leagues, Schmittou believes. "In the big leagues
you can promote individual players. You can't do that
in the minor leagues because good players get promoted and bad players get released. Only the marketing director stays there."

But what is perhaps Schmittou's greatest promotion got right to the heart of the matter: greed. What, he wondered, is the best thing money can buy? More money, he figured. The Cash Scramble. In the minor leagues Schmittou put five hundred dollars in change into a wheelbarrow and gave two fans, drawn from the ballpark crowd, sixty seconds to collect as much money as they could. But when he reached the major leagues, he decided to do it in style. "We got ten thousand brand-new dollar bills. We marked one of them with an X; that one was worth one thousand dollars. What we didn't realize was that brand-new dollar bills stick together, and that would have sort of taken the fun out of it. So we had to separate every single bill, crumple them up, and stuff them into pillowcases. Do you have any idea how long it takes to crumple up ten thousand new dollar bills?

"The ten-thousand-dollar Cash Scramble took place after the ball game. This time we made everybody stay for the entire game. We spread the money in small piles all around the infield and prayed it wouldn't be windy. The fan, a man, was selected in a random drawing. Rather than simply gathering as much cash as he could, he spent most of the time racing from pile to pile trying to find the marked bill. He didn't. He ended up with $136. It was a tremendously successful promotion. We got a lot of publicity, we sold a lot of tickets, the fans really seemed to enjoy it, and all it cost us was $136.

"Which left us with 9,864 brand-new crumpled-up dollar bills. Did you know banks will not take pillowcases stuffed with crumpled-up dollar bills? Do you have any idea how long it takes to uncrumple 9,864 new dollar bills? Trust me. A long time. At six A.M. the following morning we were still sitting in my office unfolding money."

Traditional attractions like Old Timers' Day, Father and Son/Daughter Games, and Fireworks Night always bring fans out to the ballpark. Recently some teams with full color screens on their scoreboards have begun showing movies after the game. On a Friday the thirteenth, for example, Houston followed the game with the movie *Friday the 13th*. Some fans would call an Astro game followed by a horror movie cruel and unusual punishment.

Through the years baseball teams have used special appearances by entertainers to increase attendance. Al Schacht, "the Clown Prince of Baseball," and Max Patkin did humorous baseball acts in which they made a lot of funny faces and fell down a lot. Of course, Earl Weaver used to do the same thing on a regular basis. "The King and His Court" featured legendary softball pitcher Eddie Feigner and three or four teammates playing against a nine-man team. Feigner would pitch blindfolded from behind second base, between his legs, around his back, without any fielders—and still won almost every game.

Without doubt baseball's most popular entertainer today is the Chicken. The Chicken is a man dressed in a chicken suit who waddles around the field playing with, and teasing, players, umpires, and fans. Generally everyone loves the Chicken. There seem to be a few players, however, who don't understand that this is not really a very large chicken, but rather a man doing an act. Supposedly one player being teased by the Chicken challenged him to fight. Fortunately the Chicken turned out to be a chicken.

The Chicken started life as the San Diego Chicken, a Padre mascot sponsored by a San Diego radio station. But he ran afoul of the station's guidelines and waddled off on his own. I've seen the Chicken perform a number of times, and I can honestly say I have never seen him lay an egg. Although *New York Times* sports columnist Ira Berkow did catch him eating scrambled eggs at breakfast one morning. When Berkow asked the Chicken how he could possibly do such a thing, the Chicken replied, "I'm just cutting down on the competition."

Postgame concerts by popular musicians have proven to be an extremely successful attraction. Everyone from Crosby, Stills and Nash to the Oak Ridge Boys have played baseball stadiums in the last few years.

"I can get Barbra Streisand one night, I can bring in the Beach Boys, they're all available," says Minnesota Twins promotion director Don Cassidy. "Costly, but available. But what am I in, the baseball business or the concert business? We're promoting baseball, so the things we do are geared to help attract fans to see the ball game first and the promotion second."

Even if that promotion is Captain Dynamite. *The* Captain Dynamite.

"I was home watching television one night," Cassidy remembers, "trying to figure out something special we could do on the Fourth of July. I'd hired all kinds of attractions, the Flying Wallendas, Evel Knievel, and I thought I had seen it all. Then suddenly Captain Dynamite appeared on the show I was watching. His act was very simple. He put sticks of dynamite around a coffinlike box, got inside the box, and blew himself up.

"It was the most beautiful thing I had ever seen. I dropped to my knees in front of the television set. I had been searching my whole life for that man. I had to have him perform at our Fourth of July show. What could be more spectacular than an American blowing himself up on the Fourth of July? I didn't care what it cost, I knew it was exactly the kind of thing our fans would love.

"I finally reached him in a small town in Texas, where he was blowing himself up at a county fair. I told him that I wanted him to perform in Minnesota on the Fourth of July, then added that I had a very small budget. I guessed he was going to charge me five thousand dollars. '. . . so, what'll it cost me to have you perform here?' I wondered if *perform* was the right word.

" 'Is five hundred dollars too much?' he asked.

"I coughed. 'Well,' I said, 'I don't know, with your airfare and everything—'

" 'Oh, don't worry about that,' he interrupted, 'I'll just work my way up there.'

"The closer we got to the Fourth of July, the more excited I became. I was certain that this was going to be one of the greatest things ever seen in our old Metropolitan Stadium. As soon as the Captain got into town, we started preparing for the show. 'Normally I use four sticks of dynamite,' he explained to me. 'I lie in the box and put a lot of paper all around me. When dynamite explodes, the force blows outward, so I'm perfectly safe. You don't have to worry about me at all.'

"I heard him say that, and I don't know exactly what got into me, but suddenly I heard myself saying, 'Well, Captain, as long as there's no danger . . . I mean, this is the big leagues. I realize you've worked all over, but have you ever worked in the big leagues before?'

" 'No,' he admitted, 'I haven't.'

" 'Yeah, I didn't think so. Well, let me tell you, the big leagues is different than anywhere else and, in all honesty, I just don't know if you could really consider four sticks of dynamite big league. I mean, we really want a loud explosion. Just a great big bang, louder than anything you've ever heard before. That's what big league fans expect.'

"The Captain didn't even hesitate. 'Is eight sticks enough?'

" 'Sounds great to me.'

"I just couldn't believe this whole thing. The Fourth of July arrived and we had a full stadium. Just before we started our traditional fireworks display, I brought on the Captain. He wheeled his coffin out near second base and began loading the eight sticks of dynamite. I had hired a medical team and an ambulance to help build the tension, and I put them on the field behind first base. Finally the Captain was ready. With a great big wave to the fans he climbed inside the box. Then the fans joined the countdown: Ten . . . nine . . . eight . . . seven . . . It was at about seven that a strange thought occurred to me: I've actually hired a man to blow himself up with eight sticks of dynamite.

"*Eight* sticks of *dynamite*!

". . . three . . . two . . . one . . . KAAAABOOOO-MMMM! The entire ballpark shook. Scraps of wood and paper that the Captain had stuffed into the box shot into the air. A press-box window that had been stuck open for years suddenly slammed down. People living a mile away thought something had crashed in their front yards. Some fans in the ballpark claimed they didn't hear again for weeks.

"I was standing behind first base with the medical crew, waiting for the smoke to clear and the Captain to pop out of the splintered remains of his box. And waiting. There was a lot of smoke, an awful lot of smoke. I looked at one of the medical technicians standing nearby. 'Don't worry,' I said as confidently as possible, 'he's fine.'

"The technician shrugged, and shifted his weight to his other foot.

" 'I'm sure he's okay.' The smoke finally cleared, the Captain did not pop up. The Captain did not seem to be moving at all. *Oh, my God*, I thought, *I've killed him*.

"The stadium was still vibrating as I started walking toward the hole in the middle of the field. Eight sticks, I kept thinking, I had to tell him eight sticks. I couldn't be satisfied with four sticks. As I reached the remains of the box, I screamed, 'It's okay, Captain, you can get up now.' The man did not move. The man laid there, dead still.

"I bent down over him. His eyes were closed, a thin trickle of blood was coming out of his mouth. Eight sticks, I thought, couldn't I have said six? 'It's okay, Captain,' I yelled again. 'You can get up now.'

"Finally, after what seemed like an eternity, he blinked a few times, then opened his eyes. He turned to me, cleared his throat, and asked softly, 'Was that loud enough?'

"Since we moved into the Metrodome I've thought about having the Captain back, but I don't think we can. With our pressurized roof, Captain Dynamite is one performer who can literally blow the roof off."

Naturally not all promotions are appropriate for every city. If Captain Dynamite blew himself up in Yankee Stadium, for example, people would think he was just another New Yorker having a good time. Either that or George Steinbrenner disposing of another manager.

The appeal of certain promotions is obvious. I can certainly understand the success of Twins Paper Airplane Day, for example. On Paper Airplane Day prize circles are indicated on the field and a brand-new Mercedes, with one window open, is parked near second base. Fans buy paper airplanes for fifty cents apiece and sail them from the stands onto the field. Prizes are awarded according to where the planes land. All proceeds from the sale of the paper planes go to the National Kidney Foundation, which received $62,000 from two Days in 1985. The Mercedes was hit seven times, but no one managed to land a plane inside the car.

I can understand the folksy appeal of Towel Night. One minor league team simply ran out of towels, so any fan donating a new or used towel to the team got into the park for half price. The success of Towel Night led to Chewing-Tobacco Night, on which any fan donating a stick of chewing tobacco got in for half price. The catch there was that the chewing tobacco had to be new.

I can understand the humorous appeal of Ashley Whippet World Finals, a Frisbee competition for dogs and their owners, or Jackson and Oconomowoc Night, on which residents of those Wisconsin towns come to the ballpark. I can understand the appeal of Charlie Daniels in concert, and I can even understand the appeal of French's Bold and Spicy Mustard Helmet Weekend. But as far as I am concerned, there is no rational explanation for the success of Cow Chip Throwing Contests. I don't even understand why people would want to throw them, much less why other people would want to watch people throwing them. I think that the only thing worse than being a competitor or a spectator at a cow chip throwing contest would be being a target.

Umpires are sensitive about being a target.

There are some promotions that feature the fans

themselves. One of the most successful of these is the
New York Mets' Banner Day. When the Mets were
born, fans began bringing homemade banners to Shea
Stadium. Initially the Mets discouraged this. But when
they realized these banners were helping create the
image of the team as lovable losers rather than just
losers, they began encouraging them. This was eventually institutionalized into Banner Day, their most
popular annual event. Among the most memorable
have been TO ERR IS HUMAN, TO FORGIVE IS A METS FAN,
and when Ed Kranepool was an eighteen-year-old rookie,
someone asked IS ED KRANEPOOL OVER THE HILL? and in
honor of general manager Don Grant, on the day Shea
opened, WELCOME TO GRANT'S TOMB.

Most teams acknowledge the support of their fans
with an end-of-the-season Fan Appreciation Day, at
which small gifts are given away. They do not appreciate the fans enough to let them in the ballpark at a
lowered admission cost, however. But in perhaps the
worst public relations gesture of all time, Charlie Finley,
responding to the fact that his Oakland A's had drawn
only about 400,000 people throughout the season, simply canceled Fan Appreciation Day.

The success of the Chicken as a gate attraction
has caused other baseball teams to create their own
mascots. Mascots are not new. Teams in every sport
had mascots when I was growing up, usually adorable
lions or tigers or bears or, at Syracuse, an orange. The
Brooklyn Dodgers hired circus clown Emmett Kelly as
Sad Willie the Tramp, the perfect mascot for a team
known as "Dem Bums." What is new is the type of
mascot most often seen today. What's a Yoopie? Who
is Twinkie the Loon? Can the Bleecher Creecher be
stopped? Mascots today are strange-looking creatures
with furry skin, weird faces, bizarre bodies, and peculiar legs. Basically they look a lot like umpire Kenny
Kaiser.

Next to the Chicken, baseball's best known creature mascot is Philadelphia's Phillie Phanatic. Phil
was created by the design firm of Wade Harrison and
Bonnie Erickson. The Phillies wanted the Phanatic to

resemble the consummate fan, so Harrison and Erickson gave him a furry skin, a huge bottom, an outsized head, a megaphone snout, and a silly walk. Which also sounds like Kenny Kaiser.

David Raymond, a college phys ed major, whose previous part-time jobs with the Phillies included collecting cow chips for the Cow Chip Throwing Contest, was asked to become the Phanatic. "I wasn't sure I wanted to do it," he remembers, "but my father, University of Delaware football coach Tubby Raymond, pointed out that if someone else took the job and did something special with it, I'd kick myself for not taking the chance. 'Shoot,' he told me, 'if you get inside and it's a big flop, nobody's gonna know who you are. But nobody knows who you are anyway.' So that advice, plus the twenty-five dollars a game the Phillies offered me, convinced me to try it."

The original costume cost two thousand dollars to create. "I remember the first time I saw it," David says. "It had a personality just hanging there on the rack.

"I'll never forget the Phanatic's first appearance at the stadium. The Phillies had announced that a special guest was going to appear at the park that night. The rumor was that Frank Sinatra was going to sing the National Anthem. The fans were all waiting for him. Suddenly this green creature walks onto the field. They didn't know what I was, but they knew I wasn't Frank Sinatra. They were pretty disappointed. Philadelphia fans can be pretty tough; they've been known to boo the National Anthem, so you really don't want to disappoint them if you can help it.

"I went onto the field again in the fifth inning. I didn't quite have control of the costume, so I accidentally knocked over a member of the grounds crew. Then, when I turned around, I tripped and fell over. That's it, I thought, first I'm not Sinatra, then I'm clumsy. I'm finished. But then I realized that everybody in the stands was standing up and cheering. They loved it, they thought that that was just the way the Phanatic should act. I realized then that no matter what I did, the fans in Philadelphia were going to love him."

Although Phillie Phanatic idolizes the Chicken, and considers him to be his surrogate father, or mother, he has developed an entirely different performance personality. Phil often rides around Veterans Stadium on a three-wheeled off-the-road vehicle or skates from section to section on roller skates. The Phanatic on roller skates is about as graceful as me in a ballet. He also is an accomplished ballpark dancer, and his numbers with rotund umpire Eric Gregg have been featured on national television. Eric, in fact, refers to the Phanatic as "the creature who made me what I am today." I'm told that the Phanatic refers to Eric in exactly the same way.

The Phanatic is a feisty mascot, often doing things like stealing a female fan's pocketbook and bringing it down to the field as a gift for Steve Garvey. His annual birthday party draws thousands of well-wishers to Veterans Stadium, as well as attracting other local mascots like the Philadelphia 76ers' Big Shot, the Philadelphia Eagles' Birdbrain, and, in the past, the Philadelphia Fever soccer team's Soccero.

In addition to working all home games, the Phanatic makes over three hundred charitable and commercial appearances a year at such events as corporate sales meetings, company picnics, private parties, charity benefits, children's hospitals, and parades. He has starred in a fire safety film and has made special guest appearances with the Philadelphia Orchestra and ballet. Because of his tremendous popularity, the Phanatic is currently booked two years in advance for bar mitzvahs.

That's where he and Kaiser go their separate ways. Kaiser's available on about twenty minutes' notice.

Numerous other baseball creatures besides the Phanatic and Kaiser have appeared in the past few years, each with its own unique appeal. The Baltimore Oriole Bird, for example, can blow smoke out of its ears. Although famed for his remarkable dancing ability, once, while appearing at a bar mitzvah, Bird slipped on a highly waxed dance floor and slid safely into the dessert table, ending up with the party cake on his beak.

Toronto's B. J. Birdy replaced Chum Chicken, who was fired after a single appearance. Birdy may well be the clumsiest of all mascots. He has crashed into fences, broken chairs and once, while attempting to kiss a female fan, opened his beak and accidentally swallowed her wig.

Originally the Twins' mascot was going to be the Minnesota Mosquito, but apparently they couldn't make the costume large enough. Instead, team owner Calvin Griffith decided upon Twinkie the Loon. Twinkie the Loon. That just doesn't sound like something an adult should say. The Twins actually had a contest to name their mascot. That was the *winning* name.

The loon is the state bird, known for its dramatic call, which the mascot was able to duplicate. Twinkie, who had a three-year career before going into permanent hibernation, juggled, did magic tricks, popped Ping-Pong balls in and out of his mouth, and rode around both the old and new ballparks on his Loonacycle. Many mascots have problems with fans trying to pull their feathers or twist their heads off, which is why they are usually accompanied by a mascot securityman, but when Twinkie first appeared, a fan bit him on his beak and wouldn't let go. Nearby fans started shouting, "Kill the chicken," which caused Twinkie's wife to yell back, "That's not a chicken, that's a loon. And he's my husband, so shut up!"

Once Twinkie's outfit was missing for three weeks, and everyone assumed some lunatic had kidnapped it. It turned out to have been left hanging behind the door in public relations director Tom Mee's office. Unfortunately, when anyone came into the office to search for the outfit, they opened the door.

In Houston, Astrojack and Astrodillo, creatures vaguely resembling a rabbit and an armadillo, replaced mascot Chester Charger, a cavalryman on a horse. Chester was not actually a cavalryman on a horse, he was a plaster of paris mold of a horse and rider that fit over a performer, whose head stuck through. Only in Texas, where the West was won, would they use a plaster of paris horse.

I always loved the Cleveland Duck. There was a reason to have a loon in Minnesota and an oriole in Baltimore and a rabbit in Texas, but a duck in Cleveland? Actually the Duck was an unofficial mascot who roamed in the stands. Now, honestly, wouldn't you love to meet the person who dressed up as a duck and went to Cleveland Indian games? The Indians' official mascot was Chief Wahoo, who was replaced by a bird named Tom E. Hawk when American Indians complained about Chief Wahoo's image. Tom E. Hawk was then replaced by Basebug, a round-bodied creature whose head was basically a large Cleveland Indian cap, with its brim extended to become a beak. Mostly Basebug looked a lot like a duck.

Basebug took his name from major league baseball's "baseball fever" public relations campaign. Supposedly if Basebug bit you, you got "baseball fever." Most people I know would have gotten an attorney. Unfortunately, fans kept trying to bite him. He was hit on the head with a baseball bat, parts of his costume were torn off, and New York Yankee owner George Steinbrenner complained about his antics to the league office. Basebug was exterminated eventually.

For all those people who believe a mascot has no use other than entertaining fans, there is the story of the Tacoma Tiger. The Tiger mascot is, obviously, a performer in a tiger suit. But one night their manager, Ed Nottle, was thrown out of the game by the umpire. A few innings later observant fans might have noticed the tiger dancing happily near the bullpen. But when the tiger got close enough, he whispered to relief pitcher Dave Heaverlo, "Start warming up." Ed Nottle, Heaverlo realized, was a manager in tiger's costume. The "real" tiger had taken Nottle's place in the third base coach's box.

Not many people know that the Yankees once had a mascot. He was named Dandy, and his body was

covered with a pinstriped furry wool Yankee uniform—
making him a dyed-in-the-wool Yankee fan. He had a
big round nose, a large mustache that he could unfurl,
and a hat that spun around. He looked amazingly like
Yankee relief pitcher Sparky Lyle. Maybe he was even
a little better-looking than Sparky.

Dandy was created by Harrison and Erickson in
1980. A contest was held to name the character. The
winning entry was supposed to be selected by a computer on the basis of uniqueness, but "unique" in
computer language means infrequently. So the computer picked out names that were suggested only once.
The winning entry was some fan's full name. Since it
really wouldn't serve the Yankees to have a mascot
named Frank Biondo, José Rodriguez, or Albert Williams, Dandy was chosen from the song title "Yankee
Doodle Dandy."

Dandy was scheduled to make his first appearance at Yankee Stadium in 1980. A performer had
been hired; the announcement had been made. But
two days before Dandy was to make his debut, Basebug
irritated George Steinbrenner, who complained, "These
characters are ridiculous. They don't belong in a
ballpark."

· Months later Dandy was once again scheduled to
make his debut at Yankee Stadium. Harrison and Erickson sat proudly in Mr. Steinbrenner's private box,
waiting for their creation to appear. They never saw
him. As it turned out, Dandy had been banished to
the distant upper stands, as far away from that private
box as he could be while still being in Yankee Stadium. He was not permitted on the field.

After two seasons the Yankees decided to elimi-
nate Dandy's security guard from the payroll. Wade
Harrison got a call from the performer inside Dandy,
who explained, "My mother is afraid of what will
happen if they take away my security."

"We thought his mother was absolutely correct,"
Harrison said. So Dandy was sent to live in a cardboard box in the basement of Harrison and Erickson's

office. In 1985 he was cut into little strips and put to sleep.

Dandy was the least successful of the Harrison and Erickson characters. Ribbie, a large magenta creature with a long snout, big fat body, and fireplug legs, and Roobarb, his opposite, have become extremely popular with Chicago White Sox fans. Ribbie, however, once had a bit of a problem with Kenny Kaiser, who proceeded to tie his nose in a knot and pick him up. The argument had something to do with a case of mistaken identity.

Youppi, the Montreal mascot created by Harrison and Erickson, can wiggle his nose and move his ears. The Expos wanted a name that would work for both their French- and English-speaking fans, so they called him "Yoopie," which means nothing in either language.

Not all mascots are creatures. Some are people who dress in costume. In Milwaukee, for example, Bernie Brewer, a little old brewmeister, used to stay on a platform in center field. When a Brewer player hit a home run, Bernie would slide down a pole into a barrel of beer. In 1970, Bernie's rookie season, the Brewers put a trailer on the platform and announced that Bernie would live up there until more than 40,000 fans showed up for a game. It gets pretty cold in Milwaukee in the winter, and it looked bad for Bernie. Months passed before the attendance goal was achieved.

Opposition teams believed Bernie stole their catcher's signals from that platform. He wore white gloves and supposedly, if his gloved hands were visible, the pitcher was throwing a breaking ball. If they were not visible, it was a fastball. The only thing I wondered about was what did he do if he missed the catcher's signal?

Bernie was recently replaced by a one-million-dollar speaker system set on top of a tower in center field. The system works fine—unless there is a wind blowing out of the park. If there is a wind blowing out of the park, fans inside the park can't hear. "However," one fan told me, "I live five blocks from here and when the wind is blowing in the right direction, I can hear it from my house."

"Me too," a second fan added, "and I live in Appleton, and that's 30 miles away from here."

The Atlanta Braves probably have had more mascots than any team in either league. The Bleecher Creecher is a character who looks like the ghost of Pac-Man and walks around the stands. Chief Knock-A-Homa, an American Indian in authentic costume, and his assistant, Princess Win-Alota, perform on the field and near their tepee.

Chief Knock-A-Homa is a Chippewa Indian named Levi Walker, Jr. The Chippewa translation of his name is "there he goes walking," a good name for a mascot, a bad name for a pitcher. During games he usually stays near his tepee, signing autographs for young fans or leading cheers for the Braves. Off the field he makes numerous personal appearances. During a drought in 1980, for example, a local TV station asked him to do a rain dance in their parking lot. "I did it at four o'clock in the afternoon," he remembers. "Although there had been no prediction of rain, by six o'clock it was pouring buckets.

"When some citizens of Huntsville, Alabama, heard about that, they invited me to do my rain dance there too. They were having a very bad time, it was one hundred and five or six degrees every day, their crops were dying, grass and trees were turning yellow. So I went to a shopping mall at noon to hand out autographed photographs of the players and do my traditional rain dance. There was no prediction of rain there, either, but by the time I got back home, it was raining in Huntsville.

"Two or three days later the local TV station wanted to tape me doing my dance at the ballpark. Once again there was no prediction of rain. But as soon as I finished dancing, the sprinkler system went on.

"I don't know if I had anything to do with that one. There is no such thing as a traditional Indian sprinkler system dance."

Princess Win-Alota is a recent addition to the tepee. The Braves held a contest to name her, and among the suggestions were Scora-mora, Wina-pennant, Poca-single, Poca-double, and Knock-a-homer. The suggestions might have been much worse. If she were in Minnesota, for example, they might have named her Princess the Loon.

Without doubt the worst mascot of all time was the San Francisco Giants' Crazy Crab. Until Crazy Crab, the Giants had never had an official mascot, although a number of fans had auditioned for the job. One fan showed up repeatedly at Candlestick Park dressed as a penguin, calling himself Foggy the Penguin. Someone else came dressed in a large shrimp costume, claiming to be Scampi the Giant Shrimp. A fifty-year-old woman created an ant outfit in her quest to become the Gi-Ant. None of these self-proclaimed mascots caught the attention of Giants fans, which makes you wonder what normal people were wearing.

But in 1983 a marketing firm hired by the Giants, Freeman Marketing, realized that it was futile to try to convince Giants fans they were going to have a warm and wonderful evening at Candlestick Park. They were going to freeze out there, and every fan knew it. "What we were finally admitting," admitted Giants director of business operations Pat Gallagher, "was that it took a special interest to come out to Candlestick. Rather than inviting people to the ballpark, we dared them to show up."

During the 1983 season the Giants awarded a small medal, the Croix de Candlestick, to any fan who stayed through an entire night game. In 1984 they decided to do something different. "We wanted to emphasize the fact that Giant fans had to be the most dedicated in baseball to attend a night game at Candlestick," explains John Crawford of Freeman Marketing. "And that true Giants fans would never be fooled by the same silly things that attracted fans in other cities, things as mundane as a costumed figure running around the field. That's when Crazy Crab was born.

"We started by taking a poll. Admittedly it was sort of rigged. We asked, 'If the Giants had a mascot, would you boo it?' Who had ever heard of booing a mascot? Sixty-three percent of the people we questioned said they would. We had planted the idea.

"Originally Crazy Crab was going to appear only on television and radio commercials. We didn't even consider putting him on the field. The television spot showed a reluctant Crazy Crab being pushed onto the field by his pushy manager. 'They love it in Pittsburgh,' the manager is telling Crazy. 'They love it in Atlanta.'

" 'Maybe,' Crazy responds, 'but Giants fans are different.'

" 'Believe me,' the manager assures him, 'they'll love it here too.' The next scenes show Crazy Crab being booed by fans, shunned by small children, and threatened by Giants manager Frank Robinson. In the final scene Crazy Crab is walking down a long ramp, his claws sagging as his manager shakes his head and says in a bewildered voice, 'But they love it in Atlanta.'

"The radio commercials featured a feisty Crazy Crab explaining that he had worked his way up to San Francisco. He had started in the Caribbean, he explained, where he was known as Loco Langouste, or Crazy Lobster, then studied in Montreal where, as Frenchy the Friendly Frog, he had served as Yoopie's understudy. San Francisco was his first opportunity to be the number-one mascot, and he had expected to be loved. The reaction of Giants fans had shocked and angered him. Then he became a nasty old crab and started bad-mouthing the fans and players. The commercial ended with Crazy Crab hoping that Giants pitcher Mike Krukow would be shelled on opening day.

"The campaign was so successful that we began to wonder what would happen if Crazy Crab actually showed up at a game. So a week into the season we decided to test it. Giants' owner Bob Lurie was really nervous; he hated mascots and was afraid Giants fans might like Crazy Crab and he'd be stuck with him.

"He didn't have to worry. Unannounced, Crazy Crab walked onto the field. The reaction was incredible. People instantly hated him. They started booing, they started throwing things at him. It was terrific.

"Crazy Crab became the mascot it was okay to hate. Every time he appeared on the field the entire crowd would start booing and screaming at him to get off the field. We had to give him a helmet to wear in case someone threw something from the upper deck. Little children would hit him, pull his claws, or run away from him. Players would throw the resin bag at him, one of them even picked him up and body-slammed him to the ground. If he went too close to the groundskeepers, they turned their hoses on him.

"The Crab was wonderful. The more things people did to him, the more indignant he became, waving his claws at them in a threatening manner, so they did even more things to him. He had become the Rodney Dangerfield of mascots.

"He wasn't particularly good at being a mascot either. Because he had claws rather than hands, he couldn't do anything that required manual dexterity. For example, someone sent him a scooter and he tried to ride it, but he couldn't operate the hand brake and almost killed himself.

"The local radio stations began inviting him onto their talk shows. On these shows Crazy Crab responded to the treatment he was receiving by bad-mouthing Giants fans and players. 'The fans are animals,' he said, describing them as crude, stupid, and uninformed. As far as the players went, he said, they didn't go far enough to please him. He claimed to have seen better arms on furniture than he did on Giants players. Finally he admitted that his real ambition was to go to Los Angeles, where people appreciated personalities.

"He didn't have too many defenders. A few women were sympathetic and small kids would call radio stations telling Crazy Crab not to give up. But it really wasn't easy to defend him; he had become a nasty old crab.

"The campaign was more effective than we anticipated. We had made our point, that Giants fans were too sophisticated to fall for a silly act by a performer in a costume, but what we had not anticipated was that some people began to take the whole thing seriously. One night Crazy Crab had to come into the ballpark from left field, which meant he had to walk in front of the left-field bleachers. The fans who sit out there in those bleachers are rough enough on warm days, but this was a cold night and they were fortified against the weather. As soon as Crazy Crab got within throwing distance, they started throwing everything they could get their hands on at him. Bottles, cans, game programs, beer and soda containers, someone even threw a bunch of carrots at him. It was obvious we had created the Frankenstein mascot.

"Things got worse. Anti—Crazy Crab T-shirts began appearing. I think we had a few really nasty letters. We did have some requests for appearances outside the ballpark, but naturally we were afraid to send him out. Crazy Crab had to be wary of traps."

That August, Pat Gallagher was sitting with the Crab in the dressing room before a game. "I don't remember exactly what we were talking about, but suddenly he looked up at me and asked in complete seriousness, 'You don't think anyone out there has a gun, do you?' I knew it was time to end it.

"I wanted to have a party on the field and give each fan who attended a walkaway crab cocktail. It would have been a fitting end to Crazy Crab, the first time in history the fans ended up eating the mascot. Instead, we just put him in cold storage."

Once you've seen a man dressed as a chicken being cheered by thousands of fans, and once you've seen a man wearing a crab costume become an endangered species, and once you've seen the Cleveland Duck, there is a tendency to believe you've seen every conceivable mascot. Obviously that's not true. For example, I've never seen a large fly. A fly is a perfect mascot for a baseball team. He would be round, like a ball, and called Fly Ball. And I've never seen an ancient poet mascot, who, obviously, would be called

Homer. And, most surprising of all, I've never seen a ghost.

Superstition plays an important role in baseball. "If I'm sitting a certain way and something positive happens," concedes White Sox manager Tony LaRussa, "I'm not going to move. But if something negative happens, then maybe I'll uncross my legs, stand up, and walk around.

"Once I was ejected from a game in Chicago against the Yankees and had to watch the rest of the game from the runway between our dugout and clubhouse. There were a lot of people in our dugout blocking my view, so although I could see the batter, I couldn't see Tom Seaver, our pitcher. But every inning he was getting them out one, two, three, so that didn't matter. Then, in the top of the eighth inning, the Yankees began rallying. I watched Seaver, but I couldn't figure out what he was doing wrong. Then it dawned on me—I was watching him. I could see him! It was my fault. I immediately told my pitching coach, Dave Duncan, to stand in front of me so that I couldn't see Seaver. As soon as he did that, Seaver struck out Dave Winfield to get out of the jam.

"Basically that's what managing is all about."

Almost every major league player, manager, and umpire has some superstition. Some managers won't step on the foul line when going onto the field, others won't go onto the field without stepping on it. There are players who won't change their clothes when they're on a hot streak. The Red Sox's Wade Boggs, for example, eats chicken before every game and steps onto the field for pregame practice at exactly the same time every night. There are some pitchers, Tommy John, for example, who believe it is bad luck to go out to the mound without a sharpened object of some kind. For some reason I have had bad luck with all short people named Earl Weaver.

Most baseball people will deny that they are superstitious, then they'll knock on wood three times, twirl their caps around their head twice while facing east, and mention the one exception. Or two. Or three.

Professional baseball requires such incredible skill, and luck, to succeed, that every player I've ever seen will do anything to gain the slightest advantage. When players come to the plate, for example, they always go through the exact same routine to prepare themselves. It's not superstition, they insist, just habit. They may be hitting .206, but they wouldn't dare break that habit. Why? They might not be able to hit. So with all the habits and lucky charms I've seen in the big leagues, it's surprising that no team has adopted a ghost as its mascot.

With its great tradition of legend and lore, in fact, baseball doesn't seem to have any ghosts. I've never been in or heard of a haunted ballpark. The only story of a baseball ghost I've ever heard was told by former pitcher Bill Lee, who claimed that when he was with the Montreal Expos, the ghost of Red Sox owner Tom Yawkey appeared to him regularly at Olympic Stadium in the body of a white pigeon. This pigeon supposedly told him that Olympic Stadium was built on a fault line, and there was only one spot in the stadium that would be safe when the inevitable earthquake occurred. That spot, the pigeon continued, was between second base and right field, and if Lee stood there when the walls of the stadium came tumbling down, he would be safe.

Since no other players conferred with this pigeon, and since Lee has also been known to talk to trees, this information may not be reliable.

But even if baseball teams don't have ghosts, they do have curses, jinxes, and hexes. Probably the oldest curse of all is the Chicago Cubs' billy goat hex. It began when the Cubs won the National League pennant in 1945. The owner of a tavern near Wrigley Field, named The Billy Goat, wanted to bring his pet goat to the World Series. Cub management barred the gate, refusing to admit the old goat into the ballpark. This obviously got the tavern owner's goat, because he put a curse on the Cubs, declaring, "Until the Cubs allow a goat into Wrigley Field, they will not win a pennant."

Through the rest of the 1940s everybody laughed at the curse, although the Cubs did not win again. And through the 1950s they laughed at the curse, although the Cubs did not win again. And through the 1960s they laughed at the curse, and the Cubs still did not win. There is a rumor that in 1969, when the Cubs led the Eastern Division of the National League for much of the season, a relative of the original tavern owner offered to lift the curse if the team would allow a goat into Wrigley Field. The Cubs refused, and lost the pennant to the New York Mets.

In the 1970s they weren't exactly laughing at the curse, but they weren't taking it too seriously either. The Cubs won absolutely nothing, of course. But in 1982, when Dallas Green was named general manager of the team, practically the first thing he did was invite a descendant of the goat to the ballpark on opening day. Because the hex was so old, it was evidently rusty, because Green had to invite the goat back to the ballpark on opening day in 1983 and 1984 before the hex was lifted forever, allowing the Cubs to win the Eastern Division championship.

Other teams have been similarly cursed. Notice I'm avoiding any remarks about the Baltimore Orioles. When the Cleveland Indians fired manager Bobby Bragan in midseason 1958, Bragan supposedly walked to second base, stood there, and put a curse on the Indians. Obviously it worked. The Indians have never again come close to winning anything. Finally, in 1984, Cleveland radio station WERE hired a witch to go into the ballpark while the team was on the road to try to lift the curse. Dressed in fashionable witch's garb, this witch went through an entire ceremony on the field, then announced that the curse had been removed. "However," she cautioned, "my lawyer says that I must add that there are no guarantees in this line of work."

This was certainly not the first baseball witch. In 1975, for example, a Boston radio station had hired a witch to help the Red Sox break a long losing streak. They made her task as easy as possible—they sent her

on a road trip with the club to Cleveland. Talk about
loading a spell! The Indians countered by hiring a
good fairy to ward off the witch, but as it turned out,
that fairy wasn't any good. The Red Sox ended their
losing streak and went on to win the American League
pennant.

Putting the whammy on the Cleveland Indians is
sort of like investing in IBM; you're not exactly taking
a chance. But in 1976, when the Atlanta Braves fired
their traveling secretary, Donald Davidson, his wife,
Patti, put a hex on them. "She lit candles all over the
house," Donald remembers, "we could barely breathe
in there. But as soon as she did, the Braves started
losing, and as long as they kept losing, she didn't want
to put them out. After a week Phil Niekro, a Braves
pitcher and a good friend, called to make sure he
wasn't covered by the hex, but I had to tell him the
truth. 'Sorry, Phil,' I explained, 'but this is a full-time
curse. No exceptions.' "

The Braves eventually lost thirteen consecutive
games before the candles went out.

Nobody really believes curses and whammies have
anything to do with winning and losing baseball games.
Games are decided between the white lines, by professionals who have trained their entire lives. Superstition has nothing to do with it.

Still, I myself would not mess with Chief Knock-A-
Homa's tepee.

In 1982 the Braves were leading the Los Angeles
Dodgers by a sizable margin. In July the Dodgers were
scheduled to come to Atlanta for an important series.
Normally the tepee in left field stands is left standing
until the beginning of the professional football exhibition season. But this time, in order to make more
seats available for baseball fans, the tepee was taken
down. There were warnings that with the Braves leading the league, it was not a good idea to tempt fate,
but Braves management paid no attention.

The Braves began losing as soon as the tepee was
taken down, and continued losing. It was more than a
losing streak; it was a total collapse. Braves fans began

petitioning the team to put back the tepee. The team continued losing. Marchers paraded in front of team owner Ted Turner's television station, pleading with Turner to put back the tepee. The team continued losing. The Braves lost nineteen of twenty-one games before management agreed to put the tepee back up. Management was not saying that taking down the tepee had anything to do with the losing streak, not at all, no such thing, but just in case it did, they decided to have a complete ceremony when the tepee went back up, complete with the burning in effigy of a Dodger.

The day the tepee was put back in its place the Braves started winning again, regaining the lead and clinching the Western Division championship.

They lost the playoffs to the St. Louis Cardinals in three consecutive games. Patti Davidson's hex might have been weakening, but it hadn't expired.

So I've never seen a baseball ghost and, with the exception of a little curse in Baltimore (I couldn't resist), I've never been involved with anything more unusual than Ken Kaiser. I don't really believe any of that mumbo-jumbo at all. I feel that as long as I have good luck, none of that is necessary.

But there is just one thing that I've recently seen in a ballpark that I don't quite understand—the scoreboard in Wrigley Field. I have this basic philosophy: When things work, don't change them. You don't change a light bulb before it burns out, right? In a car, for example, the two things that never caused any problems were the floor switch that operated the bright lights, and the horn. Then somebody decided to move these two things. To turn on the bright lights now you have to push or pull levers—if you can find them. To honk the horn you have to push in a turn signal or find the half square inch on the steering wheel where it's been hidden. Most people who have new cars find themselves pounding the steering wheel waiting to hear the horn, and instead hear *thud! thud! thud!* Scoreboards are the same thing.

As a fan I've learned how important scoreboard

watching at the ballpark can be. In the old days scoreboards informed people in the ballpark who was at bat, what position he played, maybe what he was batting, what the score of the game and the count on the batter was, what inning the game was in, and what the scores of all the out-of-town games were, sometimes inning by inning. Today scoreboards are multimillion-dollar television sets that are constantly flashing basic information on and off, or asking some silly quiz question that can usually be answered by knowing who the batter is, or showing a picture of the batter that often looks like it was taken by a drug-crazed police photographer. If you believe the scoreboard in Milwaukee, for example, baseball players have no foreheads. The worst thing is that the scores of out-of-town games are flashed on and off every seven or eight seconds, meaning that if you miss the score of a game you're interested in, you've got to wait through the entire cycle of other games before it comes up again. And usually, by the time that happens, I've taken my eyes off the scoreboard to call a vendor, and I've got to watch the cycle again.

Except in Wrigley Field. They still have the old style scoreboard in Wrigley Field. There are no pictures on this scoreboard; while other teams show you highlights, the Cubs tell you highlights. For example, a sign beneath the scoreboard will *describe* Don Larsen's World Series no-hitter. But the one thing that this old scoreboard can do is give the fans the progress of every out-of-town game inning by inning. But there is one thing, one small thing, that I don't quite understand.

The Cubs play only day games; everybody else plays at night. There *are* no out-of-town scores to put up there.

THE PLAYER'S THE THING

Although I do kid about my exploits, I'm proud to say that I haven't failed at absolutely everything I've tried. For example, my weight gain program has been a huge success. The bankruptcy went very well. I've got the car running again. I've been able to stay unemployed since being fired by NBC. As a fan I haven't been ejected from a single ballpark. The books I've written have been best sellers, and have been published in one language. And Ron Luciano's Baseball Game will soon be available in smart shops everywhere.

Some people get buildings named after them. Others get bridges and airports and stadiums. Casey Stengel got a deli. I get a cardboard box. Ron Luciano's Baseball Game, comes in a genuine cardboard box. It's actually two different games, one involving the use of strategy, the other a knowledge of the rules. The first time I played these games I won the rules version, but lost in strategy. Do you have any idea what it feels like to lose your own game?

Not many people are honored by having their name put on a game. Even Abner Doubleday, the

inventor of the game of baseball, didn't put his name
on it. Of course, if he had, the Yankees would be a
famous Doubleday team. Presidents of the United States
don't get games named after them. Movie stars don't
have their own games. Even Pulitzer prize–winning
author Norman Mailer doesn't have a game, and he's
even invented one.

Years ago, I've been told, the author of such mon-
umental books as *The Naked and the Dead* and *The
Executioner's Song* invented a baseball board game
which he called Norman Mailer's Cardball. Supposedly
he drew the baseball field on which the game was
played on a piece of cardboard, and colored it with
crayons. This, of course, is nothing like Ron Luciano's
Baseball Game, which is on fine quality cardboard and
has a multicolored field printed in actual ink. Norman
Mailer's Cardball was played by turning over cards
that read "single" or, more creatively, "double," which
then entitled the player to move his little plastic man
one base or two bases.

It was not a very complicated game.

Norman Mailer informed his literary agent that
he had invented a board game and asked him to try to
sell it. This senior agent told a junior agent in his
office to play the game with its creator. So the young
agent and Norman Mailer went into an office and
started playing Cardball. About an hour later the junior agent staggered out of that office and was asked
by the curious senior agent how the game was. "Great,"
replied the junior agent, "I'm winning 16–12, but it's
only the second inning."

Eventually the senior agent submitted Cardball to
one of the largest game manufacturers in the country,
with a letter explaining that it had been created by the
distinguished author Norman Mailer, winner of a Pulitzer prize, a National Book Award, certainly one of
the most important creative artists in the world.

The game came back by return mail. "Dear Senior Agent," the manufacturer responded, "thank you
for the submission of Mr. Miller's game, but . . ."

They don't kid around in the world of games.

Besides my game, the only thing I've really been successful at is writing. My two previous books, *The Umpire Strikes Back* and *Strike Two*, which I liked to call *Return of the Deadeye*, were both best sellers. People who knew me were surprised I could write a book. People who *really* knew me were surprised I could read a book. But in 1982, the year *Umpire* was published, it sold more hardcover copies than *Gone with the Wind* did. Admittedly *Gone with the Wind* had already been in bookstores for forty-four years.

The success of *Umpire* prompted my publisher to ask me to write the second half of my autobiography. The subsequent success of *Strike Two* caused the publisher to ask me to write the third half of my autobiography. This is where my real problem came in: Just when I'd finally found something I could do without putting someone out of business, I ran out of my own life.

I just didn't have any stories left to tell. I couldn't even make any good stories up. I considered writing a how-to book because how-to books are very popular. But the only thing I have really ever been very good at is failing, which caused me to wonder, if you write a book entitled *How to Fail*, and it fails, is it a success? I was told that travel books were popular, so I considered writing a travel book, but realized there probably isn't too large an audience for *Visiting Exciting Endicott, New York*. I looked at the best-seller list and saw two cookbooks listed. Yeah, I thought, I'll write a cookbook, but my editor, Peter Guzzardi, quietly pointed out that in my case it would have to be an eat book. That left me with only one possible solution— since I'd run out of my own life, I simply had to steal other people's life stories. The question became, whose?

And then it struck me: During the decade I spent at my major league calling, it became obvious to me that the not-so-great players were having just as much fun as the superstars. Sometimes, in fact, they seemed to be having more fun, perhaps because, since everyone realized they weren't stars, there was little pressure on them to star. These were the players who struggled to get to the big leagues, who lived one error or one strikeout from the minors. Players whose baseball card might read "This is Ted's tenth major league season. Why?" These were my kind of players, players who wondered about records like "What player has watched the most games from the bench?" Players that fans would look at and say "If that guy can play in the big leagues, I certainly can be a success in my business."

The players I liked best were the journeymen, people who were never going to be paid a lot of money to endorse products, but without whom there would be no major league baseball. Take Tom Paciorek, please. At least five major league teams have. Tom "Wimpy" Paciorek is one of the nicest people in baseball. He wouldn't hurt an umpire. Tom Paciorek has spent almost fourteen seasons in the major leagues, more than Joe DiMaggio or Sandy Koufax, as many as Fred "Chicken" Stanley. He was even on a first-name basis with many superstars; when he was with the Dodgers, for example, Steve Garvey often permitted him to call him Steve. Tom has played in an All-Star game, he's been in league championship playoffs in both leagues, he's played in a World Series. He has had as many memorable and humorous experiences as any major league superstar, but has any publisher asked him to write his memoirs? Noooo. Publishers want superstars. They want Steve Garvey to write *his* autobiography. They want Tom Paciorek to buy Steve Garvey's autobiography. They claim there are simply not enough people willing to buy *The Wimpy Story* to make it worthwhile to publish.

So my publisher, I realized, wanted me to write a third best seller, and I had no more to tell. That same publisher did not want Tom Paciorek to write his autobiography and Tom had quite a bit to tell. Somewhere in that equation I knew there was a perfect fit.

If Tom Paciorek was not well known enough to write his own autobiography, I decided, he was certainly good enough to have his own chapter. In this book I've asked some of my favorite players, people I consider "good guys," to write at least part of their autobiography. Doing this has allowed me to accomplish my two major objectives: first, give some recognition to deserving players and, second, complete this book without working very hard.

In selecting the players whose autobiographies would be included in this very select group, I wanted people who share my deep love for the game of baseball, people who played hard on the field, when they got to play, and had fun off the field. People who weren't playing with a fully padded glove, if you know what I mean. In addition, they had to be willing to work cheap.

After convincing these players that the publicity they would receive for writing their autobiographies was far more important than mere money, I sat and talked with each of them for a substantial length of time. Much more than 15–20 minutes. Then I took their words and helped transform them into autobiographies that briefly described their careers. For example, I spoke to one of the least known "Boys of Summer," Brooklyn Dodger catcher Dick Teed. Dick played for the Dodgers in 1953, and wrote warmly of his major league experience:

MY LIFE IN THE BIG LEAGUES
by Dick Teed

I got up. I struck out. I sat down.

Perhaps that is not the best autobiography to begin with, but it does explain how the following chapters were written. Naturally I was glad to find something I could do well. As long as I had my tape recorder, and the cooperation of the player, it was very easy. There was absolutely nothing that could go wrong.

Well, maybe there was one thing:

THE INDIAN TAKES THE BRONX

by Ron Hassey

Had the tape recorder worked, catcher Ron Hassey would have described how exciting it had been for him to come from the Cleveland Indians to the New York Yankees, become the Yankee regular catcher when Butch Wynegar got hurt, hit some vital game-winning home runs during the Yankee pennant drive, and finish the season as a Yankee star. That's what he would have written if the tape recorder had worked.

That really is too bad, because any fan who had the opportunity to sit with Ron Hassey would really enjoy it. Ron told some wonderful stories. Other players were rolling on the floor with laughter, that's how good they were. It really is a shame I couldn't get that tape recorder working. Ron, as he is known to fans, a great name, told about catching Len Barker's perfect game in 1981, about being with the Chicago Cubs during their exciting pennant drive in 1984, about the thrill of hitting his first major league home run off Nolan Ryan. And what a great story that one was.

But just because the tape recorder failed for one interview, people began hinting that I might not be so good with the play button. That maybe it was my fault that the tape recorder didn't work, rather than the entire island nation—I won't mention any names—that manufactured the tape recorder. However, except for that one failure, one small failure out of so many, every other interview and the resulting autobiographies proved to be very successful. I had no other problems, every word that every other player said was captured crisply and clearly, and transcribed into the written word.

Except for Bob Shirley.

My autobiographical team consists of fifteen people, each of whom has spent considerable time in the big leagues—except my manager, of course. My catchers are Marc "Booter" Hill and Steve Nicosia, who once didn't recognize snow. Mike Squires is my first baseman because he likes to talk to the first base umpire. Phil Garner is my second baseman because his favorite city in the world is Pittsburgh, Pennsylvania. Julio Cruz, usually a second baseman, is my shortstop because he looks like a shortstop and used to tell me that I was his favorite umpire. Darrell Evans is the third baseman because he's been in the major leagues seventeen years and people still don't realize how good he is, and because he's six-two, two hundred pounds, and he wanted to be the third baseman. Tom Paciorek is one of my outfielders because he is the greatest player ever to work for Kowalski Sausage, Thad Bosley is my second outfielder because he is the best-hitting poet-songwriter in the major leagues, and Mike Easler is my third outfielder because he may be the only player in the big leagues I can beat in a race. Milt Wilcox is my starting pitcher because his father designed what to me is one of the most important inventions in history—the modern shopping cart. Greg Minton is my relief pitcher because he admitted he almost cried when he received his first paycheck on a multimillion-dollar contract, and I can empathize with that because when I was an umpire, I'd cry when I got my paycheck too. Charlie Hough is my spot starter/long and short relief pitcher because he throws a knuckleball and my team has to have a knuckleball pitcher because I never could call that pitch a ball or a strike so I want some other umpire to suffer. Our utility player will be John Waltham. Rocky Bridges is my coach because he's Rocky Bridges. And Ray Miller is my manager because he worked for Earl Weaver and survived, and the only manager less known than him is the man he replaced, good old what's-his-name.

Naturally I am this team's biggest fan. Three hundred and six pounds.

Would we win any games? That depends entirely on what league we were playing in. But we would certainly have a good time.

LISTENING TO LUNAR TUNES

by Greg Minton

*Relief pitchers are sort of the Rambos of baseball—
they never start anything, but they're always there at
the finish. Being a relief pitcher is the worst job in
baseball. First, relief pitchers spend most of the game
sitting in the bullpen, and the bullpen is usually
situated next to the worst seats in the stadium. In
some ballparks players can barely see the field from
the bullpen. Although, considering the job of the relief pitcher, that might be intentional—they're so far
away that they usually don't know what they're getting into.*

*And second, the best relief pitchers pitch only
when the game is on the line, often when some other
pitcher has already put the tying or winning runners
on base. "There are a lot of things that go through
your head when you're coming in to relieve in a troubled spot," Yankee Hall-of-Famer Lefty Gomez once
said, "and one of them is, 'Should I spike myself?' "*

*I remember one night when Yankee manager—
former manager—manager—former manager—manager
—former manager—manager—former manager Billy Mar-*

tin brought his ace reliever Sparky Lyle in at the start
of the ninth inning. Before throwing his first pitch,
Lyle just stood behind the mound looking around the
infield. It was unusual for him to be pitching with no
runners on base. I leaned over and asked catcher
Thurman Munson, "What's wrong with him?"

"I don't know," Munson said, "maybe he's lonely."

Relief pitchers have to be a little bit crazy to
survive the daily pressure they face. The Kansas City
Royals' Dan Quisenberry once said that the main
thing he had learned from pitching in relief is that
you can't drown yourself with a shower nozzle. But
even among relief pitchers, San Francisco Giant Greg
Minton is acknowledged to be just a little bit crazier.

I can't blame him. When I first began deciding
which players I wanted to include in this book, I had
the feeling I was going to come up with a lot of
players about whom people would say, "Didn't he
used to be with Cleveland?" As it turned out, many
players who have survived a long time in the big
leagues without receiving the attention they have
earned have played in San Francisco at one time in
their career. Greg Minton has been with the Giants
his entire career.

Minton has starred as the Giants top relief pitcher
since 1979, a long time for a reliever, a longer time for
a sane person. Between the howling winds and the
howling fan, Candlestick Park is acknowledged to be
the most difficult place to pitch in the major leagues.
Roger Maris once said, "Candlestick Park was built
on the water. It should have been built under it."
"Moonman" Minton has not only survived; he has
become a star. The only problem is, nobody knows
he's a star. He's probably the best best-known unknown pitcher in baseball.

This is because night games on the West Coast
finish long after the rest of the country is asleep, and
Minton usually is pitching only at the end of the
game. The games also finish too late for the morning
papers to include their box scores. So Minton, along
with teammates like Darrell Evans and Jack Clark,

did not receive national recognition. Greg Minton doesn't seem to care about that. As far as I could determine, he doesn't even know about that.

Short relief pitchers like Minton rarely pitch more than two innings in a game, but the shortest short relief appearance I ever saw took place my first year in the big leagues. One night in Chicago, the White Sox were trailing the Orioles by a run with two out and the bases loaded in the bottom of the ninth inning. When the Orioles pitcher went to a 3–2 count on the batter, Baltimore manager Earl Weaver came out of the dugout calling for a new pitcher. Talk about coming into the game in a pressure situation. If relief pitcher Dick Hall threw one ball, the game was tied. And if he threw a pitch that was too good, the batter was liable to get a game-winning hit. "Earl," I said—we were still on speaking terms in those days—"what are you doing that for?"

He didn't even hesitate. "I don't want to lose the game on a walk," he said. I laughed to myself. You can't lose the game on a walk, Earl, I thought, a walk will only tie the score. Hall threw his first pitch down the middle of the plate, the batter hit a routine ground ball to shortstop Mark Belanger to end the game. The pitcher hadn't even had time to work up a sweat. This is what is known as short relief.

When a relief pitcher comes into a ball game, the home plate umpire is supposed to allow him eight pitches on the mound to get ready. Eight pitches, nine pitches, I never cared. I wanted to let the man get loose. Managers cared though. As soon as the pitcher made an extra pitch, they'd start screaming, "That's nine pitches, nine pitches, you can't let him do that!" as if they had discovered the secret of life. So it was nine pitches, what was I supposed to do, arrest him? Make him give one back? I can state unequivocally that I have never heard a losing manager say after the game, "I think we had the game until the umpire gave the relief pitcher that ninth pitch."

However, those warm-up pitches can cause problems. One night Lee Wyre was the home plate umpire

when Giants manager Alvin Dark brought reliever
Bill O'Dell in to pitch. After O'Dell had thrown five
warm-up pitches, Lee said politely, "That's five, you
got three more."

"Yeah," O'Dell snarled, "and you better call them
strikes, too, you !@#$%¢ !@#$%!"

Lee ejected him before he threw his sixth pitch.
Dark came running out of the dugout trying to figure
out what was going on. "He's not pitching," Lee said,
"he's out of the game."

"And what if I don't have another pitcher?" Dark
challenged.

"Then you're out of the game too," Lee finished.
Dark brought in Gaylord Perry, who took eight, and
only eight, warm-up pitches.

There were times when I would talk to pitchers
when they were warming up. Once, I remember, when
Dan Quisenberry was starting his career, he came in
to mop up after the pitcher before him had been
clobbered. As that pitcher walked off the mound, the
fans gave him a nice ovation. Quisenberry shook his
head. "Hey, Ronnie," he said, smiling, "if they liked
him, wait'll they see what I can do."

Quite often a manager will go out to the mound
and stall for time before signaling for a new pitcher.
This allows the relief pitcher to throw one, two, maybe
even three extra pitches in the bullpen. Eventually
the home plate umpire has to force the manager to
make a move.

One night I walked out to the mound to force
Royals manager Whitey Herzog to bring in his third
or fourth pitcher of that particular game. "Who you
gonna bring in, Whitey?" I asked.

He shrugged. "I might as well bring in Pattin,"
he said disgustedly. "He can hit their bats as well as
any of the others."

I always enjoyed watching relief pitchers trying
to psych themselves up while psyching out the waiting batter. The Yankees' Ryne Duren, who wore very
thick glasses, would always send his first fastball
sailing over the catcher's head, his way of warning

batters his control was not that good. Goose Gossage would stare at the batter, wrinkling his face into what looked like a large fist. Perhaps the best act of all was that of "the Mad Hungarian," Al Hrabosky. After taking his eight warm-ups, he'd go to the back of the mound, stand in silent meditation for a moment, then take the baseball in his bare hand and throw it as hard as he possibly could into his glove, and finally turn around and stomp angrily onto the mound.

But one night he went through the meditation, then took the ball in his bare hand and threw it as hard as he possibly could—and missed his glove. The ball went bouncing past the third baseman. I couldn't stop laughing, which made him even angrier. I thought to myself, if that guy can't hit his glove and it's three inches away, what is he going to do when the batter is sixty feet and six inches away?

I think the only people who don't think relief pitchers are strange are other relief pitchers. Relief pitchers really believe they are normal. "Think of it this way, Ronnie," Greg Minton explained to me. "The Giants are paying me millions of dollars to pitch a few innings every couple of days." He smiled. "And they think I'm crazy!"

Call me Moonman. Or Moonie. That's the nickname I picked up during the eight long years, the eight long, long years I spent pitching in the minor leagues. People assume I was given that name because I do strange things. That's not true. I mean, I do do strange things, that's true, but that is not why I got that nickname.

It happened one day during the eight long, long years I spent as a starting pitcher in the San Francisco Giants minor league system. I'd spent the day tubing down a river just outside Phoenix, Arizona. Tubing means you lay on your stomach on an old inflatable inner tube and drift peacefully down the river. Well, it so happened that I forgot one thing—my clothes. And certain parts of my body got very badly sunburned.

The burn was so bad, in fact, that I got big ugly water blisters on that part of my body that goes over the bullpen fence last. Big blisters. Craters. So that night, when I walked into the clubhouse and started putting on my uniform, manager Rocky Bridges took one look at me and said my body had more craters than the moon. I became Moonman. Or Moonie.

I did not grow up wanting to be the righthanded relief pitcher for the San Francisco Giants. I never even thought about playing professional baseball. I wanted to do something meaningful—I wanted to be a surfer. Although I was born in Lubbock, Texas, I did most of my growing up in San Diego, California. I had a long ponytail, and I was your typical California surfer. I'd get up at 5:30 in the morning, before school, and meet my friends at the beach. After school it was "Hi, Mom. 'Bye, Mom," grab my surfboard, and hit the waves. Or, because I wasn't that great a surfer, sometimes the waves hit me first.

I played Little League, but I wasn't one of those kids constantly throwing a tennis ball against the garage or pretending to be a big leaguer. I wasn't even the best player on my high school team. It wasn't until my junior year in high school that I began to take athletics seriously. That was when my father, who was a professional gardener, told me, "Son, I'm not paying for college for you." Well, I knew brains weren't going to get me there. So I decided to try for an athletic scholarship.

I became the six-two, one hundred forty-eight-pound shortstop at San Diego Mesa Junior College. I could throw hard, I could always throw hard, but I never had any real good idea just where the ball might be going. I'd make a nice play at shortstop, then make a perfect throw into the other team's dugout. Let's put it this way: When I was at shortstop, the seats behind first base were considered a combat zone. But because I could throw hard, the Kansas City Royals made me their third selection in the January 1970 draft.

When I reported to their rookie team manager,

John Shields took me aside and said, "Son, we think you're going to be a fine pitcher someday."

Pitcher? "Uh, excuse me," I said, "I'm not a pitcher, I'm a shortstop."

He looked right at me. "You're number fourteen, right?"

I sort of twisted around and looked over my shoulder. I was number fourteen. "Yeah?"

He nodded. "You're gonna be a fine pitcher someday."

I don't know who made that decision, but it probably saved the lives of a lot of people behind first base. I pitched one game in rookie ball and the Royals sent me to the winter Instructional League in Florida. I didn't know anything about pitching. In the first game in Florida my catcher, I believe it was Bob Taylor, who later went on to burn his uniform at home plate, came out to the pitcher's mound to go over the signals. "All right," he explained, "if I put down one finger, throw a curveball, if I put down two or five fingers, that means fastball, three's a slider, four's a change-up. Got it?"

Got it? I threw one pitch, the straight fastball. I didn't know anything about those other pitches. "Sure," I said. I figured, what could happen?

So he got down behind home plate and started wiggling a lot of fingers. I wound up and threw my one pitch. It hit him right in the chest. The next thing I knew he was standing on the pitcher's mound poking fingers into my gut. Hey, it wasn't my fault, I didn't have a clue.

When Kansas City finally got around to teaching me how to throw a curveball, I fell in love with it. I mean, my curveball didn't break at all, but it was great fun trying to throw it.

I spent my first full minor league season at Waterloo, Iowa. When I was assigned there, I thought, great, Waterloo, it has to be near an ocean. It wasn't even near a water faucet. But as a starting pitcher there I won eleven games and lost six, striking out 117 batters in 124 innings. The next season, in San Jose, I struck out 153 in 178 innings. Looking back on it, imagine what I could have done down there if I had had any idea what I was doing.

One year later I was pitching for manager Rocky Bridges at the San Francisco Giants' top farm club in Phoenix, Arizona, having been traded by the Royals for catcher Fran Healy. Also two years later, three years later, four years later, and five years later. Did I mention I spent eight years in the minor leagues? That was because I had a pleasant curveball and I could throw hard, I could get it up to ninety-two, ninety-three miles per hour, but I had no movement on my fastball at all. It just came in straight. I'd throw the first one right by a batter like Steve Garvey. He'd take it, then think, oh, you mean that fastball doesn't move? Then he'd turn up the dial a little bit and the second one would go for a ride. A long ride.

I began to believe I was never going to get out of the minor leagues. If it wasn't for Rocky Bridges, there is no question in my mind I would've quit baseball. But Rocky understood that I was a little different. Okay, a lot different. That is because he is too. Rocky has all fifty-two cards, but he just keeps shuffling and shuffling. I remember one game my first year with him when I was really getting shellacked. I'd given up something like seven runs in one inning, and the bases were still loaded. Rocky came ambling slowly out to the pitcher's mound. I assumed he was going to take me out. But when he got to me, he looked me straight in the eye and said, "Listen, Moonie, I'm gonna go into my office and fill out reports. If this inning ever gets over, you come in and get me."

He would do things like that. Once, after I'd given up some tremendous shots, he came marching out to the mound and said, "Okay, gimme the ball."

I tossed it to him. He turned it over in his hand, carefully inspecting it. Then he shook his head and said, "Well, I'll be . . . it's still round." Then he flipped it back to me and went back to the dugout.

One night he put me in as a pinch runner at first base. On the first pitch the batter hit a line drive off

my kneecap. A runner hit by a batted ball while off
the base is out. Then a few weeks later he put me in
to pinch-run at second base. This time I got thrown
out at home plate trying to score on a single. Finally,
on the last day of the season, I was sitting in the
dugout thinking about going home. I wasn't even wearing spikes. Suddenly Rocky shouted, "Moonie, come
here. You're gonna pinch-run at third base."

I didn't understand. We were winning by a comfortable margin and the runner on third was faster
than I was. "Why, Rock?" I asked.

" 'Cause," he said, "if it's the last thing I do this
season, I'm gonna get you to score one time." I went
out to third base. The batter hit a ground ball to the
infield, the play was made to first base, and I came
sliding home in a cloud of dust. Wearing sneakers.

I would have to say my career as a relief pitcher
was the result of a fluke. Fluke, not flake. In 1978 the
Giants were out of options on me. If they sent me to
the minors again, I would be frozen there for the
season and they would lose their rights to me. It
didn't look like they would have much choice, though;
I just didn't have the variety of pitches needed to win
consistently in the big leagues.

In the second to last game of spring training that
year I dived for a slowly hit ball and tore the cartilage
in my knee. That turned out to be my big break, so to
speak. The Giants didn't want to send me to the
minors because they would lose me, so they put me
on the disabled list.

I was operated on, and almost immediately started
working out with weights. About five weeks later one
of the Giants coaches approached me and said, "Look,
we know the knee's not ready, but can you land on it
at all?"

"A little bit," I said.

"Good. We'd like you to start throwing batting
practice just to get your arm built up."

Fine with me. So a few days later I went out there
before the regularly scheduled game and started throwing to our batters. Mike Sadek was the catcher. Well,

after I'd thrown about six pitches, Mike came charging out to the mound. I'd been knocked out of ball games before, but getting knocked out of batting practice was something else. "Moonie," he said somewhat sarcastically, "just what do you think you're doing?"

"Uh, throwing batting practice?" I thought it was a pretty good guess.

"Yeah, well, stop kidding around," he said. "Just throw the damn thing straight so I can catch it." Then he turned around and started going back to the batting cage.

It took me a minute to realize what he was saying. "What?" I screamed at him. "What do you mean?"

"Hey," he told me, "I don't know what you're doing, but that damn ball's dropping straight down."

And that is how my major league career was born. Before getting injured I had lifted my leg very high when I delivered the ball. Because of the sore knee, I couldn't lift the leg quite as high, which forced me to land a bit farther down on the mound. Stretching out my delivery caused the ball to sink. No question about it, if I hadn't torn that cartilage, I'd be driving a milk truck today.

That was just the first lucky break. The Giants ace reliever at that time was Randy Moffitt. Just as I was getting healthy, Randy came down with an extremely rare stomach disorder. Randy trained horses at Bay Meadows in the off season, and somehow he'd caught a virus from the horses that prevented him from flying. He was only the third person in the United States to get this virus, just to show you what it took for me to get a chance.

With Moffitt unable to pitch, manager Joe Altobelli came to me and asked, "Moonie, you ever been a relief pitcher?"

Well, when you're the tenth man on a ten-man pitching staff . . . "I SURE HAVE," I told him. That dumb I'm not.

"Fine," he said, "we're gonna put Moffitt on the disabled list and you're our right-handed relief pitcher."

As soon as he walked away, I went over to our

pitching coach and asked, "What do I have to do to relieve?"

"Throw as hard as you can for two innings," he explained.

"That's it?" Why hadn't somebody told me about that sooner! And that was it. I'm still pitching relief.

I owe everything I've accomplished in baseball to that sinker. It's a pitch that starts out just like a fastball, but as it reaches the batter, it drops straight down. I don't go out there and try to fool anybody. I throw the sinker and let them try to hit it. Even if they do, most likely they are going to hit the ball on the ground. In fact, I hold the major league record for consecutive innings pitched without giving up a home run: 269⅓ innings. Dodger catcher Joe Ferguson hit a home run off me in the last appearance I made in 1978. Four seasons later, on May 2, 1982, Met catcher John Sterns hit the next home run off me. Sterns hit what is known as a high sinker—it started at his helmet and sank all the way down to his shoulders.

So if I give up a home run, I've made a very big mistake. I actually have more problems with the short ball than I do with the long ball. The sinker is a lot less effective when I'm pitching against a team that can run and we're playing the game on an artificial surface. The ball really bounces high when hit straight down on those carpets, and fast runners can often reach base before the ball comes down. The St. Louis Cardinals for instance. One time during the 1985 season I got both Vince Coleman and Willie McGee to hit one-bouncers to me—but those balls bounced so high, they should have had a stewardess on board.

Once I became a relief pitcher I learned to love it. I'd never want to be a starting pitcher again. No way would you get me out there knowing I was going to play only every four or five days. How would you like to go to school or to the office knowing you were going to have to work only one day in every four or five?

Okay, maybe I worded that question incorrectly. What I mean is that I love the feeling of coming to my office, the ballpark, knowing that I might get into the game. The biggest adjustment I had to make in becoming a reliever was learning not to let yesterday's game bother me tomorrow. Some guys are going to take me deep—that's all there is to it. If they earn it, if they hit my best pitch, I tip my hat to them.

My problem has always been my control. I have actually walked more batters than I've struck out in the big leagues. When I am wild, there isn't too much I can do about it except suck it up and go at 'em again the next day. I'm not one of those pitchers, like Tom Seaver, who understands the mechanics of pitching and can make tiny corrections. I throw the ball, and if it doesn't go down, I say, "Gee," and start reading the employment pages.

The only thing I study about a batter is who turns his wrists over and who doesn't. If a hitter turns his wrists over, he's going to be grounding out all game. But a hitter like Warren Cromartie, who flicks at the sinker, he can hurt me. Or Garvey, who'll take a step backward when I pitch, which makes the inside pitch an outside pitch, he can hurt me. I need to know a batter's tendencies.

I have to be honest: Sometimes I haven't a clue what I'm doing out there. I'm always impressed when I see a pitcher position his fielders, then make the batter hit the ball right at them. I think, you gotta be kidding? I tried that once in 1982. I wanted to pitch someone a certain way, I don't remember who it was, so I carefully moved left fielder Jeff Leonard over about fifteen feet. He stopped, and I moved him just a few more feet, till he was exactly where I wanted him. Then I pitched—and missed the catcher.

So I gave up on positioning fielders. There was a game in 1984 when I turned around and my second baseman, Manny Trillo, yelled, "Where do you want me?"

I couldn't lie. "Oh," I said, "back there somewhere."

As long as the ball sinks, I'm going to be okay. Hey, it helps to be lucky sometimes too. I have had the old Moonman luck. Like once I had the bases loaded and a 3–2 count on Randy Bass. As I got ready to pitch, I somehow hit my thumb and lost my grip on the ball. I threw Bass the most awesome twelve-mile-an-hour change-up you ever saw. He wanted to hit that thing so badly, so badly, he waited and waited, I thought he was going to burst, and finally he just let it go right past him for strike three. I thought he was going to cry. I just turned my hat around on my head and walked off the mound.

One of the things that has helped me survive the pressure of pitching practically every day with the ball game on the line is the fact that I am what is known as a free spirit. Or as some people might say, my elevator doesn't go all the way to the penthouse. I just like to have fun. Like in Houston one year, about forty-five minutes before the team bus was scheduled to leave the hotel for the ballpark, I stole it. The bus, not the ballpark. I drove it downtown to Jerry's House of Boots and bought myself a beautiful pair of hand-tooled boots. Then I drove the bus to the ballpark and I got it there exactly on time. Without the team, of course, but hey, nobody's perfect.

The Giants fined me cab fare for the entire ball club.

Admittedly I have cultivated that flaky reputation because if batters think you might be just a little insane, you've got a jump on them. For example, if I shake off four signs from the catcher and the hitter knows I throw only one pitch . . . he has got to start wondering, what is that guy thinking out there?

And I'm not crazy. Oh, sure, maybe I'll steal an occasional bus or I'll trade baseballs to fans for undergarments, but if a relief pitcher doesn't find a means to release the tension, he will end up collecting his checks at the funny farm.

Which is why strange things happen in the bullpen. Old-time relief pitcher Moe Drabowsky used to make long distance calls to Europe from the bullpen telephone. One bullpen crew locked a relief pitcher in the john out there—then set fire to it. About the most unusual thing I've ever seen was my roommate, catcher Dennie Littlejohn, trapping spiders, then barbecuing them with his lighter and eating them. Oh, sure, they were small spiders, but still ... After the eighth spider I had no choice, I threw up.

I myself have been known to play a small prank. For example, one time the other team was bringing a relief pitcher into the game and the pitcher was standing there waiting for the car to drive him to the mound ... and waiting ... and waiting. Now, I knew that that car was not going to be going anywhere. I knew it because I had the keys in my pocket.

If you're doing a good job, you're allowed to be flaky. When I was first trying to make the ball club in 1975, I remember, the team was in San Diego and I met some old friends at the beach for an afternoon of hang gliding. I was just gliding around up there and I looked down, and who did I see lying on the beach? Manager Wes Westrum.

I couldn't resist.

I swept down on him, screaming, "Yo, Wes! Yo, Wes!" He was looking all over trying to figure out where the shouts were coming from. And finally he looked up. I waved. I was only being friendly. He waved back, then held up two fingers and tapped his backside. I didn't know what he was indicating until I got to the ballpark that night. "You were up about two hundred feet," he explained, "so that'll cost you two hundred dollars."

That was a lot of money for a career minor league pitcher. All I could do was be thankful that I hadn't become an airplane pilot.

I was back with Rocky at Phoenix soon after that. As I learned, when I'm pitching well, I can be as flaky as I want to be. But when I lost my job as the Giants number-one stopper, as I did in 1985, that meant that I had to be serious, so that I could get enough opportunities to pitch to win my old job back, so that I could be flaky again.

The best season I've had in the major leagues was 1982, when the Giants were in contention for the western division pennant right up until the end of the season. Now that was fun. I was getting to the ballpark two and a half hours *before batting practice* began, and I never do that. Everybody was just ... I simply can't explain that feeling, the high I would get every day. Every game somebody would do something that was ordinarily impossible. An infielder would dive for a ball he couldn't possibly reach, and not only would he catch it, he'd get up and throw the runner out. I'd watch the things we were doing and I'd think, hmmm, that is definitely not normal.

The most incredible things would happen. We were tied with St. Louis in the ninth inning and they had runners on first and second with one out. I got the batter to hit a perfect double-play ball to the shortstop. The shortstop flipped to second, for the second out, then the second baseman threw the ball wild past the first baseman. It looked like the winning run was going to score from second. But the ball hit a box seat railing and, when our first baseman turned around, bounced directly to him. He made a perfect throw to the plate to catch the runner, and we went on to win the ball game.

Those kinds of things were happening every single day. I wanted to pitch in every game. If we were losing by six runs, I'd be angry if Frank Robinson wouldn't put me in to pitch.

For me, the ultimate high came with four games left in the season. We were a game behind the second place Dodgers and two games behind the first place Braves. We were playing the Dodgers, leading by a run. I came in to pitch in the eighth inning and retired the side. Then in my typical fashion I walked the leadoff batter in the ninth. The second batter bunted him to second. One out, the tying run on second, Dusty Baker the hitter. Every pitcher has at least one hitter who always does well against him. I had Dusty Baker. Dusty has a quick bat and just seemed to be able to get down on my sinker. I knew he liked the ball inside, so I tried to pitch him outside, but usually ended up pitching him inside.

I was so pumped up that for the only time in my entire career I threw three consecutive pitches on the outside black part of the plate. Three absolutely perfect pitches. Dusty was waiting for the pitch inside, he knew it was coming inside, and he never took the bat off his shoulder. When the umpire called strike three, he slammed the bat down on home plate so hard that it split in half. He dropped the handle and walked away.

I stood out on the pitcher's mound and thought, eeeeeeeeiiiiiiiiiyyyyyoooooowww! I couldn't throw three pitches on the outside corner of the plate like that again if they promised me a lifetime of twenty-foot waves and a perfect beach.

The sinker has been very good to me. For three consecutive years I finished second in the league in saves to Bruce Sutter, so when my contract came up for renewal, I knew I was going to make a lot of money. I told my agent, Tom Reich, what salary I thought was fair and he negotiated with Giants general manager Tom Haller. Finally Reich called me on a Sunday and told me we had an agreement. "How much?" I asked.

"We're going to meet in Tom Haller's office Tuesday to sign it," he answered.

"How much?" I repeated.

"You'll see Tuesday." My kind of agent.

I waited until Tuesday morning to find out. It was your typical baseball contract. In it, I was forbidden to ride on any boat with more than a 110-horsepower engine, or ride a motorcycle, or do any more hang gliding, or parasailing, or ride a Brahma bull. Ride a Brahma bull? I own a horse ranch, but ride a Brahma bull? I'm just a little flaky, not a lot crazy.

In return for agreeing to all that, as well as pitching, the Giants were going to pay me $750,000 a year and $5,000 every game in which I appeared. I couldn't believe it. When I tried to sign that contract, my hand was shaking so much I couldn't write my name. Giants owner Bob Lurie said to me, "Well, Greg, if you really don't want the money, we don't have to do it."

I grabbed my right wrist with my left hand and signed that thing firmly.

Then I asked everyone except Mr. Lurie to leave the room. When we were alone, I said to him, "I want to thank you very much. I can't promise you that I'm going to be the best pitcher in baseball, but I am going to do my best. I just want to tell you something. I cannot believe you can pay a guy like me that much money for throwing a little round object at a guy who looks like he's wearing bomb-protection gear and is standing bent over like he's going to the bathroom."

He started laughing. When he started laughing, I started laughing.

I wasn't kidding him. It took me a long time to accept the fact that I could earn that kind of money doing what I was doing. I remember when I was a kid, Mickey Mantle was paid $100,000. That seemed like almost all the money that could ever be made. Now I was making $5,000 a game in bonuses.

When I got the first check, I sat in my easy chair for two hours and just stared at it. The next day I took it to the bank for deposit. When I handed it to the teller, she looked at it, looked at it again, and screamed.

Imagine how I felt.

Unfortunately, I didn't get off to the kind of start I wanted to in 1984. Let me put it this way. The Giants had a mascot, the crab. He was the worst mascot in baseball. Whenever he came onto the field, people would hit him or throw things at him. Naturally I felt sorry for the crab. So I would go over and stand by him. But I was going so badly, he would walk away from me—he was afraid *he'd* get hurt.

I understand the frustration of the fans. When I'm not pitching well, I feel the same way they do. I want the team to win at least as much, as any fan, and probably more.

There are a few things I want to do in baseball before I steal my last pair of car keys. Naturally most of these will have to wait until I'm pitching well enough to be crazy again. But, see, I own a Grand National horse, Diamond Jim. Diamond Jim is a roping horse. And what I really want to do is one day, during batting practice, I want to put on full riding regalia, all the silver breastplates, everything, ride in from the outfield, rope one of the bat boys, and drag him off the field.

And I also want to enjoy the thrills of a pennant race again. And I want to fly in from the bullpen with a jet-pack on my back.

So call me Moonman. Or Moonie.

LUCKY TO BE A ~~BRAVE~~ ~~GIANT~~ TIGER

by Darrell Evans

Name one player in baseball history who has hit over 300 career home runs, including hitting more than forty in a season twice, who has knocked in over 1,000 runs, scored more than 1,000 runs, walked more times than he's struck out—and never made an All-Star team. Name one besides Darrell Evans, I mean.

Too tough? Okay, what do you call a player with the Boston Red Sox who hits .313 with twenty-seven home runs? If his name is not Jim Rice? If his name is not Jim Rice or Dwight Evans? If his name is not Jim Rice, Dwight Evans, or Tony Armas? In 1984 Mike Easler did that for the Red Sox.

Darrell Evans and Mike Easler are probably the two least known power hitters in baseball. For some reason, certain players go through their careers without ever being well known. It may be the team they play with, it may be that they are overshadowed by their teammates, but even besides Evans and Easler there are some outstanding players in the major leagues who are simply not known.

I don't know who they are, of course. But they're there, believe me.

Umpires love sluggers. They never waste time at bat. They don't want to walk, with the exception of Darrell Evans, so they go up to the plate determined to take their cuts. They either hit the ball or strike out and they do it quickly. They don't let too many pitches go, so umpires don't have to worry about missing a pitch, and they don't waste time hitting eight foul balls. Hit or miss, next batter, let's go home.

The reason for this is that most sluggers are guess hitters. They try to guess what pitch the pitcher is going to throw, and commit themselves to swing at that pitch even before it is thrown. That was fine with me, a lot of players considered me a guess umpire. But when a power hitter guesses wrong, for example if he guesses high fastball and the pitcher throws a low change-up, he can look awfully ridiculous.

But when he guesses right . . .

Bobby Bonds took the most vicious cut I've ever seen. I remember one night at Yankee Stadium when he was guessing fastball and the pitcher threw a slow curveball. Bonds literally swung at it twice. His follow-through turned him completely around, and the bat crossed over home plate twice.

Now, was I going to let that go? The first thing that came into my mind was, it will be pretty funny if I ring up two strikes. But before I could raise my right hand once, Bonds turned and shouted to me, "That's only one strike!"

The only thing I didn't like about sluggers is that they hit the hardest foul balls. Not the most foul balls, the hardest. I hated being behind home plate when Jim Rice came to bat. Rice is usually near every pitch, so he hits a lot of foul tips. And no matter where I tried to hide, he'd foul off a pitch and hit me. Invariably, after working a Red Sox game, I'd have at least one bruise on my leg or arm. I used to refer to them as "Rice checks." During a game against the Angels he fouled one straight back off my iron mask, and my head started ringing so badly I thought maybe the hunchback of Notre Dame had rented space. I started shaking my head. Jim stepped out of the batter's box and asked, "You okay?"

I told him the truth. "How should I know?"

The strongest batter I ever saw was Frank Howard. He was so strong that he once hit a bunt triple. It was my first season in the big leagues and we were in Washington. When he came to bat, the infielders played as deep as they could without embarrassment. I was working third base and I backed up near the outfield wall. I used to umpire him deep. Howard crossed up everybody by laying down a nice bunt. The third baseman was much too deep to have a play, so the pitcher tried to field it. The ball went right past him. In frustration he took off his glove and threw it at the ball—and hit it. According to the rules, that is an automatic triple, the only bunt triple I've ever seen.

I've seen many of the greatest power hitters in baseball history. Reggie, Dave Winfield, Dave Kingman, Bobby Bonds, Rice, Evans, Luzinski, but in my entire career only once did I see a player hit three home runs in a single game—five-five, one-hundred-forty-eight-pound Freddie Patek, the smallest man in the major leagues. He hit only forty-one home runs in his entire fourteen-year career. The most he ever hit in a season was six. And yet one magical afternoon in Boston he hit three consecutive home runs. After he hit the third one, I started looking around the ballpark for Rod Serling.

His fourth time at bat he struck out, but that's what you get from a power hitter, hit or miss. The next day I spoke to him about his feat. He was a very nice person and I think maybe a little shy about his sudden show of power. "You know, Ronnie," he said, "it was just one of those days."

One of what days? And where do I go to get one of them?

(I was also there when Cleveland Indians infielder Duane Kuiper hit the only home run of his eight-year career. Players fainted in the dugout. The *pitcher just stood on the mound looking at the spot the ball had landed, probably trying to decide what he wanted to do after baseball.)*

Darrell Evans and Mike Easler both have home run trots, even if nobody knows it. Why haven't they received the attention they deserve? Evans played much of his career in the wrong time zone with the San Francisco Giants. Easler played in Pittsburgh before being traded to the Red Sox. With the Pirates he played with Willie Stargell and Dave Parker, then he gets traded to the Red Sox with Rice, Evans, and Armas.

Of course, it could have been worse. They could have been playing in Kansas City behind Freddie Patek.

My family raised me to be a baseball player. And I mean the *whole* family. Not only had my father, two uncles, and my grandfather all been ball players, but my mother and two of my aunts had played professional softball. My mom had been a fast outfielder with a good throwing arm. That was great, because after school I had someone to play catch with. I really worked to develop a strong arm because it was a little embarrassing to have a mother who threw harder than I did.

The kids in our Pasadena, California, neighborhood loved coming around to my house because they knew there was always some kind of ball game going on. If we didn't have enough kids, my mom would be the catcher; if we had too many kids, my father would umpire. We also had the advantage of having the streetlight in front of our house, so we could play till ten or eleven o'clock at night.

Not all of our neighbors liked that, which helped me become a better hitter. The neighbor who lived in right field on our street didn't want kids running into his yard to retrieve a tennis ball or wiffle ball. I batted left-handed, so rather than "pulling" the ball into his yard, I learned to hit the ball to left field, or "inside out." We didn't mind the neighbor; it was his big Doberman that scared us. So when the ball did go into his yard, we'd just have to send my little brother in after it.

Fortunately he got my mother's speed.

My family taught me the game of baseball. Other kids' parents read them classic stories at night; my father would sit on my bed reading questions from *So You Think You Know Baseball!* The only thing I didn't like about that book was that it had no pictures. But no one in my family ever put any pressure on me to either play or play well. Baseball was supposed to be fun. When I came home from a game, no one ever asked me how many hits I'd gotten; they knew I was out there playing and enjoying myself. Instead, they asked what I'd learned during the game. Why did the center fielder throw to third rather than to second? Why did I swing at the first pitch after the pitcher had just walked a batter on four straight pitches? They taught me to think, and every game was a lesson.

I've played seventeen years in the big leagues. I've hit 300 home runs and knocked in over 1,000. I'm twentieth on the all-time-bases-on-balls list. And I still learn something about this game almost every day. In spring training, for example, after I'm taken out of a game, I sit on the bench and watch the last few innings. I figure, for four months my mind hasn't been thinking baseball. Something a little unusual might take place on the field and I'll see how everybody reacts and what the result is. So if a similar play occurs during the season, I'll know how to react. The most frustrating part of baseball is that by the time you really learn how to play the game, your body is too old for it. You send all the proper signals to your muscles, and your muscles respond, "Who, me?"

I could always hit. Always. That was sort of surprising because I was playing with a minor handicap—I couldn't see. I'm sometimes asked if I can actually see the spin on a pitch as it comes to the plate. Without my contact lenses I can't even see the pitcher. I might have the worst vision in major league baseball. My eyes are so bad, I used to have to wear glasses over my contact lenses. Uncorrected, my vision is about 20/800 in one eye, 20/600 in the other. I struggled along without glasses until my junior year in high school. Then one night I was playing third base in an American Legion game and the batter hit a high pop-up. I called for it, I thought I was moving under it, the ball landed in right field. In right field! Literally.

The next day I was fitted for glasses. I still couldn't catch pop-ups, but at least I could see what I was missing. Eventually I started wearing contact lenses. Hard lenses irritated my eyes, and soft lenses couldn't correct my astigmatism, so I compromised. I wore glasses over my soft lenses. In San Francisco, when that fog rolled in over my glasses, it didn't matter what I was wearing. I couldn't see anything anyway.

I signed my first professional contract with Charlie Finley's Kansas City A's in 1967. I played only two months that season, but in three different leagues. Charlie just kept moving me up. The only problem, although I didn't realize it at the time, was that I was one league behind a kid named Sal Bando. At the end of the 1967 season Charlie Finley told me I would start the next year in Double A, but would be brought up to the major leagues in midseason. Now, I had played two months of professional baseball on the lowest levels and the owner–general manager of the ball club was telling me I was almost ready for the major leagues? Why wouldn't I believe him? I mean, does anybody ever spend more than two months in the minors?

That winter I served my Marine Reserve basic training. The 1968 season was already two months old when I was finally released. Although I hadn't touched a baseball in six months, I immediately went onto the field and tried to throw the ball through a brick wall. I felt I had to; I knew I was going up to the big leagues in a few months and wanted to be ready.

A day later I couldn't lift my arm. It hurt to wiggle my fingers. Just thinking about lifting my arm caused a pain to run through it. I'd torn all the ten-

dons in the front of my shoulder. Not only couldn't I
throw the ball from third base to first base, I couldn't
even throw it from third base to the pitcher's mound.
But when the manager asked me if I was ready to play,
I lied. "Ready," I said. I figured, if they don't hit too
many balls to third base, I'll be okay.

They hit a lot of balls to third base. I mean, a lot
of balls.

The shoulder injury also prevented me from swinging freely, and I hit only .241. I didn't want the A's to
know about my injury, so I let them think I just
wasn't hitting. That probably was not the most intelligent thing I might've done. The A's decided I couldn't
hit. There is a fact in baseball life: If you can't hit in
the low minor leagues, you can't hit in the major
leagues. This is it, I thought, six months ago I was all
set to go up to the big leagues; now I'm getting released. I was so mad at myself for trying to play before
I was ready, I would've hit myself in the head if it
didn't hurt so much to lift my arm.

Fortunately A's farm director Eddie Robinson was
named general manager of the Atlanta Braves. He believed I could play. When the A's failed to promote
me to their forty-man major league roster, the Braves
drafted me. I had played four months of pro ball. I'd
played on four different minor league teams in four
different leagues. I had been the property of two major
league teams. Baseball had been a lot less complicated
when all I had to do was take the ball out of the
mouth of an angry Doberman.

The following spring I found myself dressing next
to Henry Aaron, Orlando Cepeda, Felipe Alou, Clete
Boyer, and my absolute idol, Eddie Mathews, at the
Braves' West Palm Beach training camp. I had no idea
what I was supposed to do, so I did nothing. I kept
entirely to myself. So much so that after three days,
coach Tommy Aaron suggested I introduce myself to
the manager, Lum Harris. "It helps him to know who
his players are," Tommy told me.

After ten days of workouts we played the first
game of the spring training schedule. I didn't know

what I was supposed to do after infield practice, so I followed a group of players—I knew they were players because they were wearing uniforms—into the clubhouse. When they started to get dressed to go home, I figured, if you're not playing in the game, I guess you can go home. So I took off my uniform and got in the shower. What I didn't know was that those players getting dressed were all pitchers who were not going to throw in the game.

Five minutes before game time I came out of the shower wrapped in a towel. Tommy Aaron stood there looking at me for a few minutes, then shook his head. "Uh, listen, rook," he said, "I don't want to bother you or anything, but, uh, what are you doing?"

"Going home?"

I have never put on a uniform so fast in my life.

There were 5,000 fans in the ballpark. The only time I'd ever seen that many people in one place at one time had been at a major league ballpark. I couldn't believe that so many people were going to have to watch me play.

Lum Harris put me in at third base in the fifth inning. When I'd signed with Kansas City, I'd spent three days working out with the big club, but this was the first time I'd played in a game with major leaguers. Nervous? I would say it was probably a good thing I hadn't eaten that day.

The first pitch of the inning, the very first pitch, was popped up near the third base dugout. The problem with pop-ups is that you can't tell anyone that the ball took a bad bounce. Well, sometimes in San Francisco's Candlestick Park pop-ups do take bad bounces. Pop-ups have never been my strong point, but I really thought I was going to catch this one. "I got it," I screamed loudly, loud enough that every one of the 5,000 fans heard me. I settled under it, under it. . . . The ball landed maybe two feet from third base, certainly nowhere near where I was standing waiting for it to come down.

I started the 1969 season with the Braves, but I wasn't ready for the big leagues. After playing in twelve games I was sent back to the minors. Atlanta won the Western Division championship that season, losing the playoffs to the "miracle" Mets. I didn't mind not being a part of that championship team. I figured, they've got Aaron, Cepeda, Phil Niekro, Ron Reed, I'm going to be playing for a lot of championship teams in my career. I was absolutely right: Only fifteen years later I was with the World Champion Detroit Tigers ball club. I played seven and a half seasons with the Braves and seven and a half seasons with the Giants before signing with the Tigers as a free agent in 1984. We came close to winning a pennant with some of the Atlanta and San Francisco clubs, but we always came up a little short. It would have been wonderful, but it was not that disappointing. To me, being able to play baseball is winning. Just being there is winning. Everything else, the championships, the individual honors, are just the chocolate icing on the cake of life.

There were some great years during that time though. In 1973, for example, Henry Aaron, second baseman Davey Johnson, and I each hit at least forty home runs, the first time in history three teammates had done that. The team finished fifth.

When I first came up to the major leagues, I couldn't catch a cold, I couldn't throw that accurately, and I wasn't terrific on pop-ups or groundballs either. But I was fortunate enough to have the two best teachers in the world, Clete Boyer and Eddie Mathews. Mathews had been my idol when I was growing up. I even wore his number, and when he came back to the Braves as a coach, then as the manager, he worked with me, and worked with me. One of the first days we spent together he told me, "You know, I was just like you when I first came up." That made me feel pretty good, this was a man who had hit 512 big league home runs. Then he finished his thought. "I couldn't catch the ball and I couldn't throw either." But he was willing to work with me and encourage me. I worked harder at learning how to play third base than at anything else I've done in baseball. I'm proud

of what I've accomplished—I'm currently fifth on the
all-time list for total chances played by a third baseman.

Oh, there have been some bad days in the field,
and there was one terrible day. The way I look at it is,
anybody can make four errors in one game. I don't
think anybody else has, but they certainly could. I
proved it's possible. It was opening day, 1976, in San
Diego. The sun was shining, bands were playing, it
was a beautiful day until the game began. I fielded the
first ball hit to me cleanly, then I threw it into the
stands behind first base. That was the first error, and
it was a legitimate error. The second ball was hit to
my left, in the hole between third and short. I made a
nice play to get to the ball, but it took a bad hop off
my glove. The official scorer gave me my second error, but that one could just as easily have been called
a hit. Two errors, but it was still early. The third one
. . . that was in the third inning. With a base runner
on first, the batter hit a two-hopper down the third
base line. I backed up and made a good stop, but as I
tried to take the ball out of my glove, I dropped it.
That was the third error. Unfortunately, as the runner
from first reached second, he rounded the base. Unfortunately for me. I picked up the ball and whistled it
into right field. My fourth error and it was only the
third inning of the first game of the season. I figured I
had a long season ahead of me. I'd already had a long
season, and it was still opening day.

The Braves traded me to the San Francisco Giants
in 1976. I loved playing with the Braves, and I loved
playing with the Giants. I'm not that tough to please.
Our fans in San Francisco were wonderful, and I never
blamed them for not coming out to Candlestick Park.
We all have a survival instinct. The best thing that
can be said about the winds that blew around the
ballpark, or blew the ballpark around, is that it gave
the players something else to complain about besides
the cold. The wind taught me an important lesson
about baseball—the best team doesn't win all the time.
I've seen a lot of games lost by the best team on
wind-blown pop-ups. Imagine a Ping-Pong ball bounc-

ing around a wind tunnel, and that's what it was like when a ball was hit into the wind currents at Candlestick Park. I've literally seen eight fielders call for the same fly ball. I've literally seen a ball hit 400 feet sail over the outfield fence, and watched as the outfielder turned his back to the infield and caught the ball when the wind blew it back into play. There was no way to figure out which way the wind was blowing, either, because it went in different directions at various heights. I'd watch hot dog wrappers on field level blowing across the field from third toward first, then see a ball go into the air and be blown completely in the opposite direction.

There's nothing like an August night at Candlestick Park, except maybe a December night in Anchorage, Alaska. I'm an optimist and I liked to believe that the freezing cold temperatures at night helped make me a better hitter. When it was that cold, the one thing you just didn't want to do was hit a ball off the bat handle. The stinging in your hand would last at least until your next at bat, and maybe into the next month. So I would concentrate every at bat on just trying to make solid contact. Of course, based on this theory, I would be the greatest player in Alaskan history.

There was a hill behind the ballpark, and once a week a fog bank would just ease in over that hill. It was eerie. As it rolled in, it looked like the beginning of a monster movie. We used to watch it, and make jokes about Godzilla rising from the murky depths, and everybody laughed, but nobody took their eyes off it for too long.

After spending almost eight years in San Francisco, it was difficult for me to leave, but my contract expired at the end of 1983 and the Giants were rebuilding with younger players. It was time for me to move on. In August of that season I told the front office that I intended to sign with a contending team, and suggested they try to make a deal for me in which they might get some prospects. I told them two or three times point-blank I wouldn't be coming back.

They told me they couldn't make a deal for me, that nobody was interested. I hit thirty home runs that season, I knew somebody had to be interested. In the free agent draft following the season I was selected by eighteen clubs, including the San Francisco Giants.

I signed with the Tigers. Not only were they a contender in 1984, they were the only contender. We led the American League East from opening day to closing day. It was a truly memorable season, although it did not start out that way for me. I've always been a slow starter; for some reason it takes me some time to get going. In 1982, for example, I started so slowly that the Giants brought up Tom O'Malley from AAA to play third base. When you're thirty-five years old, as I was, and they start playing the kids at your position, you check to see how many years you have in the pension fund. I was terribly frustrated because I knew I could still play. My father knew I was depressed and put it in perspective for me. "You've been in the big leagues fourteen years," he reminded me. "There's a reason for that. Just wait your turn." He was right, I was still there when a lot of people I'd once played with were working for investment firms. Whatever the reason, I was still there. When my chance came, I produced.

But when a ball player begins getting older, every time he makes an out, every misplay in the field, is looked at with a question mark. Is he losing his skills? Is he over the hill? In 1984 I got off to my usual slow start. That would have been acceptable in San Francisco, where they can't even see the hill, and where they had learned I always start slowly. But Detroit made the mistake of looking at my normal end-of-the-year statistics at the beginning of the year. That was a mistake. Give me time, let me play, I'll hit twenty or more home runs, knock in eighty to eighty-five runs, bat around .250 and walk between seventy-five and eighty-five times. My father was right; there was a reason I was still there. But the owner of the Detroit team was quoted as saying that signing me was the worst investment he'd ever made.

I mean, the worst investment? The very worst? Wasn't there maybe an oil deal that went sour somewhere? How about just a bad investment? *Worst* covers a lot of territory.

I didn't have an outstanding year statistically in 1984, but I must have done something right because I'm wearing a World Champions ring on my finger. The thing about that team is that we had twenty-five players who knew their roles. Some of the veterans, not to mention any names, me, might not have compiled tremendous stats, but we did what we were capable of doing, and did it when it was needed. While younger players might have complained about not playing regularly, the veterans never said a word, stayed ready to play, knew how to play, and weren't upset when they got only a 1-for-4. Once you accept the fact that you are going to fail at bat seventy-five percent of the time, you learn to take joy in the accomplishments of your teammates. That's what forms the core of a successful team.

I'd been through a lot of seasons, I'd played a lot of games, but nothing had prepared me for the intensity of the American League playoffs. We knew we had the best team in baseball, but if we hadn't beaten Kansas City in the playoffs, it would have been a tremendous disappointment. We beat them three straight games. After the third game I had to lie down to relax. My heart couldn't take it. Every pitch, every play, had meaning. If I had to play with that intensity for an entire season, I couldn't make it. I'd find an easier job, like cleaning windows at the Empire State Building, or defusing bombs. And this was after we'd won the playoffs easily!

The World Series is often called "the second season." In 1984 I found out that I start the second season as slowly as I start the first one. I had a bad series at bat, but it didn't matter because we won four out of five games.

Some people believe that major league players don't get nervous. I'll tell you who doesn't believe that—major league players. There are those tense situations that arise when you're swinging the bat good or fielding well and you feel capable of doing whatever is necessary. Then there is every other time. As Dodger Pedro Guerrero said when asked about playing third base, "Sometimes I look up in the sky and say, 'Please don't let them hit the ball to me.' Then I pause and add, 'And don't let them hit it to Steve Sax at second base either.' " It's impossible to get out there every day and feel confident. The key thing is that major league players are able to play through their nervousness, or channel it into positive action.

I think the best part of the playoffs and the World Series was the parade we had in Detroit after becoming champions. There is no pressure in a parade. Detroit is a city that has had its share of ups and downs, and it has also had other cities' share of downs. It was incredible to see 600,000 people who didn't know each other, people of different colors, different ethnic backgrounds, people on all the levels of the social scale, kissing and hugging each other, sharing joy, and knowing that I had some share of responsibility for creating that happiness.

The worst moment of the year came in July, when my father passed away. At least I know he had the best seat in the house for the playoff and World Series.

In 1985 I led the American League with forty home runs, becoming at age thirty-eight the oldest player to ever win a home run title. Carlton Fisk finished second, with thirty-seven homers, but he's just a young whippersnapper of thirty-seven. I've always hit home runs in bunches, but usually not big bunches. When I'm in a hot streak, it's as if I have a special connection to the game. Whatever pitch I guess the pitcher is going to throw is the pitch he throws. Not only that, the pitch is always where I guess it's going to be. The ball doesn't look bigger, it looks slower. I seem to see it for a longer period of time, and therefore I have more time to react. Now, if I could find glasses that made that happen consistently, that would be something. What goes through my mind

when I'm in the middle of a hot streak? Playing doubleheaders. Leading off.

I'm certainly intelligent enough to know that hot
streaks have nothing to do with luck, that they are
simply a part of the game. But when I'm doing well,
I'll do everything the same every day, starting with
how many cups of coffee I drink when I wake up in
the morning. I'll eat the same food for lunch at the
same time. I'll ride to the ballpark with the same
people at the same time. I'll wear the same pants, the
same undershirt, I'll use the same bat, I'll step into
the batter's box the same way. If I happen to speak to
someone the day I start a streak, they may hear from
me a lot during the next few days. I just don't want to
change anything. Maybe a new T-shirt would be snug
and distract from my concentration. Maybe another
type of food would make me feel lethargic. I just don't
want to take any chances.

I was in the middle of a torrid streak in 1985 and
I'd worn the same T-shirt for a while, washed daily.
Then one night I came to the park and I couldn't find
it. Now, I realized that superstition had nothing to do
with my success, I knew my performance depended
on my ability, I didn't really believe that a T-shirt was
the reason I was hitting home runs. Knowing all this,
I searched through the lockers of every player on the
entire team until I found the thing.

Obviously the bat I use has something to do with
my success. And some bats are better than others. I
work with three bats: the gamer, the one I'll use in
the game; a second bat that I've used in batting practice and feel comfortable with; and the bat I'm breaking in during batting practice. When I break my gamer,
I move the other two up in the rotation. I clean my
bats every day so I can see where I'm making contact
with the ball. A ball will leave a mark on that bat and
that mark will be an indication of how well I'm swinging the bat. That and my batting average. I had a
six-week hot streak in 1983 that was the most incredible thing I'd ever lived through. Every time I got up I
hit the ball hard. I hit about .450 during that period,

even while changing T-shirts. I felt as if I could almost go up to bat with my eyes closed and I'd get a hit. I used the same bat for three weeks, a long time for a bat to survive. I cleaned it every night, and there was an area on the barrel, probably two or three inches long, and I hit every ball right there. I would've taken that bat home with me at night, but my wife, LaDonna, objects to my putting it in the bed.

When I think back on that bat, I remember happily that it broke on a base hit. That bat went out in a blaze of glory.

The hardest thing about being in the midst of a hot streak is not getting giddy. When everything is going right, this game seems almost easy, but the day you start thinking it is easy is the day it gets hard.

The worst thing about a hot streak is that it ends. And when you suddenly cool off, it seems like every time you come to bat, the winning run is on third base, or the team needs a big hit, or you're leading off both games of a doubleheader. Experience has taught me that eventually I'm going to get another hit. Sometimes "eventually" seems like "eternity," but they are different. After 8,000 major league at bats, I know that I'm not going to forget everything I've learned.

One of the things I'm most proud of in my career is that I walked more often than I've struck out. I take a lot of pitches because I know what pitch I want to swing at. A pitch may be a strike, but it may not be the pitch I can drive. If I'm going to swing at a pitch, I'm going to hit it. If I had swung at a lot more pitches, I certainly would have had more home runs, and I'd still be hitting them—in some softball league somewhere because I would have been out of baseball.

Playing in a World Series is somewhat like eating Chinese food. A half hour after you're done you want to do it again. I hit only .067 in the 1984 series and I'd like an opportunity to improve upon that before I retire.

And when I do retire, I'd like to manage a baseball team. I know more about baseball now than at any time in my life, and I'm still learning. To me, the ultimate challenge in baseball is to get an entire team, twenty-five individuals, all moving in the same direction—as long as that isn't the opposite direction the manager is going in. Managers can make a tremendous amount of difference in the success of a ball club—if the most talented team won every year we wouldn't even bother playing the schedule.

Surprisingly I'm still learning baseball from my family, only the teacher has changed. The day after we'd played a game in Chicago in 1985 my wife called from Detroit. The game had been on television and she'd seen me pull two balls foul in the ninth inning. "I can't keep the ball fair," I told her. "It's been like that for the last few games."

"Of course you can't," she said, "you're pulling your head off the ball at the last minute."

"I can't be," I told her, "because if I was, I wouldn't be hitting the ball solidly."

"I'm telling you," she said, "your head is tilted a little too much toward third base and before making contact you're pulling back."

I paused. "You really think so?"

"Absolutely. If you'd just stayed on the ball a little longer, both of them would've been fair."

That wasn't bad advice, especially since she doesn't know anything about baseball.

THE HAPPY HIT MAN
by Mike Easler

I spent ten long seasons in the minor leagues. I signed
with the Houston Astros' organization in 1969 for five
hundred dollars. It wasn't even a real five hundred
dollars, it was just a tuition payment at Cleveland
State University. Man, I didn't care, I just wanted to
play professional baseball. I spent the 1969 season
with Covington, Virginia, the 1970 and 1971 seasons
with Cocoa Beach, Florida, 1972 and part of 1973 in
Columbus, Ohio, and the rest of 1973 in Denver,
Colorado, and six games with the Astros in which I
got seven at bats, 1974 again with Denver and Houston, fifteen games and fifteen at bats that time, 1975
with Iowa, with Tulsa on loan to the Cardinals' organization and five games, five at bats with the Astros,
1976 with Tulsa after the Cardinals traded for me, and
twenty-four games with the California Angels after
the Cardinals traded me away, 1977 in Columbus,
again, after the Angels traded me to the Pittsburgh
organization, 1978 in Columbus, and finally, in 1979,
after being traded to the Red Sox in September 1978,

and traded back to the Pirates the following March, I made it to the big leagues to stay.

That's not just a long minor league career, that's a long sentence. So I was around to a lot of places before I got anywhere. Course, it was nice to know that so many teams wanted me. It wasn't so nice that so many teams didn't want me.

Not only did I play baseball all summer in order to make enough money for my family, I spent every winter playing baseball in South America. Baseball, twelve months a year for ten years, and the most money I ever earned was $22,000.

I'll tell you what, Jack, no way I could've made it without my wife, Brenda. Brenda is the sister of major league player Cliff Johnson, but she is much more attractive than he is. We got married in 1971 and she's been with me the whole trip. Brenda is a very special woman; not only can she cook and take care of our three girls, she can hit, she can throw, she can run, and she probably knows more about baseball than I do. She came from a real athletic family. When we were in the minor leagues, she would go out in the backyard with me and pitch batting practice. It was helpful to my hand—eye coordination, but honestly, she never had much of a breaking ball.

Hitting has always been my strongest point. My philosophy of hitting has always been a simple one: You throw it, I hit it. That's why Willie Stargell and my brother, Ted, hung my nickname, "Hit Man," on me. The scouting report on me in the minor leagues was that I couldn't hit the good gas; I had a jackup swing and couldn't get around on a major league fastball. That scouting report was one of the reasons I stayed in the minors so long. Man, that's crazy. I make my living off good gas. It's the junk I can't hit.

I never hit with much power until 1974, when Houston coach Bob Lillis began working diligently with me to bring out whatever talent I had. He convinced me to hold my bat lower and uppercut, and to really follow through hard on my swing. Once I started whipping that bat, I mean *whipping*, balls started flying out. Lillis was the one coach I had in the minor leagues who worked with you. Everybody else tried to change me; Lillis worked with what I was doing. And the other players didn't help me—it's a dog-eat-dog world down there, everybody's eyes are on getting to the big time.

Pittsburgh coach Al Monchak did spend a lot of time trying to turn me into an adequate outfielder. Nice try. Actually he did help a bit. Couldn't hurt.

My best season in the minor leagues was 1976. I hit .352 with twenty-six home runs and seventy-seven rbi's, and I led all outfielders with sixteen assists. I couldn't do any better than that, and the following year I still got sent back to the minor leagues. Well, hey, if they had wanted me to drive the team bus, too, all they had to do was ask. I would have done anything to get a real shot at the bigs.

Before each game that season I would sit by myself in the dugout and stare out at the field and visualize myself doing things. I would actually "see" myself hitting in my head. Then I would be ready for the game. I hit good on the field, but I never made an out in my head. What that preparation did was help me improve my concentration and my confidence.

I kept getting brief trials in the big leagues, but no one would ever give me a chance to play. I started the 1975 season with the Astros and I literally begged manager Preston Gomez for a chance. "One game, that's all, just give me four swings. Three swings, I'll settle for three swings." The only time I got to bat was when we were already out of the game and he needed a pinch hitter. One time after I hadn't batted in three weeks I got sent up to hit against Padre Randy Jones. Are you kidding me, Jack? That man was winning the Cy Young Award. I had no chance against him. Pow. Pow. Pow. See you later. Three pitches. I was just overmatched. I realized I wasn't going to get better at anything sitting on a major league bench, except at sitting on the bench, so I asked to be sent down to the minor leagues.

That was the season I became a born-again Christian, and that made the difference in my career because I had a peace about myself. I knew I wasn't supposed to be up in the big leagues at that time. But I also knew my chance would come.

By 1978 I was ready. I was practically bursting. But the Pirates had Dave Parker, Omar Moreno, and Al Oliver in the outfield and I wasn't going to make any of them sit down. I realized the only way I was going to get to the big leagues with the Pirates was as a pinch hitter. So I tried to work as a designated hitter in the minors as much as possible, because I wanted to get used to coming off the bench swinging.

One very important thing you learn while spending ten years in the minors is how to select quality rental furniture. By 1978 I could go into that rental store and pick out the very best stuff, but I just didn't want to do it anymore. I wanted to have something to show for all the time I'd spent in baseball, so we went out and finally bought our own furniture. We still have it, and I'm not ever getting rid of it. Things have gone very well since then, but you never know, you know.

I hit .330 that year and at the end of the season we decided to buy a house in San Antonio. I knew I was either going up to the big leagues or I was going to be released, because I was twenty-eight years old and making $22,000 a year, too old and too much for a minor league player. We bought that house on faith. We had to; we didn't have any money.

That was the last season I spent in winter ball too. I appreciated the opportunity to play winter ball, a lot of years it was the difference between eating hamburgers and eating Hamburger Helper. I have a deep love for the Spanish people, they are good people with good hearts and they love the game of baseball. A lot of times baseball is all they have. I can relate to that. My first few seasons in the Caribbean were difficult. Not just getting used to the language, the food, not just the riots in the stands, and the armed guards in the dugouts, but the road trips. Man, I didn't sleep for months. We'd get on that bus and drive over mountains that had 115 curves and roads about three inches wider than the bus. Every time we went around one of these curves, I would pray, O Lord, don't let us go over this. Then we'd reach another one. Lord, don't let us go over this one either. And another. Pay attention, Lord, this is a big one. But after a while I couldn't help but go to sleep. I figured, if we fell off a mountain while I was sleeping, at least I wouldn't know we were falling.

I almost didn't make it with the 1979 Pirates either. A few weeks into the season the team had to make one more cut, someone was coming off the disabled list or something, and I knew it was going to be either me or Matt Alexander. Matt Alexander was a pinch runner, that's all he did, run, so that shows you how valuable I was to the team. Matt and I used to sit in the dugout sneaking glances at each other, then pretending we weren't looking when the other one tried to sneak a glance. We knew one of us was going to be going, gone.

I was pretty sure it was going to be me. I wasn't playing at all, and I wasn't pinch-hitting worth a dog either. Manager Chuck Tanner rarely used me because he had veterans like John Milner on the bench and he had confidence in them. Oh, I wanted to play so badly. Lemme play, Chuck, put me in. I begged him to put me in. I begged coach Bob Skinner to talk him into putting me in. Let me swing my bat, give me a chance to play.

Finally, one night in the middle of May, we were tied with the Mets in the thirteenth inning. Everybody was going into the game except me. I thought he was going to use the bat boy before me. I was literally beating a bat against the metal walls in the runway between the dugout and clubhouse, bam, bam, screaming, "I wanna hit. I wanna hit." Skinner kept taking peeks at me down the runway like I was crazy. I didn't care, bam, bam, "Lemme hit, Chuck."

Skip Lockwood was pitching in relief for the Mets and I kept going into the clubhouse to watch the game on television so I could see what he was throwing. He was starting off every hitter with high gas. My pitch. That's the pitch I hit. Bam, bam. "I gotta hit, Chuck." There was nobody left on the bench still breathing when Tanner sent me up there to pinch-hit. First pitch: high gas. BOOM! That's outta here.

A week later we were playing the Mets again, this time in Shea Stadium, New York, with Craig Swan pitching. I pinch-hit again. BOOM! Home run, Easler. Good-bye, Matt Alexander, hel-lo, big leagues.

Those were the only two home runs I hit all year, but they were very important. They kept me in the big leagues, that's how important they were. A year later Tanner was using me regularly.

In 1980 I hit .338, with twenty-one home runs and seventy-four rbi's. I also hit for the cycle against Cincinnati that year, getting a single, double, triple, and home run in one game. The triple came first, then the double and single, so I came up to bat the fourth time needing a home run. In spring training of 1978 I had been fortunate enough to spend some time with Ted Williams, and he told me that when he was ahead of the pitcher on the count, he would open his hips and throw his hands open before the pitch, almost letting go of the bat. All that is a technical way of saying he was committing himself to hitting a fastball as far as he could.

Doug Bair was pitching for the Reds when I came to bat the fourth time. A fastball pitcher. First pitch, fastball outside, ball one. Second pitch, fastball outside, ball two. Two balls, no strikes, I knew he had to come over the plate with a fastball. I thought, forget it, Jack, come on, Ted Williams, here we go. Bair cocked his arm and I opened my hips and opened my hands and hit that sucker into the upper tank in Cincinnati, an upper deck home run.

I'm gonna tell you how much respect Chuck Tanner had for me. After I hit that home run, he took me out for defensive purposes. I didn't care, man, I was in eighteenth heaven. I was one happy jaybird, you can believe me.

To me, hitting is a great battle between me and

the pitcher. A challenge. And I love it. I love it most when I know he's got to come with his strength against my strength. The worst part is when the umpire makes a bad call, interrupting the battle. I just want to curl up and die, telling him, oh, man, how can you take my fun away from me like that?

Part of the battle is being able to wait until you get a pitch you can drive, and sometimes that means fouling off a lot of strikes, pitches that you won't be able to do what you want to do to them, know what I mean? In the minor leagues I was a great foul-ball hitter. I could foul off eight, nine pitches, no problem, I did it all the time. Now I'm foolish. Now I just put the ball in play all the time. I do remember one great foul ball I hit in Pittsburgh. They have these very high light towers there, and I hit an Al Holland pitch foul over those lights. Man, a foul ball out of the stadium. That was great. I knew I couldn't hit Holland anyway, so I was really pleased with that. Hitting a lot of foul balls during an at bat helps build your confidence. It means you're thinking right along with the pitcher. Even if you make a loud out after fouling off a lot of pitches, you feel good, you feel ready for the next at bat.

The best foul-ball hitter I've ever seen is Wade Boggs, then Pete Rose and Rod Carew. If they don't like a pitch that is close enough to maybe be called a strike, they just stick out their bats—flick—foul ball. Another chance. Me, I stick out my bat, that ball hits it, and becomes a short fly to left field.

Even when I was hitting .338 in Pittsburgh, Chuck Tanner would platoon me, letting me bat only against right-handed pitchers. I used to hate that with a passion, and Chuck knew how much it bothered me when he took me out because a left-hander had come in to pitch. I think the bats and helmets I threw probably gave it away. He fined me only once, and I told him, "What am I supposed to do, smile when you take me out for a pinch hitter? I wanna play, I wanna face that left-hander in a tough situation."

Chuck understood. He would tell me about his

career as a player. He had an even bigger problem than I did—he was playing behind Henry Aaron. How many at bats you think he got?

When the Pirates started rebuilding the ball club around speed and defense in 1983, I knew it was time for me to move on. Two things I'm not are fast and a good defense outfielder. At the end of that season the Pirates traded me to the Boston Red Sox. Man, I thought, this is just great, the American League, the designated hitter league. The way I field, I was born to be a DH.

When I walked into Fenway Park in Boston for the first time and saw the Green Monster, the big wall in left field only 315 feet away from home plate, I knew I was in heaven. I'm a left handed batter, but I have a natural inside-out swing and hit mostly to left field. My first season in Boston: .313, twenty-seven home runs, thank you very much.

I was a perfect Fenway Park hitter. In 1985 I found out they have Fenway Park pitchers. I was in a slump the entire year. My God, I wouldn't want to go through life being a .260 hitter. I don't know how they do it. They'd better be able to pick it in the field, I'll tell you that. Hitting .250, my, my, that's a lot of oh-fors, a lot of sleepless nights. I just struggled through the season. It seemed like every time a pitcher had to make a good pitch, he was able to make it. And when I did get my pitch, I would foul it off.

In order to change that I have to go back to working like I did in the minor leagues. Start doing the basic things I did back then, sitting in the dugout before the game and visualizing the game itself. In the minor leagues I treated every game like it was the last game I would ever play, each at bat like it was my last at bat. I think what has happened since then is that there are so many distractions in the major leagues, it is really tough to concentrate on the game itself. In the minor leagues there is one thing on your mind—get to the major leagues. That is all you think about—get to the major leagues. You ain't making any money, so you don't worry about money. You don't worry about investments because you haven't got any investments. You don't worry about your house, because you haven't got a house, just a rented apartment. You don't worry about the car payments because you ain't got no car. You don't worry about getting tickets to the game for your friends, because nobody wants to come to a minor league game. You don't worry about your shoe endorsement contract because you've got only one pair of shoes and they're falling apart. Life is simple in the minor leagues, you do your work, you grab a bat, and you hit. You hit enough, you make the major leagues.

Life changes when you make it. I've still got that furniture we bought in 1978, I'll never part with it, but it's in the back of the house now. I put a Nautilus workout machine in my garage, imagine that, a workout machine in the garage. Before I'd made the big leagues, my workouts would consist of running around the gym or the neighborhood until I fell down. When I fell down, I knew I was finished.

After spending a few seasons with the Red Sox, I've learned how totally different the American and National leagues are. Until a player has spent a season in each league, there is just no way he can understand *how* different. It's not just the ball, the ballparks, the umpiring; it's an entirely different style of play. American League pitchers have this philosophy: Whatever pitch you don't hit, they'll feed it to you until you show them you can hit it. In the National League it is gas, gas, gas. They start you off with a fastball and if the count gets to 3-0, 2-0, 3-1, or 3-2, you can bet the barn they're going to bring that gas. But the American League? No way. They throw any pitch anytime. Nobody in the National League ever heard of throwing a 3-2 change-up. A pitcher does that, National League people talk about him for years. In the American League it's always, now, what is he going to throw now? A split-fingered fastball that drops? A spitball? In the American League a pitcher will intentionally walk the winning run, actually put him on first base if he feels he can get out the next batter. If a National League pitcher did that . . . he'd soon be an American League pitcher.

I miss that National League gas. Man, I would love to hit against Dwight Gooden. I'm not complaining, I'm just so happy to be in the major leagues, I don't care exactly where I'm playing.

The hardest thing for me to learn was how to control my temper. Even after I was born again in 1975, it took me time to grow in Christianity. Just because you're an instant Christian doesn't mean everything else inside you stops. It took me five or six years to finally become a mature person. I used to break bats, throw helmets, scream, everything. In '81 I even smashed a big water cooler in the dugout in San Francisco with my bat. I was oh for 3 against the Giants, but I went like 5-for-5 on that cooler. If you can hit a water cooler for a home run, I did it. A good, nice level swing, right through the thing. Cost me nine hundred dollars out of my final paycheck to replace it too. But the players very kindly put a big piece of white tape on it and wrote, "Donated by Mike Easler."

Baseball is a game of breaks; being in the right place at the right time, getting the right pitch at the right moment, having the right manager. But I've also learned that a player can make his own breaks. If your mechanics are good when you swing the bat, the breaks come. If you hit for an average, you seem to be in the right place. The biggest break I ever got was my God-given talent. I've been very fortunate, very fortunate. There have been times when I've been down, and in those times I'll talk to my father, a great man, and he has his own way of putting everything in perspective. He'll pause, and tell me softly, "Now, son, it's very simple. If you can't hit the ball, just come home and drive a truck for the post office."

I'd rather hit for a living. I don't trust my driving.

MY LIFE IN THE ARM FORCES

by Milt Wilcox

Pitchers and umpires go together about as well as milk and beer. Maybe not even that well. For example, Red Sox and Expo pitcher Bill Lee once snarled at me, "You're nothing but a rotten vampire."

Naturally, being a college graduate with a master's degree, I attempted to correct this obvious misuse of the language. "I think you mean umpire," I explained. "Um-pire."

He shook his head. "I meant vampire," he said, "because all you do is suck the blood out of pitchers."

I don't dislike pitchers. I dislike kids. The problem is that some pitchers turn out to be kids. They stand on the mound and scream at the umpire every time he dares to call a pitch a ball. "Where was it?" they whine. Well, where did they think it was? Santa Fe, New Mexico? Or they complain, "Looked good to me." What am I going to say? Yeah, I've seen your wife, she probably looked good to you too.

The problem is a simple conflict of interest. A pitcher wants to win the ball game and the umpire doesn't care who wins. That immediately makes the umpire the enemy. Now, I've known Milt Wilcox since he came up to the major leagues with the Cincinnati Reds in 1970. Although he was in the National League, I'd see the Reds in spring training. And, at that time, I didn't like him at all. He didn't scream at the home plate umpire from the mound, as many pitchers do, but he made it obvious he didn't like umpires. At that time he was a thrower, not a pitcher, meaning he had tremendous natural ability but wasn't very smart out there. Of course, I'm quite sure he thought I wasn't very smart back there either.

But when a player survives in the big leagues as long as Milt Wilcox has, he matures. Many of them, in fact, stop blaming umpires for every problem in the world. They realize that umpires aren't responsible for every home run and . . . car accident, for example. What happened with Milt Wilcox is that he got smarter as a pitcher and a complainer. Instead of simply yelling, he would make intelligent, cutting remarks. He'd pitch and I'd tell him, "That curveball was low."

"It wasn't a curveball, Ronnie," he'd say. "It was a slider."

"Yeah, well, I meant to say slider."

"No, you meant to say strike."

He always had some kind of remark to make. It was never personal and he didn't use foul language. But he made me feel like he was in the Peace Corps and I was on parole. But as time passed, he got smarter and I got older. I remember one night, after I'd called a few close pitches balls, he walked off the mound shaking his head. I didn't like that at all, so I took off my mask and moved toward him. "What's the matter with you!" I asked.

"What do you want from me!" he replied. "I gave to the United Way."

By the time I was ready to retire, I liked Milt Wilcox as much as I liked almost any pitcher. Of course, that's about as much as children like broccoli. I respected his ability, his competitiveness, and the fact that he had survived a decade in the big leagues. And I like to think he had begun to respect my ability

too. At least on the day I announced my retirement,
he didn't complain.

I was born in magnificent Honolulu, Hawaii, in 1950,
but almost immediately my father moved our family
to Crooked Oak, Oklahoma. We were the only family
from Honolulu to move to Crooked Oak that particular year. My father also tried to turn me into a track
sprinter. He was an unusual man, my father.

His name was Theodore Lonoee Kanapoo Wilcox,
and we called him T.W., or Chief. He used to tell us
his middle names meant "God's gift to women," but
we were never too sure about that. In Crooked Oak he
worked at a place called Folding Carrier, Inc., designing
shopping carts. Next time you're in a supermarket, or
you see somebody walking in the street with all their
belongings piled into a shopping basket, stop them
and tell them that Ted Wilcox probably designed their
basket.

The Chief had run track and played football in
college in Hawaii. His mile relay team held the state
record for decades. Our backyard in Crooked Oak was
about sixty or seventy yards long and fifteen yards
wide. Other kids had a basketball court behind their
house; we had two running lanes. Every night my
father would work with me and my brother, trying to
teach us how to burst out of the starting blocks he'd
made.

He really believed he could help me develop running speed. What do you expect from a man who
moved from Honolulu to Crooked Oak?

The Chief didn't know anything about baseball,
except that I loved it. That was all he needed to know.
He bought every baseball book he could find, and tried
to teach me everything he learned. Some of it must
have worked; I was pitching in the 1970 World Series
for the Cincinnati Reds when I was twenty years old.

I was also pitching in the minor leagues when I
was twenty-five. I had a sore arm, I couldn't get anybody out, and it was beginning to look like I was just

another former *phee*nom whose future was behind him. That's when I began the second stage of my career. Only ten years later I was again pitching in the World Series. Ironically George "Sparky" Anderson was my manager in both World Series.

Some people don't realize how smart Sparky really is. Believe me, that is one smart man. He was smart enough to follow me to Cincinnati, and we went to the World Series. He was smart enough not to follow me to the Cleveland Indians or the Chicago Cubs, and neither of those clubs won anything. Then he was smart enough to follow me to the Detroit Tigers when we won the World Championship.

What's it like pitching in the big leagues when you're twenty years old? I wish I knew. It has to be great, right? But I just don't remember. The season went by in a whirl. It was like living in a dream that stopped only when I went to sleep. I vaguely remember my first game in the big leagues; we beat San Diego 5–4 and I got credit for the victory, but I couldn't give you any details. I remember pitching in the National League playoffs against the Pittsburgh Pirates. I pitched three innings in relief to get the win. I remember striking out four batters in a row in that game: Matty Alou, Freddie Patek, Roberto Clemente, and Willie Stargell. I know it happened, because I wouldn't have dared dream something like that.

I struck out Roberto Clemente on three pitches, and I can close my eyes and see each of them. Three fastballs on the outside corner. On the black. Three perfect pitches. You think that little kid inside me wasn't jumping up and down screaming when Clemente swung and missed the third pitch? The little kid inside *and* outside. Of course, at that time I still was a little kid.

I pitched that game as if I were in a trance, as if part of me were sitting in the stands watching another part of me pitch. I wasn't aware of anything going on around me. I didn't see or hear the fans. I didn't know the television cameras existed. My entire world consisted of catcher Johnny Bench and the batter. I just knew I could get those hitters out, and I did.

I was a confident kid when I was with the Reds, and eventually that caused me some problems. I really liked to run my own game on the pitcher's mound. Cincinnati had Johnny Bench catching and Sparky Anderson in the dugout, I was twenty years old and telling them what pitches I was going to throw. I was constantly shaking off Bench's signals. I felt that after the season, when I went in to talk to the general manager about my contract, Johnny Bench wasn't going to be sitting next to me saying, "Oh, don't blame him for losing that game. I called the pitch that Parker hit for a home run." It was my career and I wanted the responsibility.

For some reason both Bench and Anderson thought they knew more about pitching than a twenty-year-old rookie. No wonder we had problems. All right, maybe I was a little hardheaded, and Sparky and I did clash a bit. But was that any reason to trade me to Cleveland?

Actually I was grateful to be in Cleveland because the Indians gave me a chance to pitch regularly. In those days anybody who showed up got a chance to pitch regularly. Our pitching staff consisted of Gaylord Perry, then everybody else. We had a pitching coach who was slightly senile and very deaf. That was a bad combination, because he kept forgetting he couldn't hear. He would stay down in the bullpen with us, and had problems hearing the bullpen phone ringing. Occasionally he'd sit with his head resting against the phone so he could feel it ringing, but usually he just sat nearby. We had a bunch of good guys in the bullpen, and every time we'd see him starting to nod off, we'd scream, "Phone, phone!" He'd snap awake, grab the receiver, and start shouting, "Hello, hello. Talk louder, I can't hear you."

The best thing about Cleveland was Gaylord Perry. When I first met him, I was twenty-two and he was in his mid-thirties. I would look at him with tremendous admiration, and think, there's a great pitcher nearing the end of his career, still fighting to win a few more games in the big leagues. I knew that in ten years I'd be able to look back with fond memories about the old guy.

Ten years later the old guy was still winning in the big leagues. And by that time there were all these young players looking at *me* and thinking, there's a pitcher nearing the end of his career, still fighting. . . .

I've never seen a tougher competitor than Gaylord Perry. He would do whatever he had to do to win. He was even tough on his teammates when he was pitching. He believed that if he was out there giving 110 percent, they had better be giving 110 percent too. If they messed up an easy play, or looked as if they were dogging it a little, he'd jump all over them. For that reason he got a lot of ball players mad at him. On the other hand, if a guy knocked in the winning run or had a few hits or made an outstanding play, he'd pay them. He would give them fifty or a hundred dollars, or he'd take them out for dinner.

I never did anything like that, I was too cheap. When one of my teammates played well when I was on the mound, I'd thank him, then say, "Jeez, too bad you didn't do that when Gaylord was pitching."

I learned the fine art of pitching from Gaylord Perry. Anybody who took the time could learn from him; he was a gracious teacher. Not just how to throw a spitball, but how to carry yourself, how to attack a batter, how to use your mind as well as your talent on the mound. Of course, everybody thinks Gaylord Perry equals spitball. And everybody is right. I remember after he had pitched one day, I looked at catcher Ray Fosse's glove. There was a big old ring of Vaseline around the rim of the pocket. Either Gaylord's pitches splashed a lot, or Fosse was loading it up for him.

Gaylord tried to teach me how to throw it. Throwing it was easy. Throwing it near home plate was the tough part. Nobody could hit my spitball. Hit it? Nobody could reach it. Gaylord's spitball was so effective because he knew where it was going. I couldn't even be sure mine was going toward the plate.

Just being on the same pitching staff as Gaylord Perry made me more effective. The word gets around the league very quickly when a pitcher is experimenting with the spitball, and everybody knew I was trying to learn how to throw it. What they didn't know was that I wasn't succeeding. So I'd go out on the mound and I'd walk off the side and rub the back of my neck or reach into my glove or touch my wrist as if I were loading up, and I'd get the batter thinking. I wanted him thinking up there because most batters can't think and hit at the same time.

The amazing thing about Perry is that he would go out there every four or five days and give you his best. He never missed his turn to pitch and I tried to emulate him. Sometimes that was difficult. Once, in 1973, we were playing the Angels in California and I was supposed to start. I was warming up in the bullpen and my arm was killing me. Killing me. It was the first sore arm I'd had in my career, and I was scared. I didn't know what was wrong with it, so I decided I was going to pitch the pain away. So I did what Gaylord always did: I took two tubes of red hot balm and just covered my arm with it. Just slapped that grease all over my arm and shoulder. Gaylord told me it would burn the pain away. He was half right anyway. I felt like somebody was holding a torch to my arm.

We scored four runs in the top half of the first inning, so I took the mound with a four-run lead. Next thing it was 4–4, the Angels had the bases loaded with nobody out, and I was in the shower desperately trying to get that balm off my arm.

How do you get nobody out? It's not that easy. You have to be both bad *and* unlucky. You figure, no matter how hard they hit the ball, chances are they're going to hit at least one of them at somebody. In this particular case, the only people the Angels hit balls at were sitting in the right-field stands.

God, I hated getting knocked out of a game in the first inning. Getting knocked out in the fifth or sixth was not a tremendous thrill, but the *first* inning. You prepare three or four days for every start, building mentally toward that day. And then you get knocked out in the first inning. It's a shock. What do you do for the rest of the day? In this case, no problem. I spent most of my time trying to put out the fire on my arm.

That sore arm caused me to lose just a little off my fastball. For a fastball pitcher, losing just a little bit off his fastball is like losing just a little bit of the foundation of a house. Suddenly I was able to throw my fastball only halfway past the batters. That second half was getting me clobbered. I realized I had to change the way I pitched if I wanted to stay in the big leagues, but besides Gaylord, there was no one there to teach me how to do that. Most pitching coaches, I learned, were there because it was easier than being someplace else. They were just along for the ride. They told me what I already knew: My fastball was losing its velocity.

Cleveland did the best thing it could under the circumstances—traded me to the Chicago Cubs. I was traded for pitcher Dave LaRoche and outfielder Brock Davis. I didn't mind; I thought I would get a chance to pitch regularly for the Cubs. They did trade two players for me. After the trade was announced, the manager called me and told me I was going to be in his starting rotation in spring training and I was going to stay there throughout the season.

I didn't start a game in spring training. And when I didn't pitch at all the first two weeks of the regular season, I went in to see the manager. "It's hard to get you in a game," he explained. "You know you didn't pitch too much during spring training."

Hmmm. I could see this was not turning out to be the wonderful experience I had anticipated. I pitched for the first time twenty-one games into the season. I was the tenth man on a ten-man pitching staff, the mop-up man. It was amazing: Every time I pitched well, I wouldn't pitch again for weeks. But when I pitched badly, he'd get me in there the next day. In fact, he would keep pitching me until I did well—then I'd have to wait a few more weeks.

Finally he called me into his office. "You know,

you're not pitching too much," he pointed out, "so I spoke to the front office and we're going to send you down to the minors for six weeks. You just get yourself in shape and in six weeks we're going to bring you back and put you into the starting rotation."

I went to Wichita, the Cubs Triple A team. After getting into shape, I began pitching very well. Six weeks passed, no phone call. Seven weeks ... seven weeks and one day ... and two days ... I called the general manager. "This is Milt Wilcox," I said. "I've been here almost eight weeks."

"That's great, Milt," he said enthusiastically, "and thanks for calling. Call collect next time."

Hmmm. As I discovered, the general manager knew nothing about my being recalled in six weeks. He told me he would check with the manager, and the next day I was recalled. When I walked into the manager's office, he was thrilled to see me. He patted me on the back, told me he had heard I had pitched well at Wichita, and then said, "I'm putting you right into the rotation as our fifth starter."

The next time I pitched was twenty-one games later.

At the end of the season the Cubs dropped me from their major league roster. The following spring Wichita manager Doc Edwards told me I was going to be his opening day pitcher. All right, I thought, it is the minor leagues, but if I'm the starting day pitcher, it means they think I can still pitch. I'm only twenty-six years old; I have time to make it back to the big leagues.

I had a great spring training camp. I was throwing the ball as well as I'd thrown it in a few years. But three days before we broke camp, Doc Edwards called me into his office again. "I just got a call from the front office," he explained. "They want me to go with some of the younger kids. You're going to be the fifth starter and long reliever."

"I thought you were going to use only four starters," I said.

Edwards nodded. "Yeah," he said softly.

That's it, I thought, that's the career. I was twenty-six years old, the "younger kids" they were talking about were twenty-four and twenty-five. I knew they were trying to tell me something.

I had no choice but to get used to being the fifth starter and mop-up man for Wichita. Either that or learn how to design shopping baskets.

Breaks come in strange places. Mine came in Evansville, Indiana, home of the Detroit Tigers club in the AAA American Association. Wichita was getting beaten badly one night, and rather than use another real pitcher, Doc Edwards put me in to mop up. I did pretty well. As it turned out, the Evansville Triplets had something like eight doubleheaders to play in the next ten days and were desperate for pitching. I was a pitcher. So Wichita "loaned" me to Evansville. They didn't trade me, or sell me, they *loaned* me. It made me feel a little like a lawnmower—although a lawnmower probably had more value at that time than I did.

Freddie Hatfield was managing Evansville, and in one of the first few games, he brought me in to relieve against Denver. I struck out six men in three innings, my best performance in a long time. I was all pumped up. I knew after that that I'd get a chance to pitch in some of those doubleheaders. I might even get a start.

"I'm not going to pitch you again for a while," Hatfield told me.

I didn't know whether to laugh or cry. I thought, here we go again. "Why," I asked him, "tell me why."

"We like the way you pitched against Denver," he said, "and we're going to try to buy you from Wichita. We don't want to pitch you again because if you do too well, they'll want too much for you and we might not be able to make the deal."

Baseball is certainly a funny game. First I didn't get to pitch because I wasn't good enough, then I didn't get to pitch because I was too good. It was the first time I'd ever heard of anybody being too valuable to play. But it felt good to be wanted. Good? It was great. Wichita sold me to Evansville for some old uniforms, and a season later I was back in the major leagues.

The Tigers brought me up in 1977 and put me out there on the mound every fourth or fifth day. I had always known how to throw, but in Detroit I began to learn how to pitch. Everything came together for me on April 20, 1983, when I retired the first twenty-six White Sox batters I faced. Unfortunately it takes twenty-seven outs to make a complete game.

I had two outs in the bottom of the ninth inning. I was one out away from pitching the twelfth perfect game in baseball history. Pinch-hitter Jerry Hairston was the only thing between me and a permanent place in the record books. The Chicago fans were giving me a standing ovation.

I knew Hairston was a good fastball hitter who liked to hit pitches on the outside part of the plate, so I decided to jam him inside. As I released the ball, I knew I'd missed just a little, and the ball started tailing back over the middle of the plate. Hairston hit a line drive right at second baseman Lou Whitaker.

For an instant, for a fraction of an instant, I thought it would be caught. I had done it. A perfect game. Twenty-seven up, twenty-seven down. I turned just as the ball sailed by Whitaker, maybe five feet beyond his reach, five feet from the Hall of Fame. The next batter hit a routine groundball to first base for the final out of the game. Twenty-eight up, twenty-seven down.

I'd pitched a one-hitter. A complete game. A shut-out. We had won the ball game. I had pitched about as well as I could, almost perfectly. And I felt rotten. My teammates felt worse. The clubhouse was very quiet, as if we'd lost an important game. I think they had been pulling for me even more than I had been pulling for me.

Under normal circumstances I cannot get to sleep at night when I've pitched. It makes no difference if I've pitched good, fair, or terrible; that night I do not sleep. I replay the game in my mind all night. I try lying down, but inevitably I start tossing and turning, then I get up to watch television, maybe drink some milk; the adrenaline is still flowing and that night I just don't sleep.

The next night, though, I'm a dead man.

The night I pitched the one-hitter I didn't even bother lying down. That was the worst. I spent the night walking the streets of Chicago. I saw the sunrise the next morning. I finally managed to convince myself that the world was not coming to an end, that I had done something good, not bad. It wasn't like I'd lost the seventh game of the World Series. I'd been one batter away from perfect.

But oh, that one pitch . . .

I guess if I had been a little luckier, Hairston's line drive would've gone right at Whitaker. Of course, if I had been a little less lucky on numerous other occasions, the line drives that did go at somebody would've been hits. I've learned that luck evens out in a career; as many bloops fall in for hits as there are smashes hit right at somebody. A pitcher will have good days and bad days, and if the good days outnumber the bad days, he is going to have a good career. I have also found that the harder I worked, the more good luck I had.

Personally, I am not at all superstitious. Oh, I always eat blueberry pancakes on the day I pitch, but that's just a coincidence. And I never step on the foul line while walking out to the pitcher's mound, but that's just a habit. And I always throw eight warm-up pitches before an inning, three fastballs, then three breaking balls, then a fastball I turn over and a fastball I throw straight. That isn't a superstition, though; it's just a routine I use to help me get ready to pitch.

There are lucky baseballs, however. I'll get a baseball from the umpire and it will just feel right. Whatever I do with it turns out to be good. I'll get quick outs with it, or make a bad pitch that the hitter misses. Then, inevitably, someone will foul it off. If it doesn't go into the stands, I'll scream at my fielder, "Get that ball, get that ball." They'll think I'm crazy, but they also think all balls are the same. What happens sometimes, though, is that I'll get the ball back, make one pitch, and the umpire will look at it and throw it out of the game.

There are balls that a pitcher really wants to keep. In the minor leagues a ball can have graffiti written practically all over it and the umpires will keep it in play. But in the majors if a ball has one little spot, or one good slice in the cover, the umpire will throw it out. Balls do get scuffed, and cut, and after pitching as long as I have, I know how to make a ball like that dip or sink or run. I like those balls. Now, I have never scuffed or scratched one up myself—not because I don't want to—but because I'm so inept that I'd have to stand on the mound with a complete carving set before I could make any difference.

I've noticed that when I pitch against certain pitchers, Don Sutton or Tommy John, for example, I'll pick up the ball to start an inning and I'll find slice marks on the baseball. I don't know where these marks come from, maybe sharp infield grass, but I certainly do not complain.

All baseballs are not created equal. The seams of some balls are unusually high, or low, and some balls are even lopsided. After all these years I can instantly feel the difference in baseballs. I like a small ball, the smaller the better.

A ball that feels small is one that has high seams. National League balls feel big to me because they have flatter, lower seams. American League baseballs have higher seams, and these seams create additional wind resistance. It is wind resistance that causes a baseball to move.

I don't know why American and National League baseballs are so different; all balls are supposedly sewn at the same place in Haiti. All I can figure out is that they have one little old lady sewing National League balls, and she likes a tight stitch, and another little old lady sewing American League balls, and she favors a high stitch. I do know that the two leagues have different balls and I have a difficult time throwing a good breaking pitch with the National League baseball. I've always suspected there are more fastball and slider pitchers in the National League because of the difference in baseballs.

Generally hitters are not too bright. Most hitters go up to bat determined to wait for a fastball. It doesn't matter if they are facing a curveball pitcher, a knuckleball pitcher, a pitcher who hasn't thrown a fastball since Little League, they go up there and wait, and wait, as the pitcher throws change-up after change-up after change-up. Only then do they begin to think he's a change-up pitcher, although they still insist on looking for fastballs fifty percent of the time.

I've learned more about pitching by sitting on the bench listening to hitters discussing opposing pitchers than I have from all the coaches I've ever known. When I hear a hitter complaining that the pitcher's funky motion bothers them, or that the pitcher hides the ball so well they can't pick it up, I pay attention. If it bothers a hitter, it has to help me.

So I have this funky motion. I bounce up and down one, two, sometimes three times before I pitch. After I release the pitch, I throw out my glove hand to the side in an attempt to distract the batter. I use the biggest glove I can find because it helps me hide the ball. I'll even use a different color glove, a black one or red one, if I think that might bother the hitter.

With all that you'd think I'd be tougher to hit than I am. Every pitcher has some hitters who he simply cannot get out. It doesn't matter what he does or how he does it, he is not going to be able to get these hitters out. I know I helped Del Unser stay in the big leagues. Joe LaHoud was a lifetime .223 hitter and he probably owes me one hundred of those points. Joe LaHoud. I'll bet he hit .800 against me. He had sixty-five home runs, ten of them probably came off me. I tried everything possible against him, it made no difference. I got so frustrated, I threw him the only knuckleball I've ever thrown in the big leagues. He doubled it off the top of the left-field fence.

Conversely there are hitters who can't hit a particular pitcher. The pitcher could roll the ball down the middle of the plate and they couldn't hit it. The pitcher could tell them what pitch he is throwing, they couldn't hit it. Unfortunately I'm still looking to find the hitters who can't hit me.

Not only did I have a few batters I couldn't get out, I had an entire team I couldn't beat: the Baltimore Orioles. The Orioles beat me for the first time in the second game of the 1970 World Series; I didn't beat them for almost ten years. I pitched a lot of good games against them, I'd lose 2–1, 3–2, but I also had a lot of games in which I didn't get out of the first inning.

One reason I couldn't beat the Orioles was that the noise their fans generated in Baltimore's Memorial Stadium was the loudest noise I ever heard. It just got inside me and shook things up. It really rattled me. Of course, I couldn't beat them when we played them in Cleveland or Detroit, so it wasn't just their fans.

The finest year of my career was 1984. A lot of players who played for the Tigers that season will say that. It was a special year, a once-in-a-lifetime year. We started off the season 35–5. We weren't surprised we won thirty-five games; what we couldn't figure out was how we managed to lose five. We led the Eastern Division from the first day of the season to the last. We beat the Kansas City Royals in the American League playoffs in three straight games, and we beat the San Diego Padres for the World Championship four games out of five. Not only that, we really had a good time.

The big thing about that team was its togetherness. Thanks to Sparky, every player in the club knew exactly what his role was, and was satisfied with it. Nobody complained they weren't playing enough. We had our starters and our role players, and everybody did the job he was supposed to do. Most incredible of all was our bullpen. Our relief pitchers pounced on save opportunities like negligence attorneys fighting to represent a client hit by a city bus going the wrong way on a one-way street. They rarely missed a save.

How good were they? In 1984 I set the only major league record I hold. I started thirty-three games and completed none. I won seventeen games and lost only eight, and I never saw a ninth inning.

I could have finished one game, the pennant clincher against Kansas City. I had them beaten 1–0 after eight innings and I was throwing the ball super. When I had returned to the dugout at the end of the eighth inning, Sparky came over to ask me how I felt. "Great," I told him.

"Okay," he said, "go out there and finish up."

I sat there on the bench thinking, this is really a weird feeling. I'd love to go out there and get my complete game, but for what? I got a guy in the bullpen who can come in and shut them down. Then I had another thought. If I completed the game and won it 1–0, I had a good shot at being named Most Valuable Player in the playoffs.

My mind was really cranking, but finally I decided, so what? It's just not worth the chance. What if I went out there and blew it for everybody else? I turned to pitching coach Roger Craig and said, "Tell Sparky I'm not going to pitch the ninth."

When Sparky heard that, he smiled broadly. "I was waiting to hear you say that."

Willie Hernandez completed my shutout and, fourteen years to the day I'd clinched the National League pennant for the Cincinnati Reds, I clinched the American League pennant for the Detroit Tigers. It's a great habit to get into. I'm certainly looking forward to October 5, 1998.

It had taken me a long time, but I'd finally learned that success in baseball is not measured by what you achieve individually, but rather what heights you reach as a team. That day in the playoffs was the first time I'd realized that, and it made the victory all the sweeter.

Playing major league baseball is tough, but not nearly as difficult as not playing major league baseball. I injured my arm early in 1985 and spent most of the season on the disabled list going slowly insane. Some people go to medical school to learn how the body works; I played ball. I've had so many different problems with my elbow and shoulder throughout my career, I've become an expert on what is attached to what, and what part A does when part B is stretched. My part A was not doing it, and I spent more time in hospitals and clinics than Marcus Welby in all the reruns combined. After throwing too many pitches for too many years, my shoulder looked like my room when I was growing up. I had to have surgery to clean up the debris.

Not knowing if my arm was ever going to be strong enough for me to pitch again was a kind of torture. I couldn't watch a game, but I didn't want to miss one. All I wanted to do was go out on the sidelines and throw; the only thing I couldn't do was throw. Because of my various injuries I've learned the best feeling in the world is no feeling, and I know that my arm will never feel that again.

I'm confident my arm is going to regain its strength, but in case it doesn't, I've been working on a mean knuckleball. That pitch is definitely in my future. As I told Tiger catcher Lance Parrish, "Don't be surprised if you get a big box for Christmas, and when you open it up you find the biggest catcher's glove you've ever seen."

MY WILD WILD WAYS
by Charlie Hough

Charlie Hough is one of the rarest players in baseball. He is a knuckleball pitcher. Besides Charlie, Phil Niekro and Joe Niekro throw the knuckleball, and those are the only three knuckleball pitchers in baseball. More men have walked on the moon than make a living throwing a knuckleball. There are more Edsels still running than there are knuckleball pitchers. There are as many living former presidents of the United States as there are knuckleball pitchers. Think of it this way: I've written as many books as there are knuckleball pitchers in baseball.

If you've seen one knuckleball ... you've seen one knuckleball. No two are alike. A knuckleball is a pitch thrown without any spin on it, so it f l o a t s slo ... owly and tan ... ta ... liz ... ing ... ly toward home plate. Sometimes it $_r$$i$^{ses}, sometimes it ^{di}$_{ps}$. Sometimes it does $e_v^{er}_{yt}^{h}_{in}$$_g$. Many hitters consider it some sort of punishment and find trying to hit it as infuriating and frustrating as trying to capture a mist.

It is surprising that more pitchers don't try to throw it, because it can be extremely effective and is not that difficult to throw. It can be thrown by digging your fingernails into the ball and thrusting it out of your hand, or bending your fingers so that your knuckles rest on the ball and, again, thrusting it out of your hand. With a little practice almost anyone can throw it. Throwing it is easy.

Controlling it is hard. Nobody knows where a knuckleball is going, not the pitcher who throws it, the batter who can't hit it, the catcher who can't catch it, or the umpire who can't call it. When working behind home plate when one of the three knuckleball pitchers is on the mound, the thing an umpire must do is wait, wait, wait, then . . . wait a little longer. There are few things as embarrassing as putting up your right hand to call a strike, then having the ball suddenly shoot up and hit you right in that hand.

"It's definitely an unattractive pitch," Phil Niekro, who has won three hundred games throwing it, told me. "Sometimes when I see a batter swatting at it, I have to put my glove over my face because I really don't want anyone to think I'm laughing at them. I'm not either. I don't blame them for being unable to hit it. I've been throwing it twenty-five years and I don't know what it's going to do."

Every knuckleball pitcher in baseball—Hough, Phil Niekro, and Joe Niekro—dreams of being able to throw one, just one, real fastball. "The radar gun has clocked me upward of seventy-seven mph on my fastball," Phil Niekro claims, "and I think if I keep working at it, I might be able to get it up to eighty-two." Which, he does not add, is slightly slower than Dwight Gooden's change-up.

Knuckleball pitchers use their straight balls—it wouldn't be fair to other pitchers to call them fastballs—as a change-up. When they feel the batter has timed the knuckleball and might be just a little overanxious, they might try to slip a straight ball past him. "I throw my fastball only when I know the batter is waiting on the knuckleball," Phil Niekro *explains. "Tell you what though. I can't throw two fastballs in a row."*

What is it that turns an honest, decent human pitcher into a knuckleballer? What sort of twisted mind makes a man resort to that pitch? Desperation, usually.

I was drafted by the Los Angeles Dodgers in the eighth round of the 1966 player draft. I was a third baseman, first baseman, and pitcher. The Dodgers drafted me because I looked like a good hitter. In fact, I couldn't hit very well at all, but I did look good. I had a strange combination of talents—a home-run hitter's swing and no power. I was one of those players who would rip a little pop-up over second. That same year the Dodgers also drafted a third baseman who did have real power. He didn't look very good, and he couldn't field, but he could hit the ball over the fence. It was pretty obvious to me that they had more chance of teaching him how to pick up a ground ball than teaching me how to hit home runs.

I was assigned to the Dodger Rookie League team in Ogden, Utah, managed by a former minor league pitcher named Tommy Lasorda. I expected a professional manager on that level would be a calm man, a teacher, a man ready and willing to sit quietly with his players and listen to their problems, perhaps a small God. Instead, I walked into the clubhouse and there was this maniac, screaming at the top of his lungs that if we didn't get out on the field and kill the Giants Rookie League team, he was probably going to die.

Tommy was the man who turned me into a pitcher. He made that decision the first time he saw me run. My lack of speed combined with my lack of power convinced him I should pitch. At that point I didn't even know what a knuckleball was. I had a decent fastball, an average curveball, and reasonable control. I remember the first game in which I pitched very well. It was the fourth game of my career, and I was playing third base.

In the eighth inning we were trailing by one run. The other team had a runner on second, no outs, and their pitcher was coming to bat. Tommy called me over to the mound from third. I walked slowly to meet him, feeling very good that the manager thought enough of my ability to bring me in to pitch in this situation. "You're gonna pitch to one batter, the pitcher," he said as he handed me the baseball. "He's gonna bunt. You're the best fielder I've got. I want you to hold the runner close at second, throw a strike and let the pitcher bunt it, field the bunt, and throw the runner out at third. Don't worry about a thing. Then I'll get you right out of there."

So I took my warm-up pitches, trying not to think about the fact that the manager had put me in to pitch because I could field. Finally I was ready to pitch. I went into a stretch, held the runner close at second, and threw a strike. So far so good. On my next pitch, the pitcher laid a bunt down the third base line. Still, good. I went over to field it . . . and tripped right over the baseball. I went flying.

As I was lying there on the ground, *on the ground*, I looked up and saw Lasorda stepping right over me. I mean, he was out of the dugout before I hit the ground, calling for another pitcher and a stretcher. And he was screaming as only Tommy Lasorda could scream. Loudly.

It was my ability as a hitter that determined I would be a pitcher. Tommy figured I had no chance of making the big leagues as an everyday player, therefore I had to be a pitcher. Actually I had two pretty good seasons, then I hurt my pitching shoulder. I didn't tell anybody. There were so many good young pitchers in the Dodger organization, I was afraid to miss even one turn. So I kept going out there, and my shoulder got worse and worse. Finally I begged the Dodgers to let me go to the Instructional League to try to work out the pain.

The manager of the Instructional League team

was Tommy Lasorda. Goldie Holt was the pitching instructor. After watching me throw fastballs on the sidelines for a few minutes, Goldie looked at me and asked, "You ever think about throwing a knuckleball?"

I was ready to try anything. "No," I admitted. "How do you hold it?" He showed me and we started playing catch. It was sort of embarrassing. Goldie was sixty years old and he was throwing harder than I was. But the first few knuckleballs I threw had excellent movement. I couldn't control it at all, but I couldn't control my curveball all that well, either, so that didn't bother me. After throwing with Goldie for a while, I went into the clubhouse to find Lasorda.

"Tommy," I announced, "I'm gonna start throwing a knuckleball."

He was overjoyed. "You'd better do something," he said, " 'cause I love you like I love my own son, and if you don't start doing something right now, I'm going to have to release you."

I started throwing the knuckleball in the Instructional League and had what might be called mixed success with it. One inning I'd retire the other team in order, striking out three straight batters, and the next inning I'd give up six runs on one hit and seven walks.

The following spring I went to training camp knowing that if I didn't do well, I would probably be given my unconditional release. My real hope was that I would pitch well enough to be promoted to the Dodgers Double A team. Instead, I had a tremendous camp, I actually looked as if I had control of the knuckleball, and was assigned to the Triple-A Spokane team. I tried not to get too excited about it. I figured I was the last player on the Spokane team and was pretty sure that as soon as someone got sent down from the major league club, I was going to be demoted. The first month of the season I won nine games.

Nine games. Nine games! I hadn't been able to win consistently in the lowest division of professional baseball. I learned a new pitch, and three months later I was the leading pitcher in the Triple-A International

League. It was like winning the baseball lottery. As Tommy Lasorda says, it was as if I had taken my very last breath on earth—and woke up two weeks later on a beach in Hawaii.

The only problem I had was with my catchers. They didn't believe I was going to stay with the Spokane club very long, so they didn't bother ordering the oversize catcher's mitt used to handle knuckleball pitchers. And by the time they decided to get a glove, I was on my way to the major leagues.

Bob "Scrapiron" Stinson did most of the catching. We had only two signals; he put down one finger for a knuckleball, two fingers for a fastball. One night, with a count of two balls and no strikes on the batter, he put down two fingers. Fastball. So I threw my fastball right down the center of the plate. As I released it, I thought, this pitch has nothing on it at all, this is a home run. But the batter was so surprised, he didn't swing—and Scrapiron was so surprised, he didn't catch the ball. It hit him right in the center of the chest protector. Fortunately I couldn't throw hard enough to hurt him. He picked up the ball and jogged out to the mound. "What are you doing?" he asked.

"What do you mean? You called for a fastball."

He hesitated for a moment, thought about it, then said questioningly, "Yeah?" Then he shrugged and trotted back behind the plate. For the rest of the game, every time he gave me a signal, I'd see him looking down to see how many fingers he was showing. That made me very happy; I figured, hey, I got a guy out here who's dumber than I am.

The Dodgers decided to bring me up to the big leagues in the middle of that 1970 season, the first year I'd thrown the knuckleball. It was an almost impossible situation to believe. A few months earlier I was just about out of baseball, then I was in the major leagues. I knew it couldn't be that easy. I also knew I wasn't ready to pitch in the big leagues. Two weeks before the Dodgers called me up, my wife and I had been watching the Saturday afternoon *Game of the Week* on television. The Pirates were playing the Cubs, and it seemed to me that someone was hitting a home run every third pitch. As I watched the great Billy Williams hit one, I said to my wife, "You know, I can't imagine them not hitting the junk I'm throwing. They're hitting home runs against pitchers with talent; what are they going to do to me?"

In my first big league game Dodger manager Walt Alston brought me in to pitch against the Pirates with two out in the ninth inning. We were leading by a run and they had runners on first and second. I walked the first batter I faced, loading the bases, and bringing Willie Stargell to bat. I pitched carefully to Stargell, very carefully, and the count went to three balls and two strikes. Catcher Steve Yeager signaled for a fastball. Yeah, I thought, that's a great idea. Stargell's going to be looking for the knuckleball, so we'll fool him with a fastball. But as I went into my wind-up, I suddenly remembered I didn't have a fastball. The reason I had started throwing a knuckleball was that I couldn't get A-League players out with my fastball, and here I was throwing it to Willie Stargell with the bases loaded in the ninth inning. I couldn't believe it.

Neither could Stargell. He must have been even more surprised than I was, because he swung at it and missed. Strike three. The game was over. I stood on the pitcher's mound, saying loudly, "He missed it. He missed it. I can't believe he missed it."

That strikeout turned out to be a somewhat mixed blessing. I figured, if I can throw my fastball past Willie Stargell, it must be better than I thought it was. As it turned out, that was incorrect. I had been right in the first place. And since I was still having problems controlling the knuckleball, I spent the next two seasons commuting between Los Angeles and the Triple-A Spokane team.

In 1971 Spokane manager Tommy Lasorda sat down next to me on the bus and told me he had great news. Hoyt Wilhelm, the greatest knuckleball pitcher of all time, had just signed with Spokane. "He's gonna be able to teach you everything you need to know about throwing the knuckleball."

I looked at Lasorda as if he were crazy. I mean, I knew he was crazy, but this was more than that, this was impossible. Wilhelm was forty-seven years old and had been released by the Atlanta Braves. He was going to the Hall of Fame, not to the minor leagues. I didn't believe even Lasorda could talk him into pitching in the minors.

Wilhelm joined the ball club in Hawaii. And just as Tommy had promised, he was tremendously helpful to me. He convinced me that I was a knuckleball pitcher and only a knuckleball pitcher. "With your talent," he said, "anytime you throw them anything but the knuckleball, you're doing the batter a favor." I listened to him and started pitching better than ever. And a few weeks later, when the Dodgers needed a relief pitcher, they called up Wilhelm. I had lost my job to a forty-seven-year-old man.

It took me three seasons before I finally pitched well enough to stick in the big leagues. My problem was psychological as well as physical. I just found it difficult to believe that major league batters couldn't hit what I was throwing. Once in a while, even today, it amazes me that I can get great players out with that pitch. I remember walking off the mound in Kansas City one day after striking out George Brett, and thinking, boy, that's awfully slow; how can he not be hitting that pitch.

Hitters don't seem to mind being struck out by a macho fastball, but they hate swinging at a knuckleball. Watching them swat away at it is like watching someone trying to hit a butterfly in a telephone booth. When I was pitching in the minors, shortstop Frank Johnson once struck out swinging at a pitch that actually hit him. Sometimes batters swing so hard at the pitch that their momentum carries them around and they take a second swing at it. Big Cliff Johnson once took two swings at the same knuckleball, then fell down, looked out at me, and started laughing. I knew exactly how he felt.

Since I can't really control it, batters can't hit it, and catchers have difficulty catching it, I'm not surprised that umpires have trouble calling it. The only time I'll ever get upset with an umpire for missing a pitch is when I throw what I laughingly call my fastball, the batter doesn't swing, and the umpire calls it a ball. If I have the courage to throw that pitch in the major leagues, he should at least give me a working handicap. Besides, I don't have that many fastballs left in my right arm. I can't afford to miss with one. Young umpires in particular have difficulty calling the knuckleball because they've never seen it thrown in the minor leagues. They have to learn to wait until the ball crosses the plate, no matter how long it takes, before calling it. I've actually had umpires call the pitch and then the batter has hit it.

I have just one bit of advice for the young umpire who has never seen a knuckleball: Yes, it really is that slow.

Umpires make wrong calls both to my advantage and disadvantage, so it tends to even out. Probably the call I remember most was made by National League umpire Art Williams just after he came up to the big leagues. I was pitching in San Francisco, which is difficult enough because of the strong winds blowing off the bay, and the knuckleball was moving as well as it ever has—meaning I had no idea where it was going. Bill "Mad Dog" Madlock was batting for the Giants and my catcher was Johnny Oates. With three balls and two strikes on Madlock, I threw a knuckleball that started way outside, swerved inside, then broke outside. Way outside. Way, way outside. Oates literally had to dive to catch it. It was so far outside that it would have been behind a batter standing in the left-handed batter's box. As I looked at the plate, all I saw was batter Madlock and umpire Williams. Oates had literally dived out of my field of vision. Williams called it strike three.

Madlock reacted much better than I thought he would. He very calmly took off his helmet, and politely handed the helmet and bat to Williams. "Go ahead," he said to the umpire, "you try to hit that." Williams threw him out of the game.

I've often been asked for my definition of a good knuckleball. That's simple. A good knuckleball is one that the catcher successfully blocks. Former catcher Bob Uecker claimed that when he was catching, he never had any problem with the knuckleball. After it got by him, he'd wait until it stopped rolling, then simply pick it up.

When I first came up to the Dodgers, my catchers were Steve Yeager and Joe Ferguson. Manager Walt Alston hated to put me in a game because of what I did to them. He'd sit in the dugout and, if a pitch got past them, he'd decide I couldn't pitch. "What kind of pitcher can you be," he wondered, "if these guys can't catch you?" I had never really thought of it that way. Finally I told Yeager my career depended on his ability to catch the knuckleball. Eventually both he and Ferguson got very good at blocking it.

When Tommy Lasorda became manager of the Dodgers, he began to use me much more than Alston ever had. Tommy had a nine-man pitching staff instead of the usual ten, and because throwing a knuckleball puts less strain on the arm and shoulder than any other pitch, I tried to pick up the slack. I'd pitch an inning to save a game one night, then throw four innings in a lost game the next day just so we wouldn't have to use a pitcher who couldn't throw as often. I threw a lot of innings in 1976, '77, and '78, and finally they began to take a toll. I reinjured my shoulder and took a seat in the back of the bullpen.

I sat there for about a year and a half. The only calls for me in the bullpen were wrong numbers.

Knuckleball pitchers have to pitch regularly to be effective, so on those few occasions when I did get into a game, I was hit pretty hard. Tommy was really in a bind. He couldn't use me because I was getting hit hard every time I pitched, and unless he used me, I couldn't be effective. Since we were in the pennant race every year, he really couldn't afford to use me. And I couldn't complain. What was I going to say? Don't use the pitchers who are winning games for you.

After a while it became obvious I wasn't going to pitch in Los Angeles ... or anywhere else for that matter. Nobody wanted me. Tommy finally convinced Eddie Robinson, general manager of the Texas Rangers, to give me an opportunity to pitch. The Rangers are the team that traded away Ron Darling, Walt Terrell, and Dave Righetti, among many others ... but they wanted me. Makes you wonder. To me, this was another example of what a tremendous salesman Lasorda is—Robinson never even asked him why, if I could still pitch, he was trying so hard to give me away.

Pat Corrales was the Rangers manager. He didn't use me right away. He didn't use me after right away either. When it became obvious he wasn't going to pitch me in relief, I asked him for a chance to start a game. I figured, I wasn't getting a chance to pitch relief, I might as well not get a chance to start.

A few weeks later we went up to Toronto. As the team was going through customs, one of our starting pitchers, Ferguson Jenkins, was arrested for possession of a small amount of cocaine. It took a federal case for me to get my first starting assignment.

It was the first time I'd ever been to Toronto. My first start. I was pumped up. Ready to throw. The lead-off batter stepped to the plate, and I threw him a tremendous knuckleball.

He tripled. I was in trouble.

That runner just died there on third base. Shriveled up and died. I pitched a five-hit shutout. Man, I was happy. All I could think about was, keep Fergie in jail. Lock him up and throw away the key. After my performance I was sure I would fill his spot in the rotation as long as he was suspended. And that is exactly what happened, almost. Seventeen days later I got a chance to pitch again.

Seventeen days later. I had pitched a five-hit shutout and didn't pitch again for seventeen days. All I could think about was that it was a good thing I didn't throw a no-hitter. I might never have pitched again.

Corrales was no different from most managers.

Managers just don't understand why batters can't hit the knuckleball. I can sympathize with them; I don't either. But managers seem to believe that knuckleball pitchers are holding up a sagging roof with tired arms. That they are always close to disaster.

Eventually, though, the Rangers started using me regularly. The more I pitched, the better I pitched. The better I pitched, the more they used me. In 1984 I was the Rangers' leading pitcher, winning 18 games. I was also second in innings pitched in the American League.

Basically I throw ninety percent knuckleballs. The other ten percent are prayers. I probably could throw other pitches. The only reason I don't is that I love pitching in the major leagues. My shoulder has never really recovered from the injuries I suffered in the minor leagues and then with the Dodgers, but every once in a while I can crank up and fire my eighty-mph fastball. But it takes its toll. Once, I remember, during the 1982 season, I threw a slider to Chris Spier on a 3–2 count. He swung at it and missed by a foot. When I got to the dugout, they told me that was the best fastball I'd thrown in a year. I said, "Not only was it the best fastball, it was also the best slider too." But throwing that pitch just wrenched my shoulder. It was on fire, and by the end of the game I could barely bloop it up there.

A lot of players think they can throw a knuckleball. They know they can't hit it, so they try to throw it. Everybody I play catch with on the sidelines tries to show me that they have a better knuckleball than I do. And on the sidelines, some of them do. Larry Parrish, for example, will stand eighty feet away and whip a mean knuckleball at me. It starts dancing and I have no idea where it's going. I throw my pitch so softly that if it hits you, it's like being bitten by an apologetic mosquito. Parrish's knuckleball bounces off your body and leaves big purple bruises.

It's relatively easy to throw a knuckleball on the sidelines—it's considerably more difficult to throw it from the raised pitcher's mound. That was the toughest thing I had to learn. On the sidelines you're throwing from level ground, so you can actually push the ball up. On the mound you have to throw it down, which is much, much more difficult. I hated pitching in the Astrodome, for example, because the mound there is approximately thirty feet high, so those fastball pitchers they've got can just burn it down at the batter. I would be most effective pitching from a foxhole.

I average six or seven strikeouts a game. I don't know how, either, but I do. When I was a pitcher with real pitches, I would often get two strikes on a batter and start thinking about how to strike him out. I'd decide to throw a fastball just off the plate, then a slider inside, maybe break off a sharp curveball, then bust a fastball inside. I couldn't do any of that, of course, but that's what I'd decide. I ended up in serious trouble. Things are much easier now. I just stand out there on the pitcher's mound and think, I'm gonna throw this thing up there and it better do something or I'm in a lot of danger. And then I throw it, and I say, go ahead, hit this one—but don't hit it too hard.

(Ed. Note: Ferguson Jenkins was found guilty of cocaine possession, but the judge immediately erased the verdict due to Jenkins's community service. Today he has no criminal record.)

THE WIMPY STORY
by Tom Paciorek

In 1974 Tom Paciorek and I were both in the only
World Series of our careers. That might well have
been the most boring World Series ever played, al-
though I really don't think it was our fault. Quick:
Name the two teams that played in the 1974 Fall
Classic.

All right, slow: Name the two teams that played
in the 1974 Fall Classic. Believe me, we could wait
until my mother won a beauty contest and no one
would remember. Paciorek was with the Los Angeles
Dodgers, I was with the American League. Charlie
Finley's Oakland A's beat the Dodgers four games to
one. How boring was it? It was so boring that the
most memorable moment in the entire series was a
pick-off play.

Finley had signed baseball's first designated runner that season, sprinter Herb Washington. Washington had played in ninety games, scoring twenty-nine
runs and stealing twenty-eight bases. He had no hits,
primarily because he never batted. Never. Let me put
it this way: Eddie Gaedel, the three-foot-seven midget

that Bill Veeck hired to pinch-hit in 1951, batted more times than Herb Washington. So when A's manager Alvin Dark put Herb Washington in as a pinch runner, it was not really a secret that he was going to try to steal second base.

Mike Marshall was pitching for the Dodgers. Marshall was an extremely intelligent individual. You knew he was intelligent because he would tell you that in words that no one could understand. Marshall took the baseball and looked in for catcher Steve Yeager's sign. He checked first base. The crowd tensed for this confrontation. Yeager got set, ready to come up throwing. Washington took a four-step lead off first base. The tension was so thick you could slice it with a food processor. Marshall looked again, Washington moved off another step. I was hungry. Then Marshall threw over to first base and picked off Washington.

That was it, the highlight of the World Series. My only World Series. It made me look back fondly to the excitement of going from Endicott into Johnson City on a Saturday night to watch the traffic light change.

The series was so boring that I spent most of my time talking to the people sitting along the outfield foul lines. That upset baseball commissioner Bowie Kuhn, who warned me that if I said one more word to anybody during the World Series, he would remove me from the field. The next day Major League Baseball Films asked me to wear a microphone so they could hear me talking.

The result was that the official series film featured a conversation between me and Dodger third-base coach Tommy Lasorda. "Well, Ronnie," Tommy would say, "that Catfish Hunter is something, isn't he?"

"Yep."

"I've never seen anything like it. I can't believe he can put every pitch on the black part of the plate like that. I mean, we have guys over in our league with good control, but doesn't he ever miss?"

"No."

Then he would change the topic. "I don't like the designated-hitter rule at all," he said. "You like it?"

"No."

"It just takes too much out of the game, you know what I mean?"

"Yep."

"I like to see a manager make some moves. Like right here, see?"

"Sure."

"Walter [Alston] has got to decide what he wants to do. . . ."

Paciorek batted twice during the series, doubling for a lifetime World Series average of .500. I don't remember meeting him during that series. One of the things that happens if you spend enough years in baseball is that you forget many important moments. Quite often, in fact, players will say to me, "Gosh, Ronnie, remember that afternoon in Detroit when I got my two hundred thirty-fourth hit, a single up the middle. You were the umpire."

Remember a single up the middle? I don't remember entire seasons. Ask me about a restaurant in Oakland though.

I really have forgotten some of the most memorable moments of my major league career. In fact, I think the three most exciting things that I saw and have forgotten are . . . are . . . are going to be remembered at a later date.

I remember meeting Tom Paciorek though. It was in 1978, when he signed with the Seattle Mariners. I always remember players who smile on the field. I quickly discovered he was a fine player and a good guy. But even before I met him, there was something about him I didn't like. His name. Paciorek? I-O-R-E-K? Go ahead, pronounce that. Wrooonggg! Normal people can't pronounce that. And I never liked any name I couldn't pronounce. Spell it? Forget about that; I certainly did. Whenever he was inserted in a game and I had to write his name on the line-up card, I simply wrote down "Tom Polish."

Paciorek simply is not a great baseball name. A great baseball name is Roberto Clemente. It just rolls off the tongue. As any real fan knows, great names have nothing to do with ability. I always liked to hear someone else pronounce the name Jose Valdivielso. Val-de-ve-el-so. What a great name. Fernando Valenzuela, the most beautiful name in the world when Vince Scully pronounces it. But when I pronounce it, I make it sound like a leftover pasta dinner.

Some names are perfect, Greg Luzinski is the right name for a slugger. Reggie Jackson is an acceptable name for a slugger. But Harold Baines? Absolutely not. Harold is simply not a slugger's name.

Bobby Valentine, the Texas manager, probably the best name in baseball. The man is a sweetheart. Fred Stanley, a great name for a utility player. If you were starting a ball club, wouldn't you want a player named Cesar Geronimo? To me, Goose Gossage is the right name for a fireballing pitcher, while Phil Niekro is proper for a dawdling knuckleballer. Ralph Houk was a good, no-nonsense name for a good, no-nonsense manager. Earl Weaver is a fine name, but it's a tall name and somehow it got stuck on the wrong body. Billy Martin just sounds like it belongs to a feisty child.

I don't know how to tell this to George Brett, but he has the wrong name. The man is simply not a George. He should be Lance Parrish or Buddy Bell, although both of those are taken.

But it wouldn't be unusual for more than one player to have the same name. As the outstanding baseball statistician Bill James has pointed out, both the Met and Royals center fielders are named Willie Wilson, although the Met player is known as Mookie. No matter, it's the right name for both of them. Willie Wilson is a very fast name. It sounds like speed. Williewilssssssssson.

Probably the most famous names in baseball are Met third baseman Howard Johnson and two young players, first baseman Ronald McDonald and outfielder R. J. Reynolds.

Pitcher Ron Reed is a proper six feet six inches tall. What else could Britt Burns be except a fastballing pitcher.

Unfortunately Benny Ayala sounds like a cry for help. Ay-ala, look who's up. Al Bumbry is not the right name for a great fielder. Al Bumbry should make a lot of errors and be unfriendly. I would never have confidence in a pitcher named Al Nipper. And I don't think I need to say anything about Darryl Motley.

I always liked pronouncing the name of the brothers Alou. It sounded like I was yodeling. Matty Alouuuuuuuuuuu. If you shouted it in a mountain range, I suspect someone would shout back, "Alouuuuuuu yourself."

There was a rumor that Boog Powell was really the fourth Alou brother, but changed his name because he got tired of being called Boog Alou.

A thorough check of the major league records shows that, unfortunately, there has never been a player named Luciano. First name or last name.

And, naturally, Pete Rose by any other name would still be as great.

I still can't spell Paciorek correctly, but I can like him. "Wimpy" is now playing for his fifth major league team, the Texas Rangers. He is one of those players about whom it is said that he can roll out of bed and hit a line drive. I think more than anything else, that's what makes us different. When I roll out of bed, I'm overjoyed just to hit the floor.

My brother John was the greatest hitter in major league baseball history, getting three hits in his only three at bats for the 1963 Houston Colt 45ers. A congenital back abnormality prevented him from ever playing in the big leagues again, so he ended his career with a lifetime batting average of 1.000. Other players have gone 2-for-2 or 1-for-1 for their careers, but only John had three hits.

In all honesty, though, even if he had played again,

I don't think he could have kept up that pace for more than another season.

In my first at bat in the big leagues, in 1970 for the Los Angeles Dodgers, I topped a little nubber down the third base line for a hit, making John and me the best-hitting brothers ever to play major league baseball. That lasted until my next time up, when I hit a line drive right at the shortstop and instantly became the worst big league player in my family. It was all downhill from there.

All eight of the kids in my family played sports, mainly because we had nothing else to do. We were probably the last family in our Detroit neighborhood to have a television set, which might have made us the last family in the entire city of Detroit to get TV, because there weren't any rich people in that neighborhood.

My father worked in the Plymouth assembly plant. I didn't realize we were poor, though. I thought everybody in the world lived like we did—eight children and two adults piled into a small three-bedroom house, never having too much to eat.

It was my father's dream that none of his sons would have to work in the plant. That was a dream we all shared. I did have to work at Plymouth briefly one summer when I came home from Houston, but that was only after I got fired from the Kowalski Sausage Factory.

Getting fired from the sausage factory was pretty easy. It took only four days. I was working there with a friend and we probably weren't as serious about salami as we should have been. We did all kinds of strange jobs in the factory, but the one I liked best was lifting strings of salami onto a rack. There were about ten salamis to a string, and they each weighed about ten pounds. Doing this job made me feel as if I were accomplishing two things at one time: working for Kowalski Sausage and getting in shape for football season. For some reason my boss, I think his name was Stash, didn't like the fact that I was enjoying the job. I don't think you were supposed to like working there. He moved me to some other penny-ante chore and gave the lifting job to some really weak kid. Let's face it, the kid was a wimp. "Come on," I said to Stash, "let me do the lifting."

No. He wanted me to do something else. So about fifteen seconds after I started my new job, I heard this terrible crash from the salami racks. I went running over—there was the kid lying on the ground with a one-hundred-pound string of salami across his neck, choking him. He was close to becoming the first person ever suffocated by salami. I was laughing so hard, I couldn't pick up the string. In fact, I almost fell on top of him, which would have finished the job.

But that wasn't why I got fired.

I got fired because my friend and I were supposed to take barrels of garbage outside, roll them down a long ramp, and empty them into the dumpster. That ramp was at least fifteen feet wide, but we missed it completely. I mean, we didn't come close. There was garbage all over the place, so we started picking it up. And after we picked it up, we started throwing it at each other. We were having a great time until this man walking down the street started screaming at us. "Who do you think you are," he yelled, "throwing garbage around like that. You're incompetent. . . ."

Well, we were incompetent, but he didn't have the right to call us that; he was just some guy walking down the street. "You can't talk to *me* like that," I yelled right back, and then I yelled some other things. It turned out he could talk to me like that. He was *the* Mr. Kowalski of Kowalski Sausage. And that *was* how I got fired.

When my father heard about it, he decided to put me on the Plymouth assembly line to teach me a lesson about work. It turned out to be a great lesson: After that summer I would have rather suffered through an eternity of two-a-day football practices than ever work on an assembly line again. The plant opened at six o'clock in the morning, but my father was one of those people who always had to be the first one at work. We'd be there by 5:15. That's 5:15 in the morn-

ing. That job was so bad it even made me nostalgic for
Kowalski Sausage. I worked on the assembly line, in
the welding department and in the car-washing line.
The problem with car washing was that you had to
drive the cars and I didn't know how to drive a stick
shift. I messed up a lot of automobiles before they
caught on.

Sports saved me. I played defensive back in football. My brother John had been a great high school
football, basketball, and baseball player, and had received more than two hundred college scholarship
offers. I got a few offers, too, and accepted a scholarship from the University of Detroit because I didn't
want to go too far away from home. We did not have a
great team my freshman year. In fact, at the end of the
season the school dropped football. So I transferred to
the University of Houston, a great place to go to
school. I crammed four years of college into five and a
half years there. I wanted to stay eligible for football,
so I'd end up taking the same class two or three times.
Finally a counselor pointed out to me that I couldn't
keep taking the same courses every year, I had to do
something toward a degree. That was a shame, because I was finally getting good at some of them.

All I was thinking about was staying eligible and
signing a big-time football or baseball contract. I was a
good football player. Playing safety, I had six intercep-
tions my junior year and received honorable mention
on a number of All-American squads. Considering the
fact that I had no guts at all, that was a remarkable
achievement. I was one of those players who hit you
hard only if you weren't looking. My senior year, for
example, we were playing a really fine University of
Georgia team, and they had this big tackle named
Edgar Chandler, who later became an All-Pro with the
Buffalo Bills. Chandler was maybe six-six and tough.
He could have been six-six and weak and I still would
have been smart enough to stay away from his side of
the field. I spent most of the game running away from
him, and by the fourth quarter he was really starting
to get frustrated. You really don't want to frustrate

six-six, two-hundred-sixty-pound tackles. Finally the
Georgia quarterback called an end sweep. On that
play Chandler's assignment was to kill the safety. I
was the safety.

When the ball was snapped, he charged after me.
The running back was tackled before he reached the
line of scrimmage, ending the play, but Chandler kept
coming. Play or no play, he really wanted to kill the
safety. Suddenly, when he was maybe fifteen feet away
from me, he lost his balance and started to stumble. I
was quick to seize my opportunity. As soon as I saw
him tripping over his own feet, I went after him. I got
real low; I got my shoulder into his gut and hit him as
hard as I could. He went down hard; he didn't stay
down though. He got up and started screaming at me,
then he started chasing me. I did some serious broken-
field running to stay away from him. (One good thing
about playing football, there are always plenty of big
guys to hide behind.) He didn't catch me then, and he
certainly didn't catch me for the rest of the game.

At the team meeting the next morning I looked
great on the game films. The movies of the game did
not show Chandler stumbling, so all that anyone saw
was me going in and underneath him, blasting him to
the ground. The coaches ran that play over and over as
an example of how to play good, tough football.

After I graduated, the Miami Dolphins made me
their ninth-round draft choice. Had I been eligible for
the football draft at the end of my junior year, I know
I would have gone much higher, but I'd missed half
our games my senior year with a leg injury, and played
the rest of the games at less than full strength. The
Dolphins were really a poor team at that time, and
drafting me wasn't one of those key moves that would
turn the franchise around. Joe Thomas was the general manager, and he called me and made me a great
offer to play in Miami: a two thousand dollar bonus
and fifteen thousand dollar salary, but only if I made
the team. I told him I'd think about it.

I had also been an All-American baseball player
my junior year at Houston. We had gone to the college

World Series that year and I set the NCAA record for slugging percentage, something like 1,000. At the conclusion of the college World Series a Met scout asked me whether I had decided to play professional football or baseball. Just being asked that question by a major league scout made me feel good. "I'm going to think about it," I said modestly. "At the proper time I'll weigh the offers and see what I prefer. Anyway, I've got a year before I have to make my decision."

He shrugged. "Oh, I wouldn't worry about it too much," he said. "I think by next year you'll be carrying a lunch pail."

So much for boosting my ego.

As it turned out, he was almost right. The leg I had injured during football season had healed just in time for baseball. And in the first baseball game of the year I ran into a wall and injured my other leg. I hobbled through a very ordinary season. The Dodgers drafted me in the fifth round and offered me a twenty thousand dollar bonus to sign. That is how I became a baseball player.

The best thing about signing with the Dodgers was that I got to play for a manager named Tommy Lasorda on the Rookie League club in Ogden, Utah. I'll never forget my first day in professional baseball. I arrived alone in Salt Lake City, nobody came to pick me up, nobody seemed to care if I was there or not, but somehow I found my way to the fashionable Ben Loman Hotel in Ogden. Rooms at the Loman were two dollars a night, double occupancy. And those rooms were worth the money too. Players were assigned to rooms as they arrived, meaning the next player who showed up was your roommate. I was alone in my room until three o'clock the next morning, when the door opened and eighteen-year-old Bobby Valentine burst into the room. *Him* Lasorda had picked up at the airport at two o'clock in the morning. I immediately figured out that on Lasorda's team Italians got preferential treatment.

Bobby was the same shy person then that he is today. The first thing that he told me was that he had

originally planned to take O. J. Simpson's place as the
star running back at the University of Southern California, but changed his mind and decided to become a
major league baseball player when the Dodgers made
him their first round draft choice. As I soon found out,
though, next to Tommy Lasorda, Bobby Valentine *was*
a shy young man.

The next day we began learning how to play baseball the Lasorda way. Tommy would have us on the
field all morning, then we'd eat at the local smorgas-
bord, then go back to the field and play a game. Then
we'd do the same thing the next day, and every day. I
thought every organization worked their young players
like that. Of course, I also thought every family had
eight children and two parents living in a three-bedroom
house without too much to eat. I didn't mind working
hard. Anytime I started getting tired, I reminded myself I could be waiting in line outside the Plymouth
plant at 5:30 in the morning. It's amazing how much
energy a thought like that will give you.

With Tommy, all we did was play baseball, talk
baseball, think baseball, drink baseball, and eat. Eating was almost as important as baseball. And Tommy
taught us every aspect of the game of eating for free.
Eating for free was always a challenge to him, and I
never saw him fail to rise to the test. Even then he
accepted more speaking engagements than a politician
running for office. As long as they served a meal,
Tommy would speak. The only difference between
the now-famous manager of the Dodgers and the
Lasorda that I played for in the Rookie League is that
he is eating free steaks these days instead of free
coffee and doughnuts.

Tommy had been a pitcher during his playing
career, and to hear him talk you'd think he had almost won the Cy Young Award. Only later did I find
out that he had never won a major league game. His
lifetime major league record was no wins, four losses.
So if my brother was the greatest hitter in baseball
history, Tommy has to be the worst pitcher. He did
love to pitch though. That first day in Ogden we had

an eleven-inning intersquad game, and he pitched for both sides. That was the equivalent of going twenty-two innings. He was terrible. He must have given up sixty-seven runs. Balls were just rattling all over that old ballpark. And whenever someone got a hit, the next time they came to bat he would knock them down.

The following day he was out on the mound pitching batting practice again. With his stuff, he never had too much to lose.

His life was baseball and he made it our lives too. A lot of his players from the Dodger organization went with him to the Dominican Republic to play winter league baseball, and after night games we'd often go back to his hotel room, where he'd pitch batting practice to us with tennis balls. We'd be ricocheting those tennis balls off the walls all night, trying to hit one over the lamp. Of course, if we hit him too hard, he'd knock us onto the couch.

Tommy was one of the best known people in the Dominican Republic. I remember one night we were coming back from a fishing trip, it was very late, and we'd all hitched a ride in the back of a pickup truck. As we drove along, we didn't go more than a mile or so before we'd hear a Dominican voice shout out of the darkness, "Hey, Tom Lasorda, how you doing?" We were in the middle of nowhere, it was so dark that we couldn't even see Lasorda next to us in the truck, but somehow the Dominicans knew he was there. That man was famous.

Tommy coached a lot of famous guys in that rookie league. Bobby Valentine, Billy Buckner, Ron Cey, Joe Ferguson, Davey Lopes, Steve Garvey, Charlie Hough, Steve Yeager, even Bill Russell had been there the year before. A lot of Triple A teams never sent that many players to the big leagues in their entire existence. Tommy tried to give every player a nickname. I got mine the first time we all had dinner. All the players who got big bonuses—Valentine, Garvey, Billy Buck—ordered steaks. I didn't particularly like the taste of steak, so I ordered two double cheeseburgers. Tommy immediately named me "Wimpy," after the hamburger-loving character from "Popeye." The name stuck, and two decades later I'm still Wimpy.

The Dodgers had so much talent on the big club that it was almost impossible for a young player to break in. I had to win the Minor League Player of the Year award in 1972 just to get a chance to sit on the Dodger bench in 1973. I never got a chance to play regularly for the Dodgers. Every year I would figure, next year they're going to give me a shot, and every year they would go out and acquire another great veteran player. In 1970 I hit .326 with 101 rbi's at Spokane, the next year the Dodgers got Richie Allen. Who's gonna play, me or Dick Allen? Okay, I told myself, next year it's got to be me. In 1971 I hit .305 with 105 rbi's at Spokane, and the Dodgers got Frank Robinson. Who's gonna play, me or Frank Robinson? All right, I told myself, next year it's got to be me. They got Jimmy Wynn. . . .

Finally, after sitting on the Dodger bench for three years, I was traded to the Atlanta Braves in 1976. The Braves gave me an opportunity to play, and I hit .290. This is it, I thought, now I'm finally going to be in the lineup every day. The Braves must have been paying attention to the Dodgers, because they got Gary Matthews and Jeff Burroughs, and who's gonna play, me or . . . By 1978 it had become obvious that I had no future with the Braves. In actuality I hadn't had much of a past either. Bobby Cox was the Braves' new manager and I could see I didn't fit into his plans. I could see that because during spring training they sent me back to the minor leagues.

I went back to the minor leagues. I played one game in Triple A. In fact, I sat one game in Triple A, I couldn't even play there. I must've sat well, though, because Gary Matthews separated his shoulder that night and I was recalled. Five weeks later Matthews was ready to play. I had had a total of nine at bats. The Braves released me again. That was the second time in five weeks I had been released, a record even my brother hadn't matched.

They couldn't fire me; I quit. I went home. Being released twice in five weeks is not exactly a subtle hint. I was ready to find something else to do, but Chris, my wife, convinced me to give it one more try. "They're not hiring on the assembly lines," she pointed out. So I opened the sports section of the newspaper and looked at the standings, trying to decide which team I was good enough to play on. It was June first and I noticed that the Seattle Mariners had already been mathematically eliminated from the pennant race. There was a team I could play for.

Besides being a bad ball club, the Mariners' director of minor league operations, Mel Didier, was a good friend. "We can't pay you much," he told me when I called him, "and we'll have to send you to the minor leagues." But that was the only offer that poured in, so I reported to San Jose. Rene Lachmann was the manager there and he was super. I was awful, I stunk up the whole place. For three weeks I couldn't have hit the water if I fell out of a boat. I just couldn't hit. But when we went to Albuquerque for a short series, I got pumped up. Six years earlier I'd been a star in that town and even if I couldn't spell it, I knew I could hit there. In two games I hit four home runs and knocked in ten.

The night of the second game I played there, Seattle outfielder Ruppert Jones had an appendix attack in Boston and was put on the disabled list. The Mariners called Lachmann to find out who was hot. "Hey," Rene said, "Paciorek had four home runs and ten rbi's in the last two games alone." He neglected to tell what I had done before those two games. From his point of view he was strengthening his team by getting me off it. So I was back in the big leagues once again. I wasn't playing, but the way I had been playing in the minor leagues, that was probably to my advantage.

Slowly Ruppert Jones started getting better. Every time I walked past him, I'd give him a playful little punch in the side, but he kept improving. I knew my entire future was tied to Ruppert Jones's appendix. It looked very much like I was going to be given my third release in one season, breaking my old record. I had about nine at bats with Seattle and didn't have a hit. But two days before Ruppert was scheduled to be activated we were playing a Sunday afternoon game in Milwaukee and manager Darrell Johnson had no right-handed hitters to put in the designated hitter spot. All his decent players were either in the starting lineup or hurt. That left some pitchers, and me. Now, you know a team is in poor shape when its designated hitter is batting ninth in the order. I didn't care; I was thrilled to be playing.

Mike Caldwell was pitching for the Brewers and I thank him to this day. I went 4-for-4, including a home run, and I knocked in the winning run. The next day Johnson had no choice but to put me in the lineup again. I hit another home run. When Ruppert Jones was activated, someone else was released. I had dodged another bullet. I was happy, but the way things had been going I didn't put a down payment on a house in Seattle.

I could've signed a long-term lease though. I played four wonderful seasons in Seattle. The Mariners were the first team to give me the opportunity to play almost every day, and I responded. In 1981 I finished second in the American League in batting with a .326 average. That was the best any Mariner had ever hit. I figured that if that didn't ensure me a little security, nothing could.

I was exactly right. Nothing could. The Mariners decided to trade me while I was hot.

I loved living in Seattle and playing for the Mariners. For the first time in my major league career I really felt like I was contributing to the success of the team. Okay, we weren't very successful, but I was a major contributor to that. In addition to playing, I did a tremendous amount of public relations work for the team. Lasorda had taught us that if the organization wanted you to do something, you did it, because eventually you would be rewarded. Maybe even get a free meal. So I did everything the Mariners asked me to do. If they needed a breakfast speaker in Edmonds, I was there. If they needed someone to sign autographs at a high school banquet, I was there.

The lowest of all, though, the really lowest, was the day Bruce Bochte and I went to a Fred Meyers Grocery Store to give away Mariners pennants, hats, and schedules, and the Fred Meyers people stuck us in frozen foods. We sat there shivering, wearing parkas, trying to give away these things. Nobody came near us. I didn't blame them. Since when do you find major league baseball players in the frozen foods? We were such a tremendous success that the store asked us to leave early because we were hurting their frozen food business.

Although I was one of the Mariners' leading batters, I became better known in Seattle for my television commercials. That started when Jeff Odenwald, Mariners' marketing director, and I were asked to create a TV spot promoting the upcoming Jacket Day. We had one camera, no director, no props, and no script. We just made it up as we went along. The one thing I did find, however, was a pair of funny-nose glasses. So I sat in front of our camera wearing my funny-nose glasses and said calmly, "Hi, my name is Tom Paciorek. I'm with the Seattle Mariners and I'm inviting everybody to come out to the Kingdome on blahblah date when the Tigers come to town for Mariners' Funny-Nose Glasses Night. So come on out and be the first person in your neighborhood to get a pair of these valuable funny-nose glasses. They have many important uses and—"

Jeff interrupted, correcting me from off camera, "Uh, wait a second, Tom, it's not Funny-Nose Glasses Night, it's Jacket Night. Everybody who comes out to the Kingdome gets a free jacket."

I looked stunned. "A jacket?" I said loudly. "Who the heck wants a jacket when you can get real funny-nose glasses?"

"I know," Jeff agreed, "but that's what they get."

I really looked upset. "Then what am I supposed to do with thirty thousand pairs of funny-nose glasses?"

I asked. That spot received the Emmy Award as the best commercial of the year in Seattle.

The fans loved it. And on Jacket Night I came out on the field wearing my funny-nose glasses and got an ovation. After that Jeff and I did a series of commercials based on those funny-nose glasses. Finally we had to respond to the swelling popular demand: The Mariners scheduled Tom Paciorek Funny-Nose Glasses Night for the following season. And when they finally did have it, the only thing missing was Tom Paciorek. I was playing with the Chicago White Sox. Tom Paciorek Funny-Nose Glasses Night became simply Funny-Nose Glasses Night. They still almost packed the ballpark.

That last season I spent with the Mariners, 1981, was probably the most enjoyable year I've ever had in baseball, even including the long strike. There were two nights during that 1981 season in which it almost felt like we were a contending ball club. Two nights in a row I hit home runs in the bottom of the ninth inning to beat the first place New York Yankees. The first night I broke up a tie by hitting the gamer off Rudy May, then the next night I came right back to hit a three-run game winner off Ron Davis. Those were as sweet as any moments I've ever experienced on the field. I also made the American League All-Star team that season. No doubt about it. It was a great year.

I had two good seasons with the White Sox. And as the old joke goes, two out of four ain't bad. I hit .312 in 1982 and .307 in 1983, when we won the Eastern Division Championship. During the stretch run in '83 I hit .438 over my last twenty-five games as we eased to the title. In the American League playoffs against Baltimore I knocked in half of all the runs we scored in four games. One. O-n-e. Count it, one. But that run was also the margin of victory in the only game we won.

By mid-1985 I realized my career as a White Sox was about to end. I realized that when they put me on the "designated for assignment" list. That means that the team had ten days to trade me or sell me or they would have to give me my unconditional release.

I thought, well, this is it, the end of my career. But a few days before the end of the waiting period, the White Sox traded me to the Mets for two young players. It was incredible. I had been traded into the middle of the National League East pennant race. Rather than going full circle, my career had gone coast to coast. For me, that wasn't usually the way the baseball bounced.

During the pennant race every game, every play, was vital. Surprisingly the most important play I made was a defensive play. It was no surprise to me, but it was to the reporters who covered the team. In baseball you are always as good or as bad as your reputation. When I was a young player, I was labeled a lousy defensive player. I wasn't then, and I'm not now, but that's what I was labeled and that's what people believed. One night in Dodger Stadium, a few weeks after I'd come to the Mets, I was playing shallow in the outfield, guarding against a base hit. The batter hit a line drive directly over my head. I got a great jump on the ball, turned my back and ran to the right spot, turned and jumped, and made the best catch of my career to save at least one run.

Because of my reputation, the next day the reporters wrote that I misjudged the ball, started back on it and tripped, and as I fell down stuck out my glove and somehow managed to catch the ball.

There is no way to beat the label once it's pinned to your back. For the White Sox in 1983, for example, I played sixty-seven games at first base, fifty-five games in the outfield, and in twenty games played both positions. I made one error. To me, that's being versatile. To the reporters, that's being unable to hold one position.

The Mets finished the 1985 season in second place, three games behind the St. Louis Cardinals. The only problem playing on a team with as many exciting young ball players as the Mets is that they have so many exciting young ball players. In order to protect those players, in fact, the Mets released me. Once again I wondered if that was the end of my career.

And once again it was not the end of my career. Although I had offers from a few clubs, I decided to sign with the Texas Rangers. The Rangers are managed by Bobby Valentine. *That* Bobby Valentine, my very first roommate. The only thing I made Valentine promise me is that we wouldn't have to room together—and that Lasorda was going to stay in Los Angeles.

I know my career has to end someday. It does, right? I may not have been a Hall of Famer, but I accomplished my father's dream: I'll never have to work in the salami plant again. When my career does end, I would love the opportunity to become a broadcaster. I've done a few White Sox games and enjoyed it. I didn't mess up too badly either. And one advantage I would have over Ron Luciano, after growing up in a Polish neighborhood where my friends were named Pochewnietski, Czekinski, Wojeski, and Anjerski, I wouldn't have any trouble pronouncing ball players' names.

LITTLE BIG MAN
by Phil Garner

The thing I liked best about Phil Garner was that his uniform was always dirty. At the beginning of a game, the end of a game, in dry weather, wet weather, indoors, outdoors, it didn't matter, his uniform was always covered with dirt. The reason I liked that so much was that my umpire's uniform was always dirty too. Beginning, end, dry, wet, indoors, outdoors, it didn't matter, my uniform was always covered with mustard, ketchup, soft drink stains, and hot sauce.

Baseball uniforms have changed considerably since I first came up to the major leagues. In the late 1960s uniforms were still being made out of knitted fabrics. They were worn loose and the pants were held up by a belt. Pitchers and catchers loved these belts because they could sharpen the buckle or tongue and, by rubbing the ball against the sharp edge, slice the cover enough to make the ball move erratically. That never bothered me too much because I umpired erratically. Eventually these old-style uniforms were replaced by the new stretch double-knits. Although the double-knit pants no longer required a belt, some teams kept wearing belts out of tradition and, I suspect, because it's hard to turn down a begging pitcher. Other teams eliminated the belt, instead incorporating a colorful band around the center of the uniform to make it look like the players were wearing belts.

Double-knits allowed manufacturers to make form-fitting uniforms. I'll tell you one form they didn't fit—mine. I don't think even quadruple knits would be enough. Now, a lot of things have been written about my sartorial grace and, unfortunately, I can't deny most of it. For me, there are only two kinds of clothes—too big and too small. I'm the kind of man who thinks Popular Science is a fashion magazine. The only time my pants were creased was when all the wrinkles ran in the same direction. So it probably is not fair of me to judge how players looked in their uniforms. But I figure, they laughed at me in my uniform; now it's my turn.

One thing uniforms are not is uniform. Every player has his own way of wearing a uniform. As I said, Phil Garner, as well as Bobby Gritch, always wore uniforms that looked like "before" on detergent commercials. Gritch particularly looked as if he might have stopped on the way from the clubhouse to the dugout to change the oil in his car. On a bright sunny afternoon in Anaheim, where it might not have rained for three months, Bobby Gritch would come out to play the first inning with wet mud drops on his uniform. Where'd he get them? What did he do, buy them?

On the other side of the clothes rack, Dwight Evans, Cecil Cooper, Freddy Lynn, and Ken Singleton all would have made their mothers proud. They were the kind of players that Phil Garner's mother would point at and say to him, "Why can't you look like that?" Just looking at them, you knew that when they were growing up, they could find things in their rooms. I mean, they had creases where there are no creases. And they never got dirty. I couldn't understand that; they all played hard. Evans would go sliding into second base in a cloud of dirt and when he got up, not only wouldn't his uniform be dirty, the spot he slid over would be clean. The clean used to rub off him. Even when it rained, those four players would look great. I used to wonder if they Scotchguarded their uniforms.

Lance Parrish and Reggie Jackson wore the tightest uniforms. Their uniforms looked as if they had been spray-painted on. I always expected to see on the back of Reggie's uniform in Oakland his name, his number, and a small signature reading "Taki 183."

The two players whose uniforms never fit them, no matter which team they were playing for, were Tommy John and Buddy Bell. Their uniforms were always neat, but always one size too big. They sort of looked as if they had sent their uniforms to the laundry and while they were gone, the two of them had gone out in the rain and shrunk.

Rick Dempsey and Danny Meyers always had the tails of their shirts out of their pants. Evans, Cooper, Lynn, and Singleton, naturally, never had them out. They looked as if they were wearing jump suits.

Stirrup socks were always causing problems. These are the uniform socks without a heel or front. They are worn over the white sanitary socks, which are visible at the Achilles tendon and front of the foot. Some players liked to pull the stirrups up very high, exposing almost all of the sanitary socks beneath them. Frank Robinson and Rollie Fingers, for example, often looked as if they weren't wearing stirrups at all. For a while players believed that wearing the socks high made their knees look higher, and since umpires measured the strike zone from the top of the knee to the bottom of the team letters, this would theoretically make their strike zone smaller. Why they believed that wearing stirrup socks higher would make their strike zone smaller I never figured out. I always thought the only reason you wore socks at all was to keep your pants from catching in the sides of your shoes.

However, the entire White Sox team wore their blue stirrup socks very low. Frank Robinson played in

*five World Series, Rollie Fingers in three. The White
Sox went twenty-three years without winning a pennant. But I'm not going to touch that connection.*

Without question the best-looking uniforms in
baseball have to be the Kansas City Royals' home
uniforms. Any uniform that can make John Mayberry's
body look good has my vote.

The worst uniform of all is the Houston Astros'.
It is what is described as a "rainbow" color. This is
one of the few uniforms that actually looks better
dirty. What must have happened is that when the
team's executives were deciding what the team colors
should be, someone suggested, "Let them be the colors of the sun and the sky above." But he was voted
down and they decided on something brighter.

If I ever wore that uniform, people would mistake me for a piece of construction equipment.

Many players wear jewelry on the field, usually
gold chains with charms on them. Nobody wears
watches or rings, for obvious reasons. But when I
started broadcasting, I went down to the field and
saw Dave Parker wearing a single earring. It was the
first time I'd ever seen that. Now, personally, I'm not
the type of man who would wear an earring, but I
have a firm belief: Earrings look great on everybody
six-five, two hundred thirty pounds or over.

Phil Garner has worn the uniforms of three different major league clubs. He has played in both
leagues, so he has seen every major league uniform.
When I asked him which uniform he liked wearing
the best, his answer was the same response I'd gotten
from every other player. "I really don't care what
color it is," he said, "as long as it has the name of a
major league team on the front."

Most young boys dream about playing in the major
leagues—but when I was growing up in Rutledge, Tennessee, I dreamed about playing in the World Series.
My dream was so real I could feel the fall chill in the
air, I could hear the crowd cheering, I could see myself

making a great play to win the series. In 1979 I was
with the Pittsburgh Pirates. We won the National
League Eastern Division championship and were winning the playoffs against the Cincinnati Reds. I was
one game away from fulfilling my lifelong dream—
and that's when I really got scared.

I'd pursued that dream throughout my life. I'd
played hard every summer and worked out every day
in the winter because I wanted to play in the World
Series. I'd played with injuries and in pain, I played
when I was exhausted, I played after traveling all
night and not having a decent meal in two days, because I wanted to play in the World Series. I played
when I could have been more financially successful
doing something else, I spent a tremendous amount of
time away from my wife, Carol, and our growing
family, because I wanted to play in the World Series.
Suddenly, one game from reaching that goal, it dawned
on me: What am I going to shoot for once I've played
in the World Series?

The 1979 World Series opened in Baltimore. I
didn't sleep at all the night before the first game was
scheduled. At five A.M. I got out of bed and looked
outside—through the frost on the window I could see
sleet. I didn't care, I was ready to play. My wife didn't
understand what I was doing out of bed. I told her,
"I'm just getting ready to go to the ballpark."

"It's five o'clock in the morning," she pointed
out.

"I know," I told her, "I'm ready." That opening
game was canceled because there was too much
weather, something that had never happened in my
dream. The next day I got to the ballpark early—not
that early—and walked onto the field, looked around
at the ballpark beginning to fill up, at the media gathered around the batting cage, at the television cameras
being set up all around the field, and thought, here I
am, finally, what if I screw up? Screw up? I'd never
doubted my ability before in my life—but I'd never
played in a World Series before in my life either. I
couldn't help thinking about it: What if I make a

mistake and cost us the World Series? What if I make
the kind of mistake that people will read about forever? I really got nervous.

I took a deep breath and made the decision: If I'm
gonna screw up, by God, I'm gonna screw up big! I'm
gonna go out there and be aggressive, I'm gonna play
bull-necked out, hard as I can. And if the result is a
screw-up, then it's going to be one of the biggest
screw-ups anybody had ever seen. Deciding that, believing that, relieved at least some of my nervousness.

The Orioles loaded the bases in the first inning of
the first game, and the batter hit a routine ground ball
to me. A perfect double-play ball. I moved over and
picked it up, then calmly threw the ball about fifteen
feet over second base. Two runs scored and we ended
up losing the game.

I felt terrible. After the game, reporters asked me
if I'd thrown the ball away because I had been nervous. "No," I told them honestly, "I really wasn't
nervous on that one at all. The ball was wet, and
slippery, and I just didn't get a good grip on it. But, no,
I wasn't nervous on that one." I paused, then continued. "But on the *second* ground ball . . . I was nervous
as hell!"

We won the World Series in seven games. My
performance turned out to have been even better than
a dream come true. I hit .500 for the series, getting at
least one hit in every game, and I broke the series
record for second basemen by participating in seven
double plays. The only disappointment came after we
won the seventh game. We had to run off the field. I
didn't want to. I wanted to stay out there and cherish
that moment. I wanted to feel my dream. I wanted to
savor it, knowing I would spend the rest of my life
trying to recall that moment. Instead, we had to run
into the clubhouse.

I've been a major league baseball player for more
than a decade. I've been in a World Series, two playoffs,
and a divisional playoff. I've been on three different
teams and have represented both the American League
and National League in All-Star games. I've even hit

grand slam home runs in two successive games. But the two nights that stand out in my memory are that night we won the World Series and the night my professional baseball career began, and ended, and began again.

My hometown, Rutledge, Tennessee, had a population of about 1,500 people, a few horses, and some fine-looking dogs. Both my father and grandfather were Baptist ministers. My grandfather was an old fire-and-brimstone-type preacher. He'd stand up there and he'd tell his parishioners, "I want to throw all the beer in the river! I want to throw all the wine in the river! I want to throw all the wild women in the river! I want to throw all the cards in the river! Now, let us turn to page two twenty-nine and sing together, 'Shall We Gather at the River.'"

My father is a Calvinist, stressing knowledge, the catechism, and education. He doesn't believe in total abstinence or anything like that.

In 1970 I was an honorable mention All-American third baseman at the University of Tennessee and expected to be selected in the major league draft. Everybody at college was talking about it, the school paper ran my picture and a story, and the only question seemed to be what team would pick me and how high. Then the draft selections from the state of Tennessee were announced—my name wasn't on the list. I hadn't been picked. Man, I have never been hurt so badly in my life. I didn't want to see anybody, talk to anybody; I just wanted to be alone. I went down to the ballpark and sat there by myself, looking at a sky full of stars, and thinking, I can't believe it. I know I'm as good as at least some of those people who were picked. Why not me? Why can't I get my chance? I didn't come up with any answers; I just sat there all night, wondering.

The next morning I discovered I had been the eighth pick of the Montreal Expos. Because my parents lived in Houston, I had been selected out of Texas, and the Tennessee papers hadn't picked it up. Talk about going from the depths of despair to the top of the world in approximately one minute. If you could get the emotional bends from coming up too fast, I would've been a very sick person.

It didn't take me long to come down to earth though. When the Expo scout finally contacted me, he was less than optimistic. "Well, kid," he told me, "we drafted you, but we don't really know if you can play. You're not real fast, you don't have great power, we're not sure how well you'll hit, we don't know . . ." and so on. He offered me a plane ticket to join their minor league club. That was their offer, a plane ticket.

As I listened to him, I wondered, if I can't do all those things, why'd they draft me in the first place? I told my father, "I want to play, but I think they ought to say, 'We're a tiny bit excited about drafting you,' and maybe just give me a thousand dollars." I decided not to sign. It had become a matter of principle.

Instead, I went to Liberal, Kansas, to play in the top-caliber semi-pro league they have there. I was hitting well and Expo scout Pat Patterson showed up. For the first time he asked me how much I wanted to sign. I had never even thought about it. "I want thirty thousand dollars," I said. I don't know where that figure came from, I just blurted it out.

"That's a lot of money," he said, shaking his head. "You've gotta be able to hit home runs for that kind of money, and I don't know if you can do that."

Bert Hooten was pitching against us that night. I hit a three-run homer over the racetrack that circled the baseball diamond to win the game. Pat Patterson came up to me afterward to congratulate me. "What do you think," I asked. "Pretty good shot?"

"One home run doesn't make you a power hitter," he said.

"All right, I'll tell you what," I said, "I'll hit you another one tomorrow." Then I turned around and walked away. I had nothing to lose by saying it, since that's exactly what they had offered me.

Next night, seventh inning. I hit another three-run homer in the same spot to win that ball game. And as I crossed home plate, I looked into the stands to see the empty seat Pat Patterson had been occupying. I never saw him again, or heard from Montreal. The next year I was the number one selection of the Oakland A's. I signed.

I was twenty-one years old when I signed, and I gave myself five years to make the big leagues. Five years, and if I hadn't made it, out. Sal Bando was the A's third baseman, but I knew he couldn't last forever.

Two years later it looked like I was wrong, Sal Bando *was* going to last forever. I had had an excellent year in the minor leagues, and I knew if I had another good year, I'd still go back to the minors. I wasn't going to beat out Bando. Oakland owner Charlie Finley sent me my 1974 contract for the same six hundred dollars a month I'd made in 1973. I wanted to get away from the Oakland organization, so I refused to sign it.

This was just when players were beginning to use agents, but I had been a business major in college and believed I could represent myself. Mr. Finley called me at my parents' home and asked, "Why won't you sign this contract?"

I opened negotiations by telling him, "I can't sign it unless I get more money, Mr. Finley."

"Well, then," he said, "you can just keep your ass in Houston and sell insurance for the rest of your life, because we don't have any use for you." Then he hung up.

I could see that negotiations were not progressing exactly as I had hoped. He was certainly playing hard to get, which bothered me, because I was trying to be the one playing hard to get. Mr. Finley did not even bother asking me how much more I wanted, which was good, because I didn't know. I wanted recognition that I had done well.

In the days before free agency, ball clubs could arbitrarily renew a player's contract. Oakland renewed my contract, raising my salary to seven hundred dollars a month.

I reported to the Triple A club in Tucson, but still refused to sign a contract. About a month into the season Sal Bando got hurt and I was called up to the big leagues. Tucson's manager, Sherman Lollar, told me: "This is your chance to show them what you can do, but you'll probably have to sign a contract." Well, I admit, I didn't say I wouldn't—but I didn't say I would either. On balance, I probably sort of hinted that I would.

I joined the team in Minnesota, and manager Dick Williams put me in the starting lineup at third base. About forty minutes before game time, traveling-secretary Jim Banks came into the locker room with my contract. Meanwhile I'd learned that Bando had a bruised calf and would miss only a few games, and I would be going back to the minor leagues—and probably stay there as long as Bando was breathing. I wanted out of the Oakland organization, so I told Banks I couldn't sign.

Almost instantly Mr. Finley was on the phone screaming at me. "You told me you were going to sign that @#$%¢& contract and now you . . ."

Technically that was inaccurate. I'd never said I would. "I'm not signing it," I told him. "I need more money."

"That's it," he said. "Just go on and pack your bags and get back to Tucson."

I have to admit, the man was a tough negotiator. So I was on the verge of having the shortest big league career in history. I had been in and out of the starting lineup in approximately twenty minutes. But as I was taking off my uniform, I saw Reggie Jackson on the telephone, signaling me to come over to him. As I got there, Reggie held out the phone. ". . . SOB promised me he would sign that contract . . ." I heard Charlie Finley bellowing.

Reggie had taken it upon himself to find out what the problem was. Occasionally he would interrupt Finley to say something soothing like "Now, just calm down, nobody is trying to be authoritative with you. I'm certainly not telling you what to do, but why don't you just ask the kid what he wants."

Apparently Mr. Finley had never considered this,

because he was suddenly quiet. "All right," he finally
said, "get him on the phone."

Reggie handed me the phone. "Okay," Finley asked,
"what do you want?"

"Well, Mr. Finley," I said, trying to think quickly,
"all I'm asking for is one fifty more a month."

Have you ever *heard* a man frown? "For God
sakes," he sighed, "go ahead and sign it then. It'll cost
me that much to send you back to Tucson."

Oh, well, I figured, I could always go play for
another organization the next season. I signed the
contract and played my first game that day.

As I learned, Charlie Finley was the toughest negotiator in the world, but as soon as an agreement was
reached, he'd say, "Now, don't take any of those things
I said personally, son, it's all just business."

I never did, and I loved the man for that. Charlie
was a unique individual. I've always believed a ball
club assumes the personality of the closest authority
figure—and in Oakland that was Charlie Finley. The
A's were a truly great ball club. You had to watch that
team play 162 games to appreciate how really good
they were. They just never made a mistake, they played
tremendous fundamental baseball. Other teams might
beat them, but they never, ever beat themselves. It
was a team of supertalented free spirits, and we were
always at war with Charlie. He would draw a line just
to draw it, someone would step over it just to step
over it, and *bam!* he'd come down hard and the entire
ball club would rally behind the player. If things were
going too well, for instance, and we hadn't had a fight
in the clubhouse or on the field, and maybe were
starting to get complacent, Charlie would do something to stir the pot. Anything. Instead of taking a five
o'clock flight right after a game, for example, he'd
schedule a nine o'clock charter with cold food. We'd
get on that plane and start complaining. We'd get into
whatever city we were going to late at night, and keep
complaining. We'd have to stand in the lobby while
hotel keys got straightened out, complaining, and the
next day we'd go out and beat up on some ball club

10–0. But nobody ever took anything personally, and that was the key to the success of that ball club.

I was right about Sal Bando; he did play forever. But the A's second baseman, Dick Green, retired, Manny Trillo was traded, and I became the second baseman. I played two full seasons with Oakland. In spring training, 1977, I was traded to the Pirates in a six-player deal. Obviously it was a surprise and a shock. Pittsburgh?

After being informed of the trade, I flew all night across the state of Florida to join the Pirates at their Bradenton training camp. Pittsburgh's manager, that rotten Chuck Tanner, had me in his starting lineup that day against the Tigers. Although I regretted leaving Oakland, I did look forward to playing in a more tranquil atmosphere. It was a relief to get away from the constant fighting, and I knew the Pirates had a reputation as a happy ball club.

Jerry Reuss was pitching for us that first day, us having suddenly become the Pirates. Shortstop Tito Fuentes was batting for Detroit, and Jerry was pitching him inside. Fuentes pulled the first pitch foul, then the second, and third, and fourth. And between each pitch he would step out of the batter's box, brush off his hands with dirt, clean the bat handle, adjust his helmet, stretch his shoulders, maybe take a sip of coffee, and finally step back into the batter's box, dig a small hole, take a few practice swings, and finally be ready.

Reuss pitched again, Fuentes fouled it off. And then he got out of the batter's box, brushed off his hands with dirt, cleaned the bat. . . . I could see Reuss was beginning to get upset.

Reuss then buried a fastball in Fuentes's ear, shouting as he released the ball, "Foul that one off, you little SOB."

Oh, my God, I thought, what have I gotten into here? This was my first day with the Pirates, my first game, a spring training exhibition game, and we were having a brawl. What's it going to be like when the games count?

I never did worry about being in a fight with that ball club. Not with Willie Stargell and Dave Parker and Bruce Kison and Candelaria, all big guys. Until I joined that team I'd never realized how big Dave Parker was. I'd put him up against the French Army.

That fight wasn't even the worst part of my first day with the Pirates. The worst part was the way I played. The ballpark was crowded with Pirate fans who had come south to escape the Pittsburgh winter. I wanted to impress them right away. I made three errors right off the get-go. Three errors. These people were booing me, throwing things at me, trying to get the trade canceled. But in my third at bat I hit a long triple. I dived headfirst into third in a cloud of dust and as I got up, I started listening for the cheers. None. Not a cheer, a clap. Silence. So I called time, took my hat off, and walked over to the stands behind third base. I threw my hands up into the air and shouted, "Hey, what's the problem here?"

That's when they started cheering. After a debut like that, I knew things in Pittsburgh could only get better.

At first, I hated the thought of playing there. All I knew about the city was what I had seen a long time earlier in a Walter Cronkite report. I remembered that it looked like an old steel town, the air was filthy, the rivers polluted. You couldn't walk around without getting a thick black ring around your shirt collar. My first trip there confirmed my fears. There wasn't even one danged straight road there. Everything was up and down, over and around. The only thing Carol, my wife, had ever asked of me was that we would live wherever I played. I had agreed, but at that time I hadn't known about Pittsburgh. "Maybe we should think about this," I suggested when we got there.

We agreed to try it for one season. We bought a house and settled in. And as time went on, Carol began to meet some people who accepted her for herself, not as Mrs. Phil Garner, wife of a major league baseball player. These people didn't care who I was. Gradually, as I got to know her friends and the city itself, we fell in love with Pittsburgh. It is a great city, a wonderful, big old loving eastern city, and we're going to settle there permanently when I retire. When the Pirates traded me to the Houston Astros during the 1981 season, Carol and I didn't want to leave. We sat in the airport and cried.

My years with the Pirates were wonderful ones. I had the best season of my career during that 1979 championship year, hitting .293. It happened in a strange way. I hadn't been hit by pitchers too often in my career. Once, in Tulsa, Jim Bibby hit me in the ribs. Except for the fact that I couldn't breathe for two days, it didn't hurt at all. But in '79 I was having my usual .250, .260 season, when Donny Moore hit me on the back of my left hand with his ninety-mph fastball. He nailed me on the back of the hand, where it's all bone, and it hurt. Nothing was broken, and we were in the middle of the pennant race, so I kept playing. A funny thing happened: Because I couldn't grip the bat with my left hand, I couldn't overswing, so I was forced to start hitting the ball up the middle, or going to right field with it. And I got hot, hotter than I've ever been in my career. I ended up thirty-two points higher than I had the previous year, and thirty-four points higher than I would the following year. The obvious question is, why didn't I continue to hit the same way after my hand had healed? The answer is, I don't know. Maybe I should have been hit in the head rather than in the hand.

I never have been a great hitter, I've been ... Well, let me put it this way: When I was with Oakland, we were tied with the Minnesota Twins in the bottom of the ninth inning. We had the bases loaded and Jim Fregosi was sent up to pinch-hit. I was the on-deck batter. The Twins walked Fregosi to force in the winning run. After the game, Fregosi explained to reporters, "It's not what it seems. They were just pitching around me to get to Garner."

I did accomplish one unusual batting feat, however. In 1978 I hit grand slam home runs in two consecutive games, the first time in about eighty years anyone had done that. The first one came off the Cardinals' Bob Forsch. In the seventh inning I hit one over the center field fence in Pittsburgh.

Now, Carol rarely missed a home game in Pittsburgh, but for some reason she hadn't been there that night. When I got home, she read me the riot act. "How could you hit the only grand slam home run of your career the one night I don't come to the game?"

I was feeling pretty good, so I snapped my fingers and told her, "Hey, no problem, honey. Come on out tomorrow and I'll hit you another one." We both laughed. Tactfully she did not point out that no one had hit grand slam home runs in consecutive games in eighty years. She's that kind of woman.

In the first inning the next night I came to bat with the bases loaded against Montreal's Woody Fryman. I went to the plate remembering what I'd told Carol, and thinking how ironic it would be if I did hit another one. And I did. Oh, what a sweet feeling. Naturally I was very restrained in the clubhouse: screaming, shouting, showing everybody my power-hitting muscles. Dave Parker tried to quiet me down, reminding me, "Listen here, Slugger, when the leaves turn brown, I'll be wearing the batting crown."

Carol appreciated my thoughtfulness.

For a player who has put few exceptional statistics in the record book, I've been fortunate enough to have been selected to three all-star teams: the 1976 American League team and the 1980 and '81 National League squads. The difference between the two leagues is the way they approach the game. The National League is much more serious about winning. For example, the 1976 game was played in Philadelphia and, just as they were getting ready to start, we realized our lead-off hitter, Mickey Rivers, was missing. The National League team was on the field, the National Anthem had been played, no Rivers. We started a desperate search. And finally we found him, fast asleep in a little nook between the dugout and clubhouse. All the excitement didn't bother him at all, it didn't

even keep him awake. That sort of set the tone for the
entire ball game.

The three teams I've played on, Oakland, Pittsburgh, and the Houston Astros, have approached the
game very differently too. Oakland was a great ball
club because it was so fundamentally sound. We *knew*
we were going to win; it was just a question of how
and when. Sometimes, though, that team needed a
spark to get started, like any powerful engine. One
night, for example, manager Alvin Dark went out to
argue with an umpire. He got so angry that as he was
leaving the field, he ripped third base out of the ground
and started running. The umpire took off after him,
screaming that Dark had to put back the base. When
Alvin reached our dugout, he heaved the base into the
stands—but didn't slow down. He kept running through
the dugout, up the ramp, and into the clubhouse. That
was what that team called a "spark."

In Pittsburgh we believed we were going to win,
but we didn't have as much ability as the A's. We had
a tremendous offensive ball club, we'd just club people to death, and we had manager Chuck Tanner.
That team was an extension of Tanner, a man who
never met a day he didn't like. He loved to have a
good time, and the club reflected that. It helped to
have Willie Stargell and Dave Parker too.

Now, Houston. This team wants to win, and is
going to win, but doesn't know how to win. We just
don't have that absolute confidence. Yet.

One of the reasons they brought me to Houston is
that I've played on winning ball clubs. I've been called
a "leader," but I think that's a term that has a different meaning in baseball than in other aspects of life.
In business the leader is the man who makes the
decisions, the stubborn SOB who makes things happen. In baseball *rallier* would be a better term than
leader, because the only man who can really lead a
baseball team is the player who gets the important hit
or drives in the meaningful runs. I don't care if a man
can't lead three men in a water polo game; if he drives
in runs, he is going to be the team leader. In Oakland

we had Reggie, in Pittsburgh it was Parker. Houston has Jose Cruz, and Cheo is a great player, but he is not yet the offensive force of those other two.

I bring something else entirely to a team. A winning attitude. I expect to win because I've played with winning teams. I know how to win. Pete Rose teaches people how to win, not so much by instructing them, but by his winning attitude. That son of a buck knows he is going to win, and one of his many great attributes is his ability to make everyone around him believe that too.

One of the things that can be said about my career is that it has been colorful. I've never been with a team that wore a basic white or gray uniform. In fact, I've worn more colors than a parade. In Oakland Mr. Finley used to change uniform colors faster than he'd change lanes on the freeway. Basically we wore some combination of green and gold, with white shoes. Green and gold were okay, but white shoes? I have big feet, and those contrasting shoes made them seem even bigger. Those white shoes made me look like an albino duck.

In Pittsburgh we wore your basic bright sunburst yellow home uniforms and all-black road uniforms. I'll tell you what, when some of our bigger players put on those yellow uniforms, we looked like a fleet of taxicabs with legs.

Now, Houston. It has been said that the Astros can't decide which color to wear, so they wear them all. That's probably not entirely accurate. Maybe the Astro uniforms are a little bright, but I really see no reason for those sunglasses on our opponents' noses.

I've never cared about the color of the uniform, or how it fit, or even how it looked; as long as it was a big league uniform, it was fine with me.

Well, okay, maybe I did care about those white shoes a little bit.

HILL'S SWEET BLUES
by Marc Hill

To ensure a long major league career, the best position to play is second-string catcher. Usually the back-up catcher doesn't get an opportunity to play too often, and because he doesn't play too often, no one expects too much from him when he does play, so when he fails to produce, no one is disappointed, because he's lived up to their expectations.

Because they don't play regularly, back-up catchers often have long, unproductive big league careers. Ron Hodges, for example, didn't play for parts of twelve seasons with the Mets. Buck Martinez, who has been platooned on occasion, has been a major leaguer for parts of sixteen seasons. Among many, many others, Ray Katt didn't catch for parts of eight seasons; Matt Batts, ten years; Red Wilson, ten years; Hank Foiles, eleven years; Del Rice had seventeen seasons of nonservice; Joe Ginsberg caught only 574 games in thirteen major league seasons; Don Pavletich, twelve years; Hawk Taylor, eleven years; J. C. Martin was a big leaguer for parts of fourteen seasons; Phil Roof, fifteen seasons. Some of these players spent more time on the bench than a Supreme Court justice.

The reason that reserve catchers last so long is that every team must carry at least two dependable catchers on its roster, one to play and one to watch him play. A manager dislikes using his second-string catcher, not because he isn't good—he might not be, of course—but because a back-up catcher usually has no back-up catcher. Therefore the manager cannot pinch-hit or pinch-run for him and, if he gets hurt, a real player is going to have to risk injury by catching. Many people do not appreciate the importance of a solid back-up catcher, but to paraphrase the immortal Casey Stengel, if you need to use a reserve catcher and you don't have one, you'll have all passed balls. There are some baseball experts who believe a team can't win without a second-string catcher. Check the record books. Every team that has won the world's championship in the past twenty-five years has had a second-string catcher!

Perhaps the key to success as a second-string catcher is to have a great first-string catcher playing in front of you. Charlie Silvera, for example, served as Yogi Berra's back-up with the New York Yankees for nine seasons. The tenth year the Yankees sent him to the Chicago Cubs, who had Cal Neeman catching. That was the end of Silvera's career.

Berra was so good, in fact, that not only did he keep Silvera in the major leagues for nine years, he also kept Ralph Houk in the big leagues for eight years. I imagine that makes Yogi some sort of pin-up man for reserve catchers.

The other thing a second-string catcher must have is a sense of humor. Major league players have all been stars on some level of baseball. Even the worst player in the majors is one of the 1,000 best players in the world. So being relegated to the bench is tough. Many careers have ended because a player could not accept the fact he wasn't going to play regularly. The demand "Play me or trade me" has helped a lot of players discover new careers. Successful back-up catchers, however, live by the motto "Don't play me, or trade me."

My autobiographical team has two reserve catchers, Marc Hill and Steve Nicosia, both of whom have had plenty of time to refine their ability to take a joke. Both Hill and Nicosia have successfully not caught for championship ball clubs, not playing behind some of the finest catchers in baseball. Hill came up to the majors with the St. Louis Cardinals, where he got excellent experience not playing behind Ted Simmons and Tim McCarver. Then he went to the Giants, where he split the catching duties with Dave Rader, the result being his being sent to the Seattle Mariners. The Mariners made him play, almost ending his career. Fortunately the White Sox signed him to watch Carlton Fisk catch, which he has done successfully since 1981.

Steve Nicosia came up with the Pirates in 1978, where he would occasionally spell Ed Ott and Manny Sanguillen. Spelling Ott was easier, his name has only three letters. In 1985 Steve Nicosia became one of the very few major leaguers to play with both Canadian teams, Montreal and Toronto, in the same season. Unfortunately he also became the first major leaguer to be released by both Montreal and Toronto the same season.

Besides not playing, one of the most important jobs of the reserve catcher is warming up pitchers in the bullpen. "Unless you are crazy to begin with," Nicosia says, "life in the bullpen will make you crazy." Fortunately both Hill and Nicosia appear to have started crazy. Hill believes in literally warming-up pitchers, often sticking matches in the soles of their spikes and then lighting them. Nicosia probably gained his greatest recognition in the bullpen: During a tense moment in a 1981 Dodgers–Pirate game, television cameras focused on the Pittsburgh bullpen just in time to see Nicosia lining up a thirty-five-foot putt. He drew back his baseball bat–club, and played the bullpen green correctly, knocking a baseball into a water cup, making him the best-known golfer in baseball.

I never liked working behind the plate when the second stringer was catching. Not because I didn't like the players—reserve catchers are usually among the nicest people in a ball club—but because they often had difficulty getting together with pitchers on the signals. Inevitably the reserve catcher would signal for what he thought was a fastball, only to have a curveball bounce into the plate umpire's leg. So before a reserve catcher I didn't know was about to play, I would bend down as far as I could bend down as he warmed up the pitcher and tell him, "Just do two things and we'll get along great. Make sure that you and the pitcher agree on the signs, and don't yell at me. I hate it when people yell at me."

I always got along well with reserve catchers. I think they figured that if they were in the game, nobody could really be taking it all that seriously. They were usually concentrating so hard on doing a good job that they forgot to complain.

The best game I ever worked behind home plate was caught by California Angel reserve catcher Art Kusnyer. Nolan Ryan was pitching. Kusnyer called for a curveball on the first pitch. Ryan threw a curveball and, even though Kusnyer knew it was coming, he couldn't catch it. That ball dropped about two feet and hit him in the shin guards. For a moment neither Art nor I said anything, then he said softly, "Nobody can hit that pitch. If he throws like that, he'll pitch a no-hitter."

Ryan retired batter after batter without giving up a hit. Both Kusnyer and I knew what was taking place, but baseball superstition commands that when a pitcher is throwing a no-hitter, no one can talk about it. So we just sort of hinted at it. "No one's ever pitched like this before," I would say.

"This is probably a Hall of Fame game," he would say.

Then I would respond, "This isn't going to help their batting averages, if you know what I mean."

And he would counter with, "Can you believe how good he is?"

That was the first and only no-hitter I ever worked in the major leagues. There was only one ball hit hard off him, a ground ball right at the shortstop. And after that first pitch, Kusnyer didn't miss a ball the entire game.

Good second-string catchers accept that position. One night, I remember, a reserve catcher I will not name (it was Marc Hill), surprised me by coming out to start a regular game. As he crouched down to take the warm-up throws, I asked, "How come you're playing tonight?"

He didn't even hesitate. "I've got to. The regular second-string catcher has a strained ligament."

Many players believe their rookie year in the big leagues is the most difficult because everything is so new and there is so much pressure on them to perform. Other players believe their second year is even more difficult, because they've been around the league long enough to have their weaknesses exposed. I agree with everybody. For me, every one of my twelve years in the major leagues has been the toughest.

Twelve years, four teams, two leagues. During that time I've been a starting catcher, a second-string catcher, a third-string catcher, I've played first base, I've played third base, I've warmed up relief pitchers in the bullpen, pitched batting practice, pinch-hit, pinch-run, and, if they had asked me to, I would have mowed the outfield grass on Saturday mornings.

You have to do everything that is asked of you when your team's press guide lists among the *highlights* of your career: "Hill did not appear in the '83 playoffs against Baltimore."

Of course, that same press guide fails to mention that I was the on-deck batter when the last playoff game ended. To a player who has spent most of his major league career on the bench, those details are important.

I was born in Ellsberry, Missouri. My father had pitched in the minor leagues and my mother was a standout softball pitcher. Naturally my family was very sports-minded and we were always playing some kind of ball game in our backyard. We played everything from hardball to wiffleball to badminton to croquet. Croquet was really my kind of sport. That big wooden ball just laid there begging to be hit. And there are no curveballs in croquet.

I made all-Missouri in both basketball and baseball, but I realized there wasn't much future in basketball for a six-three forward who couldn't jump. Jumping ability really didn't matter; I couldn't run either. What I could do was throw. I had a great throwing arm. Of course, the one skill that has no value in basketball is a great throwing arm.

I didn't want to be a catcher in baseball. It seemed dangerous. I always wanted to play third base or shortstop. But a man by the name of Doc Evans, who had been in the Yankee organization, saw me hit and play the infield and said, "Son, the only way you're gonna get to the big leagues and stay there is to go behind the plate and catch." Eventually I grew to love catching. I felt like I was in control of the entire game. And I had the batter and the umpire to talk to.

I was selected in the tenth round of the 1970 pro baseball draft by the St. Louis Cardinals. That was a tremendous thrill because it meant that when I made the big leagues, my parents could drive over to Busch Stadium to watch me play. Or, as it turned out, drive over to watch me sit on the bench.

I was assigned to Sarasota in the Gulf Coast Rookie League. That was a tough league. I'll tell you how tough it was. I hit .192 and made the All-Star team. It was in Sarasota that I learned those two horrible words that were to plague me throughout my career. *Curve* and *ball*. But it was there that I began to learn how to handle pitchers and call a game, how to set up a hitter for a certain pitch, and how to throw out attempted base-stealers.

I had my best minor league season in St. Petersburg in 1972. I hit only .247, but I met my future wife, Cheri. One day at the ballpark a little kid called me

over to the stands. I assumed he wanted my autograph. I had signed . . . maybe two autographs in my
career. Instead, he said to me, "My sister likes you."
Then he pointed to a very attractive woman sitting in
the stands.

Well, I thought, I'm young and strong and I didn't
look *that* bad in my uniform. I could see why she
might find me attractive. "Oh, yeah?" I said shyly.

"Yep," he said firmly. "You're wearing her favorite number." When they had arrived at the ballpark,
he explained, he asked her what number she liked
best. It turned out to be number nine, my number. So
that, plus the fact that I looked good in my uniform,
got us together.

After the game I motioned for her to come down,
and we started talking. Eventually I asked her to have
dinner with me and she said, "You'll have to come
home and meet my parents first."

Meet her parents first? I thought, if I have to meet
her parents before taking her to dinner, what am I
going to have to do before I kiss her? I'm sure she
thought that condition would turn me off. It didn't.
She was very attractive. And, I figured, what could her
father be, a weight lifter?

The amateur weight-lifting champion of the state
of Florida to be precise. I was very glad I asked permission to take her out. And she could order anything she
wanted for dinner too.

We were married a year later, the same year I
came up to the big leagues for the first time. The
Cardinals brought me up at the end of the season,
when major league rosters are expanded to forty players.
They already had two exceptional catchers, Ted Simmons and Tim McCarver. Being third-string catcher
behind those two is like being back-up pianist to Van
Cliburn—you just aren't going to get too much playing
time.

I caught one game that season, a two-hit shutout
against Philadelphia pitched by Mike Thompson and
Diego Segui. The first runner who tried to steal on me

was Mike Schmidt. I threw him out. My first big league plate umpire was Tom Gorman.

Gorman was a tremendous help to me that day. I was nervous, I didn't put the mask on inside out or anything, but inside I was launching butterflies. When I got behind the plate in the first inning, he said, "Hey, kid, I've heard a lot about you. They say you're a good catcher. Just give me a good target so I can see the pitch and we'll both be fine."

Wow, I thought, he knows all about me. He even knows my nickname, "Kid." Only later did I find out that every umpire says that to every catcher before every first game.

The following season I played ten games for the Cardinals. That was enough for them to see my potential—they traded me to the San Francisco Giants. It was at San Francisco that I came closest to being a superstar; I had the locker next to Willie McCovey. Mackie was one of the truly great human beings I've ever had the privilege of knowing, and it didn't take me long to learn that one of the most valuable things a semi-regular player can do in the big leagues is get the locker next to a superstar. Superstars are given all sorts of great things and some of them are just naturally going to fall off into your locker.

Back-up catchers get very few requests to endorse products. Besides seat cushions, there aren't a whole lot of things we get to be experts on. It was my very good fortune to have the same size feet as Willie McCovey, so he used to give me all his extra baseball shoes.

Another thing he gave me that I still have was a new nickname. Call me "Booter." And that has nothing to do with my fielding ability. Nothing. One day Willie said that everybody had heard of Bunker Hill, and everybody had heard of Boot Hill, but nobody had ever heard of Marc Hill. So on that day I became Booter. It could have been worse, I suppose. I could have become Bunkie.

I played regularly for the first time in San Francisco and we had a pretty good ball club. The weather just made it so difficult to play there. I'd get to Candlestick Park at ten o'clock in the morning and the sun would be shining and there would be no wind and I'd think, oh, my, what a wonderful day to play baseball.

Day games started at 1:05. By two o'clock that cold wind would be blowing off San Francisco Bay and I'd be thinking, oh, my, what a wonderful day for ice skating. When that wind was blowing, trying to catch a fly ball was like trying to play badminton in a hurricane. There was no such thing as a routine fly ball or pop-up in that ballpark. When a ball went into the air, every player on the field had to be ready to catch it. One time, I remember, Jack Clark hit a long drive to center field. The right fielder started running toward center to back up the play. Suddenly he had to stop short, turn around, and start racing for the right-field foul line. The center fielder was only a few steps behind him. The right fielder caught the ball near the line.

When I was catching and someone hit a foul pop-up, I'd get under it and turn around, and around, and around. I'd move to the left, the third baseman would come in, I'd go around, the first baseman would come in, around again, and finally I would—*dive!* for the ball and catch it. And that was a routine foul ball. But I never complained about the ballpark. It was a major league park and that was all that mattered to me.

I had my best year in 1977 when I hit .250 with nine home runs and fifty rbi's. The following year I slumped to .243 with only fifteen rbi's, but I did steal the only base of my career. It was against my old teammates, the Cardinals. Ted Simmons was catching. No, I was not trying to get even with him. Since I had never stolen a base in the major leagues, they didn't expect me to run. Actually I didn't expect me to run either.

Johnnie LeMaster was the batter, and manager Joe Altobelli put on a hit-and-run play. Johnnie was hitting only about .230 then, so with his hitting ability and my speed, this was a very ambitious thing for Altobelli to try. LeMaster swung and missed, but with my blinding speed, assisted by the element of surprise and a superb hook slide, I stole the base.

People fainted.

To commemorate this historic event Giants owner Bob Lurie, one of the finest men in baseball, had Lou Brock actually present the base to me before a game a few days later. It is mounted on a plaque reading: FIRST STOLEN BASE IN THE BIG LEAGUES. There's an optimist.

There were many frustrating moments for me with the Giants. We had good players; we just couldn't seem to put all the pieces together. At that time in my career I really let the frustrations get to me. I wanted to win so badly that I took every loss and every bad play home with me. One time, I remember, we were tied with Cincinnati in the ninth inning. Joe Morgan was on second base with two outs. Our pitcher failed to hold him close enough and he took off for third base. I had no play on him at all. I shouldn't have thrown. I couldn't resist.

I threw a bullet—about thirty feet over the head of third baseman Steve Ontiveros. We lost the game.

I went home that night and put my fist through the bathroom door. Not exactly through it; I never had that kind of power. I just smashed the outside of it. But I *wanted* to put my fist through it.

It took me eight years to realize the game is supposed to be fun. I still want to win as badly as anyone, but after sixteen years in pro baseball I have learned that there is always another game the next day, while there is only one bathroom door.

My contract with the Giants was due to expire at the end of 1980, making me a free agent, and in midseason I sort of got the hint they didn't intend to offer me a contract for 1981. They sold me to the Seattle Mariners.

That half season in Seattle was the most unhappy time I ever had in baseball. For the first time in my life I lost my enthusiasm for the game. I figured I would play out the remainder of the season, or watch the remainder of the season, then retire.

But when the season finally ended, I decided to wait until after the free agent draft before deciding if I wanted to play anymore. I looked over the rosters to see which teams needed a good defensive catcher as a back-up. I made a list. It was a short list, but definitely a list. As it turned out, it wasn't even necessary for me to announce my retirement. All twenty-six major league clubs decided they didn't need me. I wasn't drafted by a single team. Let me tell you, there is nothing as free as a free agent not drafted by a single team. This was doomsday. I thought my baseball career was really over.

And then suddenly all the old enthusiasm for the game returned. I wanted to play. I knew I could still play. And a few days after the draft Chicago White Sox manager Tony LaRussa called to invite me to spring training. He made me an excellent offer. "We'll give you a tryout and see what happens."

At that point that was an excellent offer.

Within a few days two more teams called and matched the White Sox offer. I knew Chicago had only one catcher, Jim Essian, and figured they had to carry at least two. I might not be a mathematical genius, but it wasn't difficult to figure out that me and Essian added up to two. I accepted the White Sox offer.

That must have shaken up the Sox. They immediately signed Carlton Fisk, perhaps the best hitting catcher in baseball.

I still wasn't a mathematical genius, but I knew that Fisk, Essian, and Hill added up to three. I went to Sarasota with the White Sox, expecting to be cut. The day before the team broke camp and headed north to open the season I stopped by LaRussa's office to say good-bye. "I'll save you the time cutting me," I said. "I'll just go ahead and pack my stuff and leave."

LaRussa was surprised—but not as surprised as I

was when he answered. "That's a lot of bull, partner," he said. "We're carrying three catchers this season. You're going with us." No math necessary—I was still a major league baseball player.

I hit oh-for-the-entire-season. No hits in six at bats. I did hit four balls hard, however. I must have, because at the end of that year the Sox gave me a five thousand dollar raise for the '82 season. I've often wondered, if they gave me a five thousand dollar raise for going oh-for-6 what would they have done if I had been oh-for-20? If I had had fifty at bats that year, I could've been rich!

Early in August we were desperate for starting pitching. Our general manager, Roland Hemond, explained to me that the team had to make an "adjustment."

I figured I was the adjustment.

"We just signed pitcher Lynn McGlothen," he explained, "and we have to make room for him on the roster. You've got more than five years in the major leagues, so we can't send you down to the minors without your permission." He agreed to bring me back to the big club in nineteen days, when major league rosters expanded to forty players.

I was a terror in the minors. In the two games I played I had three hits in seven at bats. My last time up I just missed hitting a home run. Most of the outfield fence at Glens Falls is about 360 feet from home plate, similar to a major league park. But there is one section in center field that's only about 280—there's a tennis court right behind it—and I really got into a pitch and backed the center fielder up to the 280-foot mark. The White Sox must've been impressed. Jim Essian was gone in 1982, and I appeared in fifty-three major league games.

For the first time in my big league career, I played some third base and first base. I remember the first time Tony LaRussa played me at third base. I'd taken some ground balls in infield practice, but there I was standing there at third base against the New York Yankees. It suddenly occurred to me that I wasn't wearing any protection. Without all that catcher's gear I felt naked. I kept telling myself, if the ball is hit to me, get my body in front of it and block it. Fortunately I had a lot of body.

Bobby Murcer hit the first ball to me. At me, rather. I started to go down on my knees to block it, then I remembered, I'm supposed to catch it. I did, I caught it. Then I stood up and threw him out.

The hardest part of the play was standing there and looking calm, as if I made that play every day. In fact, I hadn't done it one day in the major leagues.

A few weeks later I was playing third against Oakland. Danny Meyers bunted on me. I thought there was some kind of law against that. I came charging in. I must've looked like a killer whale charging in for that bunt. I managed to pick up the ball, but I couldn't throw him out.

I felt a lot more comfortable at first base. There, when a ball is hit, the first thing you do is run away from it. My kind of position. Unless the ball is hit right at you, I was told, just turn and run for the base. Seemed simple enough to me.

Nobody said a word about cut-off plays.

This is what is known as on-the-job training. We were playing Boston and they had a runner on first when Rick Miller hit a line drive over my head down the right-field line. I didn't have the slightest idea where I was supposed to go. I started going to the outfield, then stopped, then started backing up. Miller rounded first and headed for second. People were running all over the place, so I felt I had to at least look like I was doing something. I headed for the pitcher's mound—it seemed like the safest place at the time. Miller rounded second and headed for third.

The relay throw came right to me.

It was almost too easy. I cut it off, turned, and fired to third to get Miller. And that's the way we do it in the big leagues.

My best year in the major leagues was 1983. Carlton Fisk and I combined to set a record for White Sox catchers by hitting twenty-seven home runs. I had one. That record stood until 1985 when we hit thirty-seven. I hit none. The '83 team won the Western Division championship by twenty games, an American League record. I was sitting in the dugout when Harold Baines hit a sacrifice fly to center field to score the winning run against Seattle to clinch the championship. I ran onto the field and started jumping up and down. I poured champagne in the clubhouse. I can't explain what I was feeling. I just couldn't believe I was on a championship ball club. Finally. After all those seasons, after all those disappointments, after almost being out of baseball, I was on a championship team.

I thought to myself, this is something I should do every year.

Everybody on that team contributed to the championship. I think I realized one night in May at Yankee Stadium that it was going to be a special season. We had the bases loaded, I was on second, and Greg Walker was hitting. He hit a long fly ball to center field. I mean a *long* fly ball. After the catch was made, I tagged up and ran as hard as I could to third base. When I got near third, I received the biggest surprise of my career—coach Jim Leyland was waving me to keep going. Keep going? Somebody must have fallen down, I thought. No, it had to be worse than that. I put it in whatever gears I had left, I turned on the afterburners, I steamed toward the plate. Have you ever seen a tank sprint? The faster I ran, the farther away the plate seemed to be. Finally, somehow, I reached home plate and slid in safely.

For a player with my speed, scoring from *third* base on a sacrifice fly is an accomplishment. But from second base? It was one of the few times in baseball history that base runners on first and second have advanced two bases on a sacrifice fly. So I think right then and there the entire team realized this was going to be a very special season.

Obviously a player doesn't survive more than a decade in the major leagues unless he has some ability. I pride myself on my ability to call a good game and I have a fine percentage against base stealers. In San Francisco I caught Vida Blue when he won something like eleven consecutive games. And I have been able to get an important hit from time to time. The pitcher's book on me is curveball, curveball, curveball. I've seen enough of them, and I've actually hit some of them. I once went 4-for-5 against the Yankees—that's more hits in one day than I've had in entire seasons—and would have been 5-for-5 except that center fielder Dave Collins made a diving catch of a line drive I hit off Goose Gossage. And many of my home runs have been off top pitchers. I've homered off Tom Seaver, Steve Carlton, Jerry Koosman, Tug McGraw—the best pitchers. My most memorable hit, however, was not a home run.

Not even close. I was with the Giants and we were tied with San Diego in the bottom of the ninth inning. We had two men on and two outs, and the Padres brought Rollie Fingers in to pitch to me.

This is what is known as a classic overmatch.

He threw me a fastball for strike one.

Then he threw me a wicked slider. It should be illegal to throw a pitch that good to a hitter like me. A slider starts out coming straight at you, then breaks, or slides, across the plate. When I saw that pitch coming at me, I stepped back, way back, halfway into our dugout—and then the ball started sliding. I lunged at it, realized I couldn't hit it, and tried to check my swing. The ball hit my bat and shot down the first base line. It hit first base and bounced away as the winning run scored.

When you've had a career like mine, those are the thrills.

Part of the job of a part-time player is keeping things loose on the bench and in the clubhouse. I'll play all the little jokes, giving players a hotfoot, putting shaving cream in their hats. Once, I remember, I filled Jerry Hairston's hat with shaving cream and he put it on. Suddenly Jerry paused and took it off. I asked him how he knew the shaving cream was there. He looked at me and said, "I could hear it fizzing when it started evaporating."

I'm probably the biggest cheerleader on the ball club. As I remind our players in crucial situations, "Hey, don't wait for me to do it. If you do, we'll be here all night."

I think I give the most trouble to the people who write the backs of baseball cards. After all these years, what more can they say about me? My cards used to say things like "Marc Hill went four-for-five to beat the Yankees." Or "Hill hit a two-run homer to beat the Indians." Lately it says things like "Marc Hill's father pitched in the St. Louis Browns organization."

In the last few years I've started saving souvenirs of my career. I've gotten bats signed by the greatest hitters I've seen play—Yastrzemski, Winfield, Brett. I have some meaningful baseballs and I have some unusual things—first balls. Whenever a celebrity throws out a first ball, someone has to catch it. Often that someone has been me. So I have a collection of first balls signed by singers and actors. How many people have a baseball autographed by Frank Sinatra? All right, then how many have one signed by Vic Damone? Or Henry "Fonzie" Winkler?

When you've had a career like mine, those are the souvenirs.

I do know what it's like being a superstar, believe me. That's because I've often been mistaken for one by fans. When I had a beard, people would often mistake me for Greg Luzinski or LaMarr Hoyt. My reaction depended on how well the player for whom I had been mistaken had done that day. Let me tell you, when Hoyt won the Cy Young Award in 1983, I signed a lot of autographs. On the other hand, when Luzinski struck out three times, people would get all over me when I left the clubhouse. That's when I'd admit, "Hey, I'm Hill."

"Who?"

"Booter."

Then they'd smile. "Oh, yeah, I know who you are."

When you've had a career like mine, that's nice to hear.

LOOKING BACK, OVER MY SHOULDER

by Steve Nicosia

I pitched one game during my sophomore year at Miami Norland High School in Miami, Florida. I hit the first batter with my first pitch and the second batter with my second pitch. I walked the third batter on four straight pitches. The clean-up batter hit my next pitch for a grand slam home run. Seven pitches, four runs. So I could see I probably wasn't going to make the big leagues as a pitcher. The big leagues? I couldn't even make the second inning.

The following year I transferred to North Miami Beach High, which had just opened across the street from my house. On the first day of baseball practice the coach gathered the squad and said, "To start with, we need someone to catch." Either that or a very strong backstop, I realized. Since I was the only player on the team with varsity baseball experience, I decided to try it. That was the best decision I ever made. Catching became my ticket to the major leagues.

I was the Pittsburgh Pirates' first selection in the 1973 player draft. Instead of assigning me to their rookie league team, the Pirates sent me to the West-

ern Carolina A League to fill in for an injured player. I
was seventeen years old and I was naive. Chuck Cottier was the manager, and in the eight weeks I played
for him, I learned more about life than I did in my
next ten years in baseball.

He taught me the basics. I mean basics. As basic
as wear shower shoes in the shower. There were puddles up to your knees in minor league shower rooms. I
think there were things living in them, but I didn't
know anything about shower shoes. Cottier was always telling me, pull your pants up. Don't wear that
shirt, it looks bad. Comb your hair. About the only
thing I was good with were shoelaces. I had shoelaces
down good. Without Cottier there is no way I would
have made it.

I'd never really been away from home in my life,
so almost everything in the minor leagues was new to
me. For example, I'd never seen snow. Ever. When I
was playing in Double A, we were in Rocky Mount,
North Carolina. One night the temperature went down
to twenty-five degrees and I got excited because it
looked like I was going to see snow for the first time.
After I went to sleep that night, my teammate, John
Candelaria, took a fire extinguisher and sprayed foam
over the entire surface of the motel swimming pool.
Then he pounded on my door, screaming, "Nick! Nick!
It snowed, it snowed. Come look at the pool."

Who could fall for that, right? If you've never seen
snow before, a lot of things could be snow. It was
white and it was wet. As far as I was concerned, it was
snow. You ever try to make a snowball with fire
extinguisher foam?

The Pirates had some serious talent in their minor league system. For example, every starter on our
1976 Charleston, West Virginia, club in the International League eventually played in the major leagues.
We had Tony Armas, Craig Reynolds, Mitchell Paige,
we had Rick Langford, Doug Bair, and Odell Jones
pitching for us. We finished sixth. That was some
strong league that year.

The best thing about looking back on the minor

leagues is being able to look back on it. If you realized what you were doing while you were doing it, there is no way you would do it. For example, I hurt my knees so badly in the minor leagues, I had to have them operated on. Not from playing; I never got hurt playing. I had "bus-ride knees." Sitting in a cramped bus seat for sixteen, seventeen hours at a time really did a job on them. One way you can identify a person who has played a long time in the minors is that he'll be walking around hunched over, knees bent, like he's been sitting on a counter stool for three years.

The most surprising thing I learned in the minor leagues is how little I learned. I've never understood that. An organization signs a player for a huge bonus, the future of the franchise might depend on him, then they pay somebody nine thousand dollars a year to instruct him. And they got exactly what they paid for. I would ask, "What do you do in this situation?"

The answer would be: "That situation hasn't come up yet."

Okay, what is the proper way to block home plate on a play at the plate?

The answer would be: "Here's the plate. When the guy is coming in, block it. Put your face in front of it."

Okay, what do you say when you go out and talk to the pitcher?

The answer would be: "Everybody's different. It depends on the situation."

Okay, here's the situation.

"That situation hasn't come up yet."

I finished second in the International League in batting in 1978 and came up with the Pirates in 1979, the "We are family" season. I was the only rookie on that team. Donnie Robinson and I were twenty-three years old; the next youngest player was about thirty. Some of those guys had kids in college. The thing I remember best about that team is how confident they were that we were going to win. We were in third place at the All-Star break, five games out of first. I was thinking, hey, we've got a shot at being in contention. As I was packing to go home, Dave Parker said to me, "You don't know how lucky you are. You're gonna play in the World Series your first year in the major leagues." Not win the pennant, not win the playoffs, play in the World Series.

That attitude came from manager Chuck Tanner. He was the most confident man I'd ever seen. We'd be ten runs down with two out in the ninth inning with the pitcher batting and he was sure we were going to come back to win. And every move he made that season seemed to work out. One night I remember in particular was my birthday. We were playing Philadelphia and were tied 9–9 in the bottom of the ninth inning. We had the bases loaded and I was due to hit. It had already been my greatest day in baseball: in four at bats I'd hit a home run, two doubles and a single, and I'd knocked in three runs. The Phillies brought in left-handed relief pitcher Tug McGraw to pitch to me.

As I started walking to the plate, I heard Tanner calling my name. I couldn't believe he was going to pinch-hit for me. I refused to look back over my shoulder. Later in my career I got so good at looking over my shoulder for a pinch-hitter that people thought I had a twitch. But this time I refused to look back. Eventually I had no choice. Tanner sent left-handed-hitting John Milner up there, and there wasn't room at home plate for both of us.

I was 4-for-4 on my birthday, with a chance to knock in the winning run, a right-handed hitter facing a left-handed pitcher, and he was pinch-hitting for me. There were 45,000 Italians in the ballpark and they wanted to kill him. They were screaming at him, throwing things on the field.

Milner hit McGraw's first pitch into the upper deck for a game-winning grand slam home run. Those same 45,000 Italians suddenly thought Tanner was the greatest manager in the world.

After the game reporters came up to me and asked, "You were four-for-four and he hit for you. Aren't you mad?"

I told them the truth. "A guy like me," I said, "what are the chances of it being five-for-five?"

Then they went to Tanner and asked him the same question. "A guy like that," Tanner said, "what are the chances of him being five-for-five?"

That was some powerful ball club. We weren't just good; we were big. We had Willie Stargell, Dave Parker, Jim Bibby, Bruce Kison, Kent Tekulve, Bill Madlock, Bill Robinson, Jim Rooker, every one of them was a big, strong guy. After I went to the San Francisco Giants, Mike Krukow told me, "We always hated to play you guys. What killed us was the way you walked out of your dugout with your chests in the air. I mean, we knew we were gonna get beat, but you didn't have to make it look like you knew we knew we were gonna get beat."

Just as Parker predicted, we won the Eastern Division championship and the playoffs. The Orioles won the American League pennant, and the World Series was opening in Baltimore. The few days between the end of the playoff and the beginning of the series were the most hectic I've ever lived through. The hype was unbelievable. There were always two hundred reporters in the clubhouse, and representatives of every type of baseball-equipment manufacturer were making deals with players to use their products. One day Billy Madlock wore two different spikes, a Nike on his left foot for something like fifteen thousand dollars and an Adidas on his right foot for ten thousand. Bill Robinson wore a different pair of shoes every day. A number of players signed with a company that made a spiked shoe so uncomfortable they couldn't wear them, so they painted their old shoes black and put tape on them to resemble that company's logo.

As the only rookie on the team, nobody was paying me to wear anything. It didn't bother me; I was thrilled to be in the World Series. I was scheduled to catch the first game, and the day before, our clubhouse man, John Halloran, came over to my locker and asked, "You wanna make a thousand dollars?"

A thousand dollars? I was making $23,000 for the entire season. "What do I have to do?"

He took out a device that looked like a small fan. It had four little blades surrounding a hole in the middle. "You put this over the end of your bat when you're on deck," he explained. "When you swing, the wind causes the blades to turn, creating resistance, making it tougher to swing. When you take it off, the bat feels much lighter and you swing better. All you gotta do is use this when you're in the on-deck circle in the opening game."

A thousand dollars for that? How tough could that be? I agreed and Halloran gave me a check for one thousand dollars.

The opening game was snowed out. By then I'd become almost an expert at identifying snow. The following day was even worse; it was freezing and there were patches of ice on the field, but we had to play. I was batting seventh in our order, and when I came out on deck, I was cold and I was nervous, but I took out my little fan and slipped it over the end of my bat.

Well, one thing I didn't figure was that I was using an S-2 model bat, which happens to have a very thin barrel. So I put the fan on and took a very hard swing—sssssssss. That fan went flying off the end of the bat. It must've caught an air current, because it took off like a piece of paper in a hurricane. It sailed about twenty-five rows into the stands and hit a woman in the side of the neck. I figured, there goes my thousand dollars.

But I already had the check in my locker and I wanted to keep it, so I had to get my fan back. I was trying to signal people. *That's my fan, can I have my fan back? I need my fan.* Meanwhile, they're playing the World Series behind me.

The ushers finally went up into the stands and got the thing back for me. I put it back on, real tightly this time. Then I turned around and swung—sssssssss—this time it goes flying into the fourth row.

That was enough for me. Now I didn't want anything to do with it. I tried to pretend it had nothing to do with me. People are shouting at me, "Hey, buddy, Nicosia, here's your fan."

I'm going, "It's not my fan. I never saw that fan before." What I didn't realize was that the batter ahead of me, Madlock, had grounded out. The game was being held up while I was arguing with people in the stands, insisting I had never seen that fan before in my life.

Suddenly I heard Tanner screaming at me. "What the heck is going on? We're in the World Series. What are you doing, kid, signing autographs?"

I was so embarrassed, I went running up to the plate, no practice swings, no nothing. The one place I didn't want to be was exactly where I was, on television in front of the entire country. I struck out quickly and quietly.

I caught the first, third, fifth, and seventh games of the series. On a travel day between Pittsburgh and Baltimore I remember Willie Stargell telling me about playing in the 1971 World Series. "The thing I kept wondering about during the playoffs and the series," he remembered, "was, how am I gonna react when we win the whole thing? What am I gonna do? Am I gonna jump in the air? Scream? Yell? I was trying to plan my reaction. Finally the last out was made and we were World Champions and the next thing I knew I was in the clubhouse celebrating. I didn't even remember that I had been on the field."

In the ninth inning of the seventh and deciding game we were beating the Orioles 4–1. Kent Tekulve was pitching for us and I didn't care who Baltimore sent up to bat; they were not going to hit him. So while I was putting down the signals, I started thinking, how am I gonna react when we win the whole thing? What am I gonna do? Fling my mask? Jump up and tap my feet? Scream? Yell? I decided I was going to be restrained.

When Pat Kelly flew out to end the game, I ran out to the mound and started hugging Tekulve and we got mobbed and the next thing I knew I was standing in the clubhouse. I forgot everything else. I didn't know how I had gotten there.

Even today, when I watch those series films, I see myself doing things I don't even remember. Usually when I've played in a game, I remember every detail— foul tips, double plays, everything. I don't remember entire innings of the series.

I was excited when we won, but I think I was happiest for people like Bill Robinson, and coaches Joe Lonnett and Al Monchek, who had been in baseball so long without reaching this peak. They were crying from happiness.

I was happy for me, too, but it was my rookie year and I didn't realize what an incredible experience it was. I was a kid, it was my first year. Wow, this is easy, I thought. We can do this every year. The big leagues are really great. You play and at the end of the season you get a bonus check for thirty thousand dollars.

Obviously it didn't turn out that way. Eventually I went to the San Francisco Giants, then to the Montreal Expos. I never played in another World Series. The years I spent in Pittsburgh were the happiest of my career. The fans were wonderful and the people I played with were great. We really were a family, and our leaders were Willie Stargell and Dave Parker. Stargell was such a class act. Once, when he was coming back to the dugout after batting practice one day, I saw him take off his spikes and give them to a young fan. When we'd lose a few games in a row, or have some problem, he would call a team meeting and decide, "I don't like what's going on. I think we have to have a party."

Parker learned from Stargell. He made the clubhouse a fun place to be. He was always teasing somebody, or being kidded by somebody else. The year after we won the series, for example, he reported to spring training two weeks late and twenty-five pounds overweight. The moment he walked into the clubhouse Phil Garner was all over him. "I can't believe it," Garner yelled, "I just cannot believe it. Look at you, you come in two weeks late, you're twenty-five pounds overweight, you can't hit, you can't throw, you've got bad knees, a bad wrist, a bad everything. Instead of getting here two weeks late, you should have been here two weeks early. I mean, I was down here February first working out . . ."

Parker looked at Garner and said softly, "Hey, if I had your talent, I would've been here at Christmas."

I spent my first two seasons in Pittsburgh platooning behind the plate with Ed Ott. It worked out well; we won about 190 games those two years. Meanwhile, a young right-handed hitting catcher named Tony Pena was turning heads in the minor leagues. Because I also hit right-handed, it looked like I was going to be traded, and Pena and left-handed-hitting Ott would be the catching platoon. But Ott was a free agent and there was some clause in his contract the Pirates wouldn't agree to, so he ended up in California. I opened the 1981 season as the everyday catcher and hit .128 for the month of April.

If the rest of the team had been hitting, we could have survived my slump, but the whole team was struggling. Finally Chuck came to me and said, "You're doing a good job behind the plate and the pitchers like throwing to you, but we've got to score some runs, so I'm going to give Pena a shot."

Pena went 4-for-4 his first game; the next day he got three hits, the next day four hits, the next day three hits—he had something like fifteen hits his first five games. Tanner told me, "Just be patient. There's no way he can stay this hot."

That was May 1981. He's still that hot.

I did get one more shot to play that season. Three weeks after Pena became the regular catcher, he was hit in the wrist by Cincinnati's Mario Soto. I started playing and hitting. I hit about .380 for a month, then we went on strike. When we started playing again, Pena was healthy and Chuck put him back in.

It was difficult for me to get used to sitting on the bench. I'd come to the ballpark and I didn't want to be there. My attitude went bad. I'd play once a week and go oh-for-4 and I wouldn't care. Finally Bill Robinson took me aside and told it to me like it was. "You're not helping anybody with your attitude," he said, "especially yourself. That's gonna change right now. From now on we're gonna start coming in early, do some running and some exercises, and we're gonna be mentally prepared to play when the chance comes."

That's what we did. Bill Robinson and I would get to the park at two o'clock and do our work. When the game started, I was ready to play. Robinson probably saved my career right there.

One thing I don't do on the bench is yell at players on other teams. Not unless I really know them. I figure, hey, they're playing, I'm on the bench—I'm gonna tell them they're no good? There really aren't too many bench jockeys in baseball. One I did play with in Pittsburgh was Kurt Bevacqua, who was always yelling and screaming at the other team's players. One night against Houston he was just ripping the Astros' 6'8" pitcher, J. R. Richard. At that point Richard was the hardest-throwing pitcher in the league and nobody liked hitting against him even when he wasn't angry. Kurt was getting him angry. I think it was Phil Garner who went over to Kurt and asked him to maybe cool it down a bit. "Hey," Kurt said, "that big guy doesn't scare me."

" 'Course not," Garner said. "You don't have to bat against him."

The ironic thing is that it was while I wasn't playing that I suffered the most damaging injury of my career. In order to keep my arm in condition, I'd pitch batting practice. One day in Chicago I felt a little twinge in my arm. Rather than stopping, I decided to throw a few more minutes. That was it. From that moment on, my arm got progressively worse. During the next few seasons I often had to take pain pills just to get through a ball game. I've worked with weights to rehabilitate the arm, and there are days when it feels as good as it once did, but it is just never going to be as consistently strong as it once was. I guess that makes me one of the few major leaguers to suffer from both "bus-trip knees" and "batting-practice arm."

Since that first day in high school when I got behind the plate, I've loved catching. There is nothing quite like the feeling of sitting back there when you are working with a pitcher in complete command of his pitches. Like Candelaria when he wanted to pitch. Candy had as much natural talent as anyone I ever caught. He was as good as he wanted to be. One day during warm-ups, I remember, he told me he was going to pitch a two-hitter that day. Whoever the other team was got two hits in the first inning—and that was it. Nothing. *Nada.* He shut them down completely for the remainder of the ball game.

I believe Candy could have won thirty games if he would have concentrated, but a lot of times he just wanted to have fun. If we were winning 5–0 and Dave Kingman came up with two out in the ninth inning, he'd throw a fastball down the middle just to see how far Kingman could hit a baseball. He didn't care about pitching a shutout; he wanted to see everyone in the stands get excited. One night he pitched a three-hitter against the Expos. This was when they had Andre Dawson, Ellis Valentine, Gary Carter—an entire lineup of hitters. Their pitcher, Bill Lee, got all three hits. And each time he got a hit I'd go out to the pitcher's mound and scream at Candy. And he'd smile sheepishly and tell me, "Okay, I'll try now."

Bert Blyleven was another pitcher who could just embarrass hitters. I'd signal for a breaking ball, and when he dropped it in the strike zone, nobody could hit it. What a power surge it was to catch him on those days.

If working with a great pitcher was the best part of catching, plays at home plate were the worst part. I didn't really mind "putting my face" in front of the plate as I had been taught in the minor leagues—it was just that the rest of my body was attached to my face. Early in a game a catcher can cheat a little, and give a runner coming home more of the plate to aim at, but when the game is on the line, a catcher has to make the runner earn it. Sometimes that means making him go through you. There are catchers that enjoy that—Mike Scoscia, Ed Ott—they come up the line to force a collision. Me? My ambition is to see my kids grow up.

I had a memorable collision with Steve Garvey in 1984. At least I remember it. Outfielder Joel Youngblood made a perfect throw to the plate, and just as I caught it, Garvey hit me in the side of my head with his elbow. It was a clean play. I held the ball and he was out.

But to this day I have this strange creaking in my jaw. Right after that I couldn't eat or talk for two weeks. It wasn't so much having to drink soup through a straw that bothered me, but not being able to talk was a killer. So one of the few souvenirs I have from my career is this strange sound that makes my mouth sound like a door that needs oiling.

The catcher's equipment can prevent most injuries —for the catcher. The only time I was ever seriously hurt in a collision I was the runner. I was with the Giants and we were playing the Dodgers at Candlestick Park. In the fourth inning I was on second base and Manny Trillo singled to left field. First of all, me running on the soft dirt at Candlestick is like an aging water buffalo running uphill on a treadmill. I had no chance anyway. But I came around third and looked up—and there was Mike Scoscia standing twelve feet up the line. Grinning. I'd say he looked to be about the size of, oh, maybe a batting cage. I couldn't even see home plate. Home plate? I couldn't even see our dugout. When I got about two-thirds of the way down the line I thought, jeez, if I try to slide, he's gonna embarrass me. I'm gonna hit his shin guards and end up lying there thirty-five feet from home plate. I decided I was just going to have to run over him. No big thing.

A team of doctors took three sets of X rays but there was so much swelling they didn't find any problems. But the fact that I was spitting up blood, and had trouble breathing for a week, bothered them. I had to sleep sitting up in a chair for two weeks. A full season later I started getting chest pains and had more X rays taken, and that is when they discovered the two broken ribs.

A catcher often has to function as a psychiatrist on the field. Like when the other team had scored three or four runs and I hadn't caught one pitch, I had to go out there and say something to boost the pitcher's confidence. What could I say? The only thing I had ever been told was "Don't be negative, don't let on to a pitcher that he's losing his stuff." So I'd just go out to the mound and make up something. "I think you're dipping your shoulder," or "You're not following through on your breaking ball." I knew I didn't know what I was talking about, but the pitcher didn't know that. He was getting hit pretty hard and would listen to anything. Dipping my shoulder? Oh, yeah, that's why the guy hit the ball into the upper deck. But if he somehow got the next batter out, he'd feel the problem had been solved and he would regain his confidence.

Tanner used to say success in baseball depended on your attitude. I believed him. The only pitcher I ever told he was horsebleep was Candy. We'd played together in A ball for two years, in AA, in Instructional League, winter ball, and five years with the Pirates, so I knew him pretty well. I'd go out there shaking my head and tell him, "Jeez, Candy. You stink. You're getting your ass kicked, you jerk. Let's go."

He loved that. He'd laugh, then say, "Okay, I'll try now."

I knew him so well, there were times I'd go out to the mound and I wouldn't have to say a word. I'd just go out there and give him a dirty look. He'd say, "I know, I know. I stink." I'd just turn around and go back behind the plate.

Of course, I couldn't talk like that—or not talk like that—to the wrong guy. If anyone said anything negative to Enrique Romo, he'd want to fight you. I was always afraid he was going to pull a knife out there, so I'd go out to the mound and say, "Boy, they're sure getting some lucky hits today. You think maybe you might want to try following through a little more, but only if you want to."

The people a catcher gets to know best of all are umpires. I always got along well with umpires. I figured, even if I did hit .300, I'm getting only three out of ten—these guys are supposed to get ten out of ten. That's tough. I never really complained too much on ball-strike calls, but what I would do when I wasn't happy with a call was to ask the umpire where the pitch was. That was my way of asking him to concentrate a little more. Only once did that cause any problems. We were beating Philadelphia 1–0 in the ninth inning. Jim Bibby was pitching, Bruce Froemming was the home plate umpire, and Pete Rose was the hitter. Bibby's first pitch was on the outside corner. It was close, but I expected to get a strike called.

Ball one.

"That was a pretty good pitch, Bruce" was all I said. He grunted. The next pitch was right on the outside corner, maybe the best pitch Bibby had made all night. No question it had to be called a strike.

Ball two.

I grunted. "Bruce," I said, "that ball was right on the corner."

"No, it wasn't," Bruce said.

I said, "Well, was it low, then?"

"No."

"Okay. Was it high?"

"No." Just that one-word answer.

I was getting curious. "All right, was it outside?"

Froemming paused. "What the hell is this," he asked, "a quiz?"

Rose was laughing so hard he had to step out of the batter's box. It was the first time I'd ever seen a batter call time out for laughter.

After playing in Pittsburgh, where it seemed we were fighting for the pennant every year, it was a big adjustment moving to the San Francisco Giants. I played considerably more with the Giants than I had in Pittsburgh, but the attitude was so different than I had experienced. In Pittsburgh we were embarrassed if we weren't in first place. With the Giants we'd be in sixth place and people would be saying, "Come on, if we win three more in a row, we can move up to fifth." Fifth? What's that?

I had a fine 1984 season with the Giants, hitting .303 before crashing into the Scoscia wall. My contract expired at the end of the year and I became a free agent. I thought I could move somewhere else, but I was beginning to like it in San Francisco and wanted to stay there. I knew Bob Brenley was going to be the regular catcher, but I believed I could help that team. So I went to see general manager Tom Haller and told him: "There's a lot of things I can do to help this ball club. I'm making only $170,000 a year, but if you sign me for two years, I won't go through the draft."

Only $170,000? Haller didn't hesitate before suggesting I go through the draft. That was some negotiating ploy.

I was drafted by six clubs, more than my agent, Tom Reich, or I expected. I wasn't looking for a lot of money; I just wanted a place where I could play some and maybe make a little something. One by one the teams dropped out without making an offer. Finally only the Montreal Expos were interested in me and they wanted to sign me to a Triple A contract with a forty thousand dollar pay cut. I thought, this is free agency? This is when teams throw millions of dollars at you? Gee, I'm a lifetime .250 hitter, I hit .300, and nobody wanted me. Three hundred, that was it, I can't do any better than that.

I signed and made the Montreal ball club. Now when I hear players like me, who aren't stars, talking about free agency, I smile and walk away.

I stayed with Montreal through most of the season. In August we had a difference of opinion: I wanted to play; they didn't think I could play. We compromised. They released me and I went home.

A week later I signed with the Toronto Blue Jays, becoming one of the very few players to be with both Canadian teams in the same season. I hit .267 for Toronto, not preventing them from winning the American League Eastern Division championship. Unfortunately I'd joined the club too late to be eligible for post-season play. But watching them celebrate certainly brought back memories of 1979.

At the end of the season Toronto also gave me my unconditional release. I immediately began hoping that baseball would expand to Vancouver. I went back to my home team, my wife, Pam, and my daughters, Kimberly and Kelly. At least I'm having a good career with that club.

For players with limited ability, like me, baseball is a very different game than it is for the Winfields and Rices and Parkers. I'm one of those people who always gets letters from fans reading, "Dear Mr. Nicosia, You are my favorite player in the whole world. Can you please get me Willie Stargell's autograph? Love——"

I CALL IT STRATEGY
by Ray Miller

*For the last few seasons my favorite baseball trivia
question has been: Name the manager of the Minnesota Twins. People I asked would look at me as if I'd
asked them to name the nutritional elements in wheat
germ. Meanwhile, that unknown Twins manager
brought the team from seventh place in 1982 to second place, just missing winning the division championship in 1984. That manager's name was Billy
Gardner. Bill-ee Gard-ner. And when the Twins got
off to a poor start in 1985, he was fired. This time
Twins management decided to hire a big name to run
the ball club, so they went out and signed Ray Miller.
Ray Miller!*

*Although much has been written about my trou-
bled relationship with Baltimore Oriole manager Earl
Weaver, particularly by me, the fact is that there were
certain things I always liked about Earl. The man's
spikes were always laced. He never dribbled on his
uniform while spitting at an umpire. And he had Ray
Miller as his pitching coach.*

The main responsibilities of a major league pitch-

ing coach, as far as I've been able to determine, are to make sure the pitchers either run or don't run, and to take the blame off the manager. The only time the pitching coach comes onto the field is when a pitcher is in a jam. The manager sends the pitching coach out to give him advice. This is the manager's way of saying don't blame me because the pitcher can't throw the ball over the plate, blame the pitching coach. If, after talking to the pitching coach, the pitcher doesn't get out of the jam, the manager then goes to the mound to take him out. This is his subtle way of saying I tried, but the pitching coach couldn't do his job, so now I'll have to take charge. But don't blame me.

The thing about pitching is that nobody really knows what makes a great pitcher. And that's what a pitching coach teaches. Some pitchers with great ability never reach their potential; other pitchers with less natural talent become superstars. Every pitching coach has a different theory about pitching. Some coaches try to teach their pitchers a new pitch, others work on their mechanics (the way they pitch). Ray Miller believed that the key to turning talent into performance was mental; and with his own pitching ability he knew he had to be crazy to stand out there unprotected.

The Orioles, first under George Bamburger, then Miller, were known for their ability to develop young pitchers. Part of that, obviously, is being able to detect when a pitcher has lost his edge in a ball game, and being able to give him that advice that would enable him to sharpen his control. For example, one night in Chicago with the Orioles leading by one run, Baltimore relief pitcher Don Stanhouse walked the bases loaded, then threw two balls to the batter. On the Oriole bench Weaver screamed at Miller, "Get out there and tell him what to do."

Miller walked slowly to the mound, wondering what he was going to tell Stanhouse. About all he could think of was, don't throw any more balls. When he reached the mound, Stanhouse said, "What are you gonna tell me, Earl doesn't want me to throw any more balls?"

Miller shook his head. "I just wanted to tell you your fly's open." Then he returned to the bench. The batter hit Stanhouse's next pitch into a game-ending double play.

I always got along very well with Ray Miller. He would get just as irritated as I would when Weaver started screaming at the home plate umpire. His concern wasn't for the umpire, of course; he was worried that the screaming would cause the pitcher to lose his concentration. So he would go out to talk to his pitcher, and eventually I would stroll out to the mound to tell him he'd been there long enough. When I got close enough to hear him, he would say without looking at me so the fans would never know he was complaining, "Looks like you're missing a few, Ronnie."

What am I going to do, lie? If necessary. "What do you mean by that?"

"Look," he'd say, "I'm going back to the dugout and tell that little !@#$%¢ to stay off your back," (meaning manager Weaver) "so you just take your time and gimme a good look at the pitch, and if he doesn't lay off, go ahead and throw him out of the game. You'll be doing everybody a big favor."

Then, of course, he'd go into the dugout and tell Weaver, "The pitcher's okay. And I told Luciano off. That big ⊕¢%$$#'ll call a better game now. Just give him a few pitches." Then he'd pray.

He took charge of the Twins in midseason, 1985. He told me that the thing he liked best about the ball club was that the players were so talented and so young. "Tell you what, Ronnie," he said, "they just haven't been here long enough to know when I've screwed up. I just tell them it's strategy."

Ray Miller is my kind of manager—I always thought it was strategy too.

I grew up on a small farm in Forrestville, Maryland, near Washington, D.C. My father was a very serious man who worked construction seven days a week, so everyone in the family had chores that had to be done. That didn't leave too much time for playing. But one day, when I was nine, I rode my bike through the woods, although I was not supposed to leave the county road, and discovered this Little League team working out. I stopped to watch and, because I was pretty much the biggest kid in the area, the manager asked me how old I was. When I told him, he explained that I was too young to play, but asked if I wanted to pitch batting practice.

I struck everybody out. That changed the rules; the manager wanted me to pitch for his team. I told him my father would never let me. And at first, he wouldn't. Somehow, though, my mother convinced him to let me try. Not only that, she got him out there to watch me the first time I pitched. During the game I kept glancing at him, but he just sat there, not saying a word. I pitched five innings and struck out all but two batters.

After the game the only thing he said to me was "How could you let those two guys hit the ball!"

I always had a good fastball. I thought that was all you needed to pitch in the big leagues. I signed with the San Francisco Giants in 1962, and in spring training that year I got an opportunity to pitch against the big club in an intra-squad game. The first batter I faced was Willie Mays. I threw him my good high heater and he swung and popped it up. I couldn't believe it, I'd gotten Willie Mays out. I wanted to call time, run off the field, and phone my dad and tell him, "You ain't gonna believe this . . ."

Willie McCovey was up next. I struck him out. The third batter grounded out. Three up, three down, two of them future Hall of Famers. Hey, I thought, this is easy. At this rate I'll be pitching in the big leagues in a few weeks.

That was just about the highlight of my career. The next inning the three Alou brothers, Felipe, Matty, and Jesus, were the batters. I figured that with my fastball I'd just blow them away. *Pschooo. Zzzzzoooo.*

Whizzzzz. Three line drives went shooting past my ear. Ten years later I was still pitching in the minor leagues.

Although I averaged a strikeout an inning until the last two weeks of my career, I never made it to the majors as a pitcher. If there is one thing I'm bitter about, that's it. Part of the reason I didn't make it might be that for the first five years of my career I also averaged a walk an inning, but I spent a lot of time in the Cleveland organization, and the Indians were a last-place ball club. I couldn't have done that much to hurt them. I always said I wanted to throw just one pitch in the big leagues, then walk off the field. A friend of mine has pointed out that with my ability, chances are that I would've thrown that pitch and then would've had to back up third base in case the relay throw from the outfield got by the third baseman.

I never made it to the big leagues, but I did make it to the airport once. At the end of spring training one year I had made the squad and was ready to fly to Cleveland. Then the Indians made a deal for a veteran pitcher. They told me I had a great spring, but they had a chance to get a proven major league relief pitcher. I couldn't argue with that; the man was a proven reliever. Then I looked over his stats. His lifetime won-lost record was below .500. The Indians didn't tell me that the thing he had proven was that he wasn't a very good relief pitcher.

After ten minor league seasons it became obvious I was never going to be a big league star. So when Joe Altobelli, then managing the Oriole Triple A team in Rochester, asked me to become his player-coach, I accepted. The Orioles gave me a thousand dollar raise which, based on my salary, was a tremendous percentage increase. I taught Jesse Jefferson how to throw a slider that year, which got him to the big leagues and convinced the Orioles to offer me a full-time job as minor league pitching instructor.

During my career I'd played for a lot of different pitching coaches, most of them from the old school. About all they would do was hit you ground balls in spring training, and tell you over and over, "Drop and drive, drop and drive, throw the ball hard. You've got a great arm, son, you've got a great arm." If you were pitching well, they would remind you, "You've got a great arm, son, remember everything I told you." If you weren't pitching well, they'd leave the room when you walked in.

I decided when I became a pitching coach the thing that would impress me least was a guy who could throw hard. I could throw hard and all it got me was ten years in the minor leagues. I'd learned that to win consistently in the big leagues a pitcher has to have a good arm, a good delivery, and he has to be able to change speeds. As a pitching coach I tried to simplify the game for my pitchers. I tried to break it down into separate aspects and focus on each one. The pitching coaches I had had never tried to do that with me. They simplified the game by saying, "Either you get better or I'm gonna drop a dime in this phone and your ass is gone!"

I was determined to prove that if a pitcher with a good delivery could learn how to change speeds, he could be a winning pitcher. That belief, plus a lot of luck named Mike Flanagan, Sammy Stewart, Dennis Martinez, among others finally got me to the major leagues.

I learned a lot from Earl Weaver. Earl was pretty calculated in everything he did. Even yelling. He yelled at everybody about everything. At first it bothered me, then I began to understand that that was just the way he communicates. Sometimes when the team was going bad, and he knew that everybody was sick of hearing his screaming voice, he'd pick a close play and intentionally get thrown out of the game. He figured his getting ejected would, one, charge up the club, and two, make everyone so happy that they didn't have to listen to him that they would play better.

Earl Weaver is the primary reason so many people from the Baltimore organization have gone on to become managers. He forces his people to manage with him. He makes his coaches keep notes on every team in the league. He is always talking about what this player can and can't do, why he didn't run in a certain situation, why he did run in another situation, what other managers like to do on a 2–1 count, why he doesn't like to bunt. When a new player came into the league, the Orioles would have forty different reports on him, then Earl and the coaching staff would run onto the field early to watch this player take batting practice to see if the reports were accurate—if he liked to pull the ball or go to the opposite field. When that player came to bat in a game, we probably knew as much about him as his own manager.

Earl forced me to think: What would I do in this situation? For three years I made notes in a rulebook each time a situation came up. I carried that rulebook with me all the time. Once Earl got in an argument with an umpire over a rules interpretation and ordered a bat boy to bring him a rulebook. Before I could make a move, the bat boy picked up my rulebook and ran it out to Earl.

Stay calm, I told myself, he's going to use it only to look up a rule. Earl waved it high above his head then, to show the umpire what he thought of the call, then ripped it in half.

Stay calm, I told myself, it's still only in two halves. I sent the bat boy running onto the field to get the two halves. "C'mon!" I shouted, as he got closer, and closer, and closer and . . . and just as he got there, Earl bent over and picked up the two halves—and proceeded to rip them into tiny pieces and throw them at the umpire. Earl giveth and Earl ripeth into pieces. That was him. I didn't realize it at the time, but it was all part of the Earl Weaver management training course. And when I finally did get hired to manage the Minnesota Twins, I was prepared for the job.

As a minor league player the only way I could afford to stay in baseball was to play winter ball in the Caribbean. For ten years I pitched year-round. I pretty much killed my arm that way. But it was in the

Caribbean that I first got the chance to manage. Managing a club in the winter leagues can be a lot of fun as long as you don't let the death threats bother you. I will guarantee one thing—it is the greatest testing ground in the world for a man who wants to manage in the big leagues.

The first day you get down there, the owner of the club gives you a big hug and then warns you that it is only a sixty-game season and if the team loses more than three or four in a row early in the season, he can't be responsible. He does not tell you what he can't be responsible for, however. But you don't expect to lose three or four in a row anyway; no new manager does. So you set up an elaborate organizational plan. For example, before every game each player is going to get fifty swings. Then the team goes out on the field with three dozen new balls, the first batter hits a line drive, and thirty-five kids jump out of the left-field stands, pick up the ball, and run away with it. The batter hits the second pitch, thirty-five kids jump out of the right-field stands and steal that ball. So the first thing a manager learns in the Caribbean is that he has to either cut down on batting practice or hire armed guards.

The teams are made up of a combination of native and American players. Each team usually has a few native-born players who have become stars in America. They've just finished playing a full major league season and don't want to play winter ball. The only reason they play is that they know their family will be held hostage or something if they don't play in their home country. So they play; they don't want to play, but they do. Motivating those people is no picnic.

Each team also has a number of promising native players, usually AAA players in the States. These people want to play, and resent it when the manager has to play, the stars who don't want to play in front of them.

Each team also has some American players who signed a multiyear contract while still in the minors.

Some of them have subsequently made the majors and don't want to play, but must fulfill their contracts.

And finally each team has a number of young native players who can play a little bit, but the owner wants them on the team because if they grow to become big leaguers, he'll own their winter league rights.

So the job is to manage a team with major league stars who don't want to play but have to, players with less ability who do want to play but have to watch players who don't want to play playing, American players who don't want to play but are needed, and young players who can't play that the owner wants to play. It makes for an interesting juggling act, complicated by the fact that if a team loses more than three or four in a row, the manager is in jeopardy.

But I learned to manage down there; I certainly learned how to manage. The most difficult thing I had to learn, any young manager has to learn, is not to overmanage. The first time I had a team down there, every time somebody got on base I wanted to put a play on. At first, the fans liked it, they called me an aggressive manager. But when we started getting our base runners thrown out and hitting into double plays, they started calling me a stupid manager. I learned that most of the best plays are the ones you don't put on.

I also learned how to argue with umpires down there. Of course, I had a master teacher in the States, but I had to learn for myself. I got thrown out of a game for the first time as a manager in Puerto Rico. It was the second game of a doubleheader. In the first inning of the game the umpire in the field suddenly keeled over as if he were having a heart attack. They rushed him off the field only to discover that between games he'd been eating burritos and drinking warm soda and was suffering from terrible indigestion. Finally he made it back onto the field.

My team was on defense. With the bases loaded, the batter for the other team tripled. As soon as he slid into third, I saw my third baseman, Cal Ripkin, call for a pick-off on the first pitch. A good play. My pitcher threw, my catcher made a perfect throw to Ripkin, and the runner was caught off base. Ripkin tagged him, then looked at the umpire. The umpire was belching and looking into the stands. Meanwhile the runner had fallen down and was trying to crawl back to the base. Ripkin tagged him again, and again, the runner kept crawling, and the umpire kept belching. Finally the umpire turned around and realized he'd missed the play—so he called the runner safe.

I went crazy. If Weaver had been there, he would have been proud of me. That umpire and I stood there spitting at each other. Finally he threw me out of the game, and when he did that, I picked up third base and heaved it into the stands.

Four days later we had the same umpire again. This time he was working second base. Again a close play went against me. My players started jumping up and down and I knew I had to go out there. But as soon as I left the dugout, that umpire threw his arms up in the air and as fast as he could ran over to second base and stood on top of it. That day I learned how hard it is to argue when you're trying not to laugh.

When the offer came to manage the Twins, I was ready. It was not the first time I'd been approached. I'd always listened, but I didn't jump at the other jobs. When second division teams offer you a one-year contract and start telling you how good their minor league players are, you know you're not going to be there long enough to unpack. But the Twins had good new management and good young players.

The timing was right. And probably the most vital lesson I'd learned in my career was the importance of timing. Weaver taught me that. Joe Altobelli, the man I consider my mentor, stressed that. Pick your spots, Altobelli used to tell me over and over; timing is everything. When a player goes into a batting slump, for example, the most important thing is not to confuse him. He's already confused enough. Rather than offering more advice, Altobelli taught me to wait until he is going to play against a pitcher he usually hits well. Then make your move. "I don't want you to be worried about hitting the ball hard," Altobelli would say, "but I don't think you're seeing the ball well. Come out early for some extra hitting before the game."

Before the game the next day you let him hit a few easy balls, then tell him he looks like he's overcome his problem. Then in the game he goes 3-for-4 against a pitcher he should go 3-for-4 against. He has his confidence back and begins to believe you know what you're talking about.

The same reasoning holds true when scheduling a team meeting. For example, it is not a good idea to hold a rah-rah-we-can-do-it team meeting just before going out to play against Dwight Gooden. Chances are you can't do it. What a successful manager does is pick his spots—he holds the team meeting before the team is going to face someone like . . . like me. The time to work with a player, or a team, is when the odds for success are the greatest.

I took over the Twins in midseason, not the ideal situation. But the time I'd spent in the Baltimore organization made it possible. After looking over my notebooks, about the only thing I didn't know about the Twins players were the first names.

I had two problems when I took over. The first was with the pitching coach, Johnny Podres, whom I respect. When I was hired, I decided to keep all of former manager Billy Gardner's coaches. It wasn't as if these people hadn't done a good job; the Twins had been a contender in 1984. But when I was working as a pitching coach, one of the things I constantly complained about was that I never had an opportunity to work with our relief pitchers. I couldn't work with them before the game because they might have to pitch that day, and during the game I had to stay in the dugout to work with the pitcher on the mound. So I wanted my pitching coach to spend at least a few games every two weeks in the bullpen. I tried to explain that to Johnny Podres, but he didn't agree with me. I ended up firing him.

The second problem was also tough: I couldn't correctly spell second baseman Tim Tuefel's name. I couldn't remember if it was *ue* or *eu*. Finally I got it right, but then I couldn't remember how to spell Tuesday. As it turned out, it didn't matter. We traded Teufel, or Tueful, to the Mets.

Without question the single toughest thing about a manager's job is making decisions about other people's lives. In any other business if you fire somebody, he is going to find another job. When you get rid of a player in baseball, you are murdering a dream. Telling a man who has spent his whole life playing baseball that he isn't good enough anymore is no fun. It's almost impossible to just wash your hands, but to be a successful manager you have to be cold-blooded enough to get the best twenty-five players you can get.

I know from experience how tough it is to be on the other end of the conversation. My dream was never exactly killed; it just died of a hanging fastball.

THE CALL
by Thad Bosley, Jr.

Pinch hitting is one of the most difficult jobs in base-
ball. A player sits on the bench for an entire game,
minding his own business, and then, with the whole
game on the line, the manager sends him up to pinch-
hit. He gets only one at bat, against either a pitcher
who has been in the game for a while and is loose, or
against a fresh, hard-throwing relief specialist. If the
pinch hitter fails—and the best ones in baseball his-
tory failed seven out of ten at bats—the fans blame
him for the loss. Hey, if that player was so good, he
would have been in the game in the first place.

Traditionally pinch hitters have been overweight
veterans who could no longer run fast enough or field
well enough to play regularly. But they could still hit.
Players like Smokey Burgess or Rusty Staub. That is
beginning to change now as high-salaried veterans
who bat only once a game are getting to be a luxury,
and younger players are getting an opportunity to
pinch-hit. The Cubs' Thad Bosley is a perfect example
of this. In 1985 Bosley was voted the best pinch hitter
in baseball. For him that was both the good news and

the bad news. He is one of the few players in baseball
too good to play regularly. The Cubs need his bat on
their bench. The ironic thing about that is that as a
pinch hitter Thad Bosley can easily play ten more
years of major league baseball, but if he played every
day, he might be done in five years.

The pressure on pinch hitters to produce is incredible. I remember one night Nolan Ryan was pitching
a three- or four-hit shutout against the Orioles and
Earl Weaver sent Terry Crowley up to hit in the late
innings. Ryan had just been overpowering. I don't
know exactly what Crowley was thinking, but I can
guarantee that he did not run up to the plate. I know
what I would have been thinking in that situation: Is
Weaver kidding? The good players haven't been able
to hit him in eight innings, and he expects me to be
able to hit him?

Terry Crowley came out of the dugout swinging
some bats over his head, stretched a little, then flipped
two bats away and got comfortable in the batter's
box. Ryan wound up and threw. Whoooosh. Fastball.
Crowley never moved his bat. Strike one.

Crowley stepped out of the batter's box and took
a few practice swings. He looked down at the third
base coach; maybe he was looking for a reprieve. But
he had no choice; he stepped back into the batter's
box. Ryan threw again. Whooosh. Fastball. Again
Crowley never moved his bat. Strike two.

Crowley repeated the entire process, stepping out,
swinging, and when he stepped back into the box, he
started digging in. And he gripped that bat. And he
focused his eyes on Ryan. I could see he was determined to get at least one swing at that fastball. There
was no way he was going to come off the bench,
watch three pitches go past him, and sit down. He
knew he was swinging at this pitch wherever it was. I
knew it. And unfortunately so did Ryan.

Nolan Ryan threw him one of the most beautiful
curveballs I've ever seen. Crowley had no chance to
hit it. About the best he could hope for was that he
wouldn't break his back trying to hold up his swing.

He managed to hold up, but the ball broke right over the center of the plate. Strike three! I rung him out.

Crowley turned around and started walking back toward the bench. And as he did, I heard this fan sitting in the first row behind the dugout whine, "Hey, Crowley, if that was all you were going to do, why didn't you just mail it in?"

Actually there are situations in which a player almost could mail his appearance in, because baseball rules state that when a player is announced as a substitute, he is officially in the game. For example, against a right-handed pitcher a manager might send up a left-handed-hitting pinch hitter, and when the manager of the other team brings in a left-handed relief pitcher to face the left-handed hitter, the first manager might substitute a right-handed pinch hitter for the left-handed pinch hitter. Clear? The first pinch hitter didn't take a swing, didn't touch a ball, maybe he didn't even walk on the field, but he is out of the game. As many players have proven, you don't have to play to be in a ball game.

So, five players have been involved in the strategy, and the original hitter and pitcher, the left-handed pinch hitter, and perhaps the right-handed pinch hitter are all out of the game. And what was accomplished? Even the best pinch hitter is going to fail seven out of ten times. Chances are it will have taken five players to get the same pop-out the original batter would have hit.

Do you ever wonder what the player on the bench who has been pinch-hit for is thinking? My guess is: I could have done that. Whatever the pinch hitter does: I could have done that. If he gets a hit: I could have done that. And if the pinch hitter makes an out, I know that's what the original hitter was thinking.

Almost every pinch hitter I ever saw come to bat had something to say to either the umpire or to the catcher. Always something like "How's he throwing?" Or "Is his ball moving?" What kind of answer do they expect? "Oh, he's got absolutely nothing, he's been very lucky to no-hit your teammates for eight innings." Or "Boy, is he lousy. Are you lucky to be coming up to bat against him." But catchers always play it straight. "Mmmm," they mumble, "throwing good." I always wanted to say softly, "Are you kidding? If I were you, I'd go back to the dugout and come back up here with a guitar, because that's the only possible way a hitter like you can touch this guy."

Every pinch hitter prepares differently for his at bat. Thad Bosley sits on the bench visualizing himself being successful at the plate. And every few innings he goes into the clubhouse and does some stretching exercises and swings a bat to stay loose. Richie Hebner, another fine pinch hitter, sits on the bench the entire game, then when he is put into the game, he picks up his bat, bends over once, stretches his arms, swings the bat a few times, then goes up to bat and hits a line drive.

Thad Bosley is the new breed of pinch hitter. He wants to play every day, and is used by the Cubs as a spot starter. And as young as he is, Bosley has a chance to set a lot of pinch-hitting records before finishing his career. But only if they don't let him play.

I played my first major league game when I was twenty years old. I was in center field for the California Angels and the great Nolan Ryan was pitching for us. I couldn't believe I was there. The big leagues, Nolan Ryan pitching, my family in the stands. I was too scared to be excited. But just as Ryan wound up to throw his first pitch of the game, I heard this terrible *Aaaagggghhhh* cry coming from somewhere. I jumped. My heart started beating a hundred miles a minute. Oh, God, I thought, what was that? It sounded like something awful had happened to somebody. But as I looked around the stadium, everybody seemed to be all right. I shook the sound out of my head. Maybe in all the excitement, I decided, I was hearing things.

Ryan wound up to throw his second pitch. *Aaaag-gggghhhh!* There it was again, even louder than the

first time. Then suddenly I realized what it was. Nolan Ryan was grunting as he threw his fastball. I could
hear him all the way out in center field. Wow, I
thought, they're really serious up here in the major
leagues.

Later, Angels coach Andy Etchebarren explained
that Ryan grunted only when he was throwing his
fastball—his change-up was just a loud growl.

I didn't really intend to be a professional baseball
player when I was growing up in California. So many
different things interested me. For a time I wanted to
be a writer. Even today I keep a book of thoughts and
write poetry. I also wanted to be a musician, and
learned how to play the piano well enough to compose my own songs. But more than anything else, I
wanted to be an inventor. I remember, when I was
very young, I read a biography of George Washington
Carver, the great inventor who spent his life develop-
ing peanut derivatives. Man, I thought, an inventor,
that's what I want to be. I wanted to invent something really useful, like a car that would go four hundred miles an hour. I thought I might power it with
rubber bands.

I've had a rough career in baseball. I've spent parts
of seven of my nine major league seasons in the minor
leagues, I've had a number of serious injuries, I've
been sent up to Canada and down to Mexico to play,
and I've never really gotten the opportunity to prove I
could play every day. I don't think I would still be in
baseball if not for my brother Greg, who died of Par-
kinson's disease in 1979. He believed in my ability as
much as I believed in his. And sometimes, when I
really got discouraged, I'd try to remember the deter-
mination with which he fought his disease, and I'd
force myself to go out there and try again. I promised
him I was going to play in the big leagues, and I just
couldn't give up.

My career started out extremely well. I was the
fourth round draft pick of the Angels in 1974. While
growing up in southern California, I'd been to Los
Angeles Dodger games and San Diego Padre games,

but for some reason I'd never been inside the Angels' ballpark, Anaheim Stadium. After the draft I would drive by that stadium and promise myself, I'm not going inside that ballpark until I can go there as a player. In 1976 I hit .324 and stole ninety bases in the California League, A ball, and was named Player of the Year. When I started the following season in Triple A hitting .326, the Angels promoted me to the big leagues.

I was one of the youngest players in the major leagues, and certainly the most naive. My teammates just loved to play practical jokes on me. I'd like to say I never fell for them, but there was the day I spent hours trying to find the key to the batter's box. And then there was the first time the ball club went into New York City. *New York City!* My teammates warned me about all the terrible things that had happened to young ball players in that city, and told me how careful a visitor had to be in New York. They suggested the best thing I could do was to lock myself in my room and put all my furniture against the door.

That night I shoved one of the chairs in my room under the doorknob, as I'd seen in movies, and the other against the door. Then I took the little table and jammed that against the chair. Then I double-locked the door and pulled the security bolt. And sure enough, that night nothing happened. I had survived a night in New York.

The next day the maid came into the room to clean and saw everything out of place. "Excuse me, sir," she said, "but is there something wrong with your room? Is there a reason you've put all the furniture over there by the door?"

"I had to," I confided in her. "I wanted to protect myself. I know all about what happens in New York." It's possible that woman is still laughing today.

I had played high school baseball with Lance Parrish. I'd been drafted in the same group as Gary Templeton and Lonnie Smith. I played side by side in the minors with Julio Cruz. I broke the minor league stolen base record that had been set by Gene Richard.

And I beat all of them to the major leagues. I hit .297 in my first big league season. It looked as if I was going to have a long and successful major league career. But I just kept getting hurt and I kept getting sent back to the minor leagues. I split the 1978 and '79 seasons between the White Sox and their Iowa farm club. In 1980 I tried to stop my swing on a Mike Flanagan curveball and a season and a half later doctors finally discovered I'd ripped the tendons in my hand. But by that time I was playing for the Milwaukee Brewers' Triple A club in Vancouver, Canada. From Canada I went south, to Seattle, Washington, and then I just kept going. I ended up being assigned by the Chicago Cubs to the Mexico City Tigers.

They didn't tell me what I was getting into in Mexico City. The playing conditions in the Mexican League weren't bad—except for the heat. That's like saying that the first voyage of the *Titanic* wasn't bad—except for the iceberg. It was so hot in Mexico in summer that the flies just quit flying. It was so hot that breathing took too much of an effort, so everyone panted a lot. It was so hot that players who wore eyeglasses used tiny windshield wipers to keep perspiration from fogging their glasses. About all you could do was try to stay in the shade, dress light, drink plenty of liquids, and live underwater.

When I first got there, the ball looked so much bigger coming to the plate. I thought that the thin air in Mexico City must have affected my eyesight, I'd never seen a pitch so well. Then when I started throwing the ball, I realized it actually was bigger, about a quarter-inch bigger than balls used in America. It also was a mushball; you could crush that thing and it would be a routine pop-up to center field.

The best thing about playing in Mexico was the people. The Mexican baseball fans were wonderful. I would watch them come into the ballpark and see the joy on their faces at being there. Those people had nothing but baseball, and they loved it. That filled my heart. One game I really remember was the day I hit a home run to beat the Diabolos team. The fans passed the hat around for me, and after the game gave me about two hundred dollars. That filled my wallet. Now, if I could just convince them to do the same thing at Wrigley Field in Chicago. . . .

The worst part about being there was being there. The Cubs had sent me there because I'd joined their organization late in spring training in 1983 and all their Triple A teams were set. They told me they wanted me to play every day, and I could play every day in Mexico. But after I got there, I began to wonder if they remembered I was there. Being sent to the minor leagues was one thing, but how many ball players get sent out of the country? There were times I got terribly frustrated. I ended up doing a lot of writing in my notebook. I tried to keep my thoughts positive, reminding myself, "If you have the mind to see it, then you have the spirit to become it." Writing down these thoughts, and every once in a while taking a baseball and throwing it as far as I could out of the stadium, helped me keep my sanity.

I had been warned when I arrived in Mexico City that the thin air was going to make me light-headed. I accepted that, but as time passed, I began taking in my belt more and more. First one loop, then a second, a third. I was losing a lot of weight. I'd never heard of a thin-air diet, but I was hitting about .330, so I didn't complain. Until I ran out of belt loops. I lost twenty-three pounds in six weeks. That's when I found out I had contracted a virus and had to return to the States to recover. I finished that season with the Chicago Cubs, being used mainly as a pinch hitter.

I've finished almost every season in the major leagues. I just wasn't able to stay there. As each season passed, I tried to find a major league team that would give me a real opportunity to show what I could do. By 1984 I had finally had enough. I had been leading the Triple A American Association in hitting when the Cubs called me up—and sat me on the bench. Before a game in Cincinnati one Sunday I decided I just couldn't take it anymore, I was going to quit. I knew I'd miss baseball, but I believed I could get a recording contract and, even if I didn't, I didn't care. I figured, hey, if you've played in the Mexican League, you can survive anything. So before the game I put my belongings into my duffel bag. After the Cub game I was going home.

Every Sunday every big league ball club holds a chapel meeting, a prayer meeting. I've always believed in God, but I had worked out an agreement with him as far as baseball was concerned. A season earlier I'd been going up to bat against Philly pitcher Larry Anderson. We had been teammates on the 1982 Seattle Mariners and I knew he believed in the same God I did. And as I walked to the plate, it suddenly occurred to me that Larry was out on the mound thinking, all right, God, I want to throw my cut fastball past this guy . . . while I was thinking, okay, God, he's gonna try to throw that cut fastball past me. . . . I had to stop myself from laughing. I knew God wasn't up there saying, sorry, Thad, this time I'm going to make you pop up to third base. I realized that God gave both of us our talent and our ability to use it; the rest was up to us.

So I went to that chapel meeting in Cincinnati, but as a pessimist. As the chaplain was leading us in prayer, I was thinking, sure you love me, God, but you have a strange way of showing it. I've had a blood clot, I've pulled both groin muscles so I couldn't run, I've had to have my wrist operated on, and you'll notice I'm not even mentioning Mexico City. I was ripping God up and down. I was on him like a bad suit.

After the service I spoke privately with the chaplain. I didn't tell him I intended to quit, but I said I was really troubled in my mind and needed an answer from God. "I know that God has given me talent and ability, but I don't understand what He is trying to show me. Maybe I'm not supposed to be here, maybe he wants me to do something else with my life."

The chaplain said, "You're in a situation right now that no matter what I said to you, I couldn't console you. I know you need an immediate answer." Then we prayed.

I went through my regular routine that day, taking batting practice, then finding my seat on the bench. In the sixth inning, with the score tied 6–6, we had two runners on and two outs. Manager Jim Frey sent me up to pinch-hit. A few weeks earlier I'd jammed my wrist in a game against San Francisco, but I hadn't told anybody. The Cubs had already sent me to Mexico City; I didn't even want to guess where they might send me the next time. But the wrist prevented me from getting any real power into my swing.

If this had been a fairy tale, I would've hit Reds pitcher Jeff Russell's first pitch into the upper deck for a three-run home run. It wasn't. I hit Russell's first pitch into the second deck for a three-run pinch-hit home run. Now, I'm not saying that God hit that home run for me as an answer, but if He happens to be reading this, I'm not saying He didn't either.

I love the challenge of hitting. When I go up to what I call "the dish of opportunity," I'm saying to the pitcher, I'm gonna get you, and he's coming in with his bag of tricks, and may the best man win. I just love that challenge.

Naturally some at bats are more memorable than others. The first time I faced my former teammate Nolan Ryan for example. I went to the bat thinking, this is the dish of opportunity, and may the best . . .

Strike one. Fastball on the outside of the plate. I swung and missed.

I stopped thinking and got ready to hit. I tensed, waiting for his telltale grunt. He went into his windup, around came his right arm, and I heard, *"Ggggrrrr."* *Ggggrrrr?* What's *ggggrrrr?* What happened to *aaaagggg-hhhh?* *Ggggrrrr* turned out to be another fastball on the outside corner. Once again I swung and missed. Strike two.

I stepped out of the batter's box and looked at my bat. I was looking for the hole in it. I had seen both of those pitches, I knew my mechanics were good, but I'd swung right through both pitches. I knew Nolan was out there on the mound thinking, what's wrong with Bosley now? He probably thinks his bat has a hole in it. Why can't he just admit he's missing the fastball?

I stepped back into the box. Nolan wound up and threw—a hanging curveball. I lined a base hit to center field. I couldn't understand why he threw me a curveball. He blew two fastballs past me, why a curveball? Now, I certainly don't want to say that God wanted me to hit Nolan Ryan, but . . . a curveball?

I started pinch hitting on a regular basis in 1980, when I hit .346 in twenty-nine pinch-hit at bats for the White Sox. Next to playing regularly in the big leagues, I enjoy pinch hitting in the big leagues. I've had to learn how to pinch-hit, and there are a lot of little things that make a difference. When I'm on the bench waiting, and waiting, I'm constantly stretching, talking to myself to pump up my confidence, trying to visualize myself being successful, going back into the clubhouse and swinging the bat. I'm always moving around, getting ready, trying to gain that edge.

One thing I never do when coming up to bat is look at the scoreboard. I just don't want anything to affect my concentration. If I look at the scoreboard and see that my batting average is .325, I might think, hey, .325, I'm some hitter, I can hit this guy easy, I don't even have to concentrate. On the other hand, if I'm hitting .205, I might think, hmm, .205, what's that, the interstate highway? I can't hit this guy at all.

Fortunately I've never hit .205. Exactly. I did hit .174 in forty-six at bats with Seattle, but that was with a badly ripped tendon in my hand. I remember when I was growing up and I'd see players coming to the plate hitting a buck eighty-five and I'd think, I can do better than that and I'm only eleven years old. So today, if I were to look at the scoreboard and it showed a low batting average next to my name, I would know some fan is saying, "Look at that Bosley. He can't even hit his weight."

I also don't look at the scoreboard in case they've put my picture on it. I hate to see my picture up there.

The thing that has helped me most with my hitting is my piano playing. As far as I'm concerned, there are eighty-eight keys to success at the plate. I play the piano well enough to compose. I'm not Beethoven, for example, but there are people who think I play the piano better than I play baseball. Those are baseball fans, though, not music critics. Besides, Beethoven couldn't hit a fastball on the outside corner either.

Seriously, though, I believe there is a very strong relationship between playing the piano and hitting well. The right side of the brain is the creative side, the side that controls rhythm. I can tell by playing the piano how good my rhythm is at a certain time. So I'll sit at the piano and go through different movements and chord progressions and I'll find out where my rhythm and balance is. If it's off, experience has taught me that my hitting will be off, too, so I'll get to the ballpark early and take extra batting practice. If I'm playing the piano well, if I'm hitting the proper note right on the beat, I'll probably take less batting practice than usual.

This works only when the team is home, obviously, unless I can figure out some way of taking my piano on road trips. It would be very difficult to squeeze it onto the team bus, however.

When I'm sitting at the piano, I visualize myself hitting a pitched baseball. In my mind I "see" the pitcher winding up, I "see" my feet in position, I "see" the slider breaking. I can "see" my level swing and I "see" the bat meeting the ball. Although physically I'm playing the piano, my mind is concentrating on hitting every bit as intently as it would if I were standing at the plate. So when I finally get to the ballpark to take my swings, my body is reacting to what is already programmed in my mind. My mind knows what I want my body to do.

I started visualizing as a means of keeping my attention on the game while sitting on the bench. I've found that the more I visualize, the less I have to practice physically to achieve the desired results. I believe that if I could get to a mental level where I was absolutely confident I could hit the ball, I wouldn't even need to take batting practice.

I'm not the only athlete to approach sports this way. There used to be a place kicker in professional football named Booth Lustig, who believed in something called psycho-cybernetics. The theory behind psycho-cybernetics is similar to mine, the idea being that when you visualize yourself doing something perfectly, the mind sends signals to the proper muscles, so when you actually do it, the proper muscles react. One day Lustig was sitting on the bleacher steps staring out at the field, visualizing himself kicking long field goals. One of his teammates walked up and asked him what he was doing. Booth looked at him and said softly, "Practicing."

The essence of music is sound, and a baseball game also has its music, its special sounds. Most fans never get the opportunity to hear this song. On the bench you always hear the manager shouting encouragement. "Come on, get this hitter." Sitting next to him is the pitching coach, who is constantly shouting instructions to his pitcher. "Breaking ball, throw him the breaking ball." Occasionally, if the pitcher is hit hard, you can hear the pitching coach mutter under his breath, "How could he throw him that pitch in this situation?"

The sounds a player hears on the field are completely different. There is the roar of the fans, but that fades in and out. It has always amazed me that it is possible to ignore 45,000 screaming people, and sometimes impossible to ignore one. Occasionally one fan will get a player's attention and that voice will be the only thing he hears on the field. In the outfield I hear the center fielder, who positions the right and left fielders. Then, in some parks, there is the incessant *buzzzzzzzzzzzzz* of the electric scoreboard, which often sounds like the world's largest bug light. But the very worst sound of all is the reverberation of the public address system. "Now *aargggggggggggging* for the *grgggrahhhhhh . . .*" That sound kills me. It sounds like a cat running its claws over a record with the amplifier turned to full volume.

A sound outfielders often hear in later innings is the thud of relief pitchers warming up. There are times you can even tell which pitcher it is just from the sound of the ball hitting the catcher's glove. On the Cubs, if I hear *pow! pow! pow! pow!* I know Lee Smith is getting loose, but if I hear *sssspptt, sssspptt,* I know it's Warren Brusstar. I've been told that if you don't hear anything, it's a knuckleball pitcher warming up. Either that or some pitcher visualizing a tremendous relief effort. And the worst sound you can hear coming from the bullpen is *roommmm, roommmmm,* as the car that will bring in the new pitcher revs its engine.

The most difficult part about being a bench player is maintaining your confidence. When you're not playing regularly on a ball club, you begin to question your ability. At least I did. But that changed for me one day when I was sitting on the bench for the Chicago White Sox. Before the game I ran my usual twenty wind sprints, took twenty minutes of fly balls in the outfield, and batting practice. I knew I wasn't going to play, so I went all out, and I was tired. Maybe forty-five minutes before game time, manager Tony LaRussa told me I was in the starting lineup. Man, I was beat, but I went 3-for-5, including a home run. After that game I never questioned my ability again.

I can play major league baseball, I know that. I've learned that the difference between players on this level is their mental approach to the game. This game of baseball is played from the inside out, not vice versa. When I go to the plate as a pinch hitter, my insides are talking. I start concentrating on the baseball from the moment I leave the dugout. I don't care who's on the mound; it doesn't matter. I don't have to hit the man throwing the ball, I have to hit the ball he's throwing.

Except if it's Goose Gossage. If he's out there, forget everything I've said. Him I can't hit.

What does it feel like to go to bat late in a game,

knowing you have one chance, and the outcome of
the ball game may depend on your ability? For me, it's
like this:

THE CALL

Sitting in the stadium,
Forty thousand strong
Waiting for your chance to come
When you get the call
All your movements you've rehearsed
Endless in the mind
Goose bumps running down your spine
Two out in the ninth
Visualize the outcome
Must see the ball hit bat
Breathe in deep, let it out
Lock-in, lock-in, lock-in.

MY ROYAL CAREER
by John Wathan

Utility players are the "water hoses" of baseball. Most people simply do not appreciate their importance. Most people do not appreciate the importance of a water hose either—until their car radiator breaks down at three A.M. in a deserted neighborhood.

Every season every team is going to break down at a few positions. Since no team can afford to carry a backup at every position, having a utility player who can fill the hole, or plug the leak, or stop the gap until the regular player returns can be the difference between winning and losing the pennant. Utility men are players not good enough to play regularly at several positions. They are baseball's "many others." For example, before Kansas City goes into Baltimore for a series, the Oriole scoreboard might advertise, "Come see George Brett, Bret Saberhagen, Willie Wilson, and many others."

The Royals' John Wathan and the White Sox' Mike Squires have been among the best "many others" for a number of years. Although Wathan caught regularly for Kansas City, he has been a catcher—first-

baseman–outfielder–designated-hitter for the Royals
since coming to the majors in 1976. Squires has also
played four positions, some in record-breaking style,
and even pitched an inning.

Most players who stay in the big leagues for any
length of time get to play more than one position
during their careers, although few of them are really
utility men. They are usually stuck at a position when
their manager has used his entire team in an extra-
inning game, or wants to give some players a rest in a
rout. For example, what position other than the outfield did Babe Ruth play? Correct, pitcher. Now, what
position other than the outfield and pitcher did Babe
Ruth play? The Babe played thirty-one games at first
base during his career.

I didn't know that.

In fact, it is surprising how many superstars have
played positions other than the spot at which they
gained stardom. Willie Mays, for instance, may be the
greatest center fielder in history, but he also played
eighty-four games at first base, two games at shortstop, and one game at third base. And if Willie isn't
the best center fielder ever to play, it might be Mickey
Mantle—who also played 262 games at first base,
seven games at shortstop, one game at second base,
and one game at third base. And if neither Mickey
Mantle nor Willie Mays qualifies as the best center
fielder, it certainly must be Joe DiMaggio, even though
he played one game at first base.

Lou Gehrig, without question the best-known first
baseman in baseball history, played nine games in
the outfield and one game at shortstop for the Yankees. First baseman Steve Garvey somehow managed
to play one game at second base during his long
career. Roberto Clemente played two games at second
and one game at third. Al Kaline played almost three
thousand major league games—two of them at third
base. Most people know that three-time Most Valuable Player Yogi Berra moved from behind home plate
to left field late in his career, but not too many people

know that he also played two games at first base and one at third base.

And home-run-king Henry Aaron played first, second, and third as well as the outfield during his twenty-three-year career.

On the other hand, Luis Aparicio played every game of his career at shortstop.

Besides Mike Squires, many other big leaguers share the fantasy of the fans—to pitch in the majors. Ted Williams, for example, played 2,151 games in the outfield for the Red Sox—and pitched two innings. He gave up three hits, didn't walk a batter, struck out one, and gave up one earned run, for a lifetime earned run average of 4.50. The great Ty Cobb played 2,943 games in the outfield, one each at first, second, and third, and pitched five innings over three games. During his stint on the mound he surrendered six hits, finishing his pitching career with an earned run average of 3.60, no wins, no losses, but one save.

Hall of Famers Tris Speaker and Honus Wagner also got their chances on the mound. Speaker gave up two hits and one run in one inning, for an ERA of 9.00, while Wagner pitched 8.1 innings, walked six, struck out six, and didn't give up a run, for a perfect lifetime ERA of 0.00.

More recently Rocky Colavito, an outfielder noted for his tremendous throwing ability, pitched 5.2 innings in two games, giving up a hit, striking out two, and walking five. Obviously he could throw hard, but not straight. He didn't give up a run, ending his pitching career with an ERA of 0.00 and a perfect record of one win and no losses.

Vic Davalillo, who played sixteen seasons in the major leagues, was not as fortunate. He pitched in two games in 1969, and still hasn't gotten anybody out. His first time on the mound he gave up two hits and two walks, and at least one run, for a lifetime earned run average of . . . infinity. Infinity! My question is, if he gave up infinity the first time, why did they let him pitch the second time!

Larry Biittner did almost as poorly during the

inning he pitched for the Chicago Cubs in 1977, giving up five hits and a walk for an ERA of 54.00. The good news is that he also struck out the side. Of course, it's important to remember that he was pitching in Wrigley Field, a hitter's ballpark.

Big Dave Kingman pitched two games for the San Francisco Giants in 1973. In four innings he gave up three hits, walked six, struck out four, and surrendered four runs, for a neat 9.00 ERA.

Sal Bando, who played every position except catcher during his career, pitched three innings for the Brewers in 1979, giving up three hits and two runs. Sal's brother, Chris, incidentally, is a major league catcher. Naturally.

And Matty Alou pitched two innings during his fifteen-year career, surrendering three hits and one walk, striking out three batters and shutting out the other team.

Certainly Pete Rose must be the patron saint of utility players, having made All-Star teams as a first baseman, second baseman, third baseman, and outfielder. But Bert Campaneris in 1965 and Cesar Tovar in 1968 beat him in quantity, if not quality. Both men played every position during one nine-inning game. Campaneris gave up one run in the inning he pitched; Tovar was perfect.

Most often, position players get to pitch during a blowout. A blowout is a game after which someone will look at the final score and remark, "Well, at least they missed the extra point." It's a game in which the losing team can't possibly catch up, so they put Ted Williams in to pitch. I hated working those games. The players on the winning side tended to get embarrassed when they went more than ten runs ahead. Not as embarrassed, however, as the team that was losing. I remember one night when the Brewers were getting clobbered, and everyone wanted to go home. Suddenly Milwaukee catcher Darrell Porter turned to me and said, "Hey, Ronnie, I got a great idea. Let's choose up new sides."

There really is no explanation for a blowout. Ev-

erything good happens for one team, everything bad happens to the other. Every ball lands two inches fair, every checked swing results in a bloop over the infield. One really hot afternoon in Texas the Rangers were just getting blasted, and as the fourteenth Red Sox runner touched home plate, Texas catcher Jim Sundberg sighed, "Maybe it was something we ate."

Generally I like utility players. Most of them have had to struggle to get to the big leagues and appreciate being there. Also, because they spend much of their time on the bench, they make the best bench jockeys. The fine art of bench jockeying—that is, insulting an opponent—had started to disappear by the time I got to the big leagues. I really never heard that many clever remarks, unless something like "Hey, elephant ears, you !@#$" is considered a clever remark. But probably the best putdown came from the mouth of Fred "the Original Chicken" Stanley, during a game in which a young shortstop made three bad errors. After the third error Stanley yelled out in a compassionate tone, "Hey, kid. If I were you, I wouldn't give up the paper route."

John Wathan and Mike Squires were both players I really liked. They never yelled at me. Squires was the best cheater I ever saw. Not only could he pull his foot off first base just a fraction before catching the infielder's throw; he could also look as innocent as an altar boy on Christmas Eve.

John Wathan will always occupy a special place in my heart. One year I umpired the Royals' annual Father and Son Game, and John's son was the catcher. As Amos Otis's son batted, I leaned down over John's son to call the pitch. John's son blew a big bubble through his mask and a photographer snapped a great photograph. As much as I don't like any child under twenty-five, even I have to admit this was a really cute picture.

So cute, in fact, that John Wathan's mother sent me a ten dollar bill to say thank you.

That was the only bribe I ever received in baseball. And I took it. Now, I don't want to say I ever

*cheated for John Wathan—what kind of man would
cheat for ten dollars?—but you'll notice he is still
playing in the major leagues.*

*Copies of that photograph are available at ten
dollars each, by writing to the publisher and enclos-
ing a stamped self-addressed envelope.*

I came up to the major leagues with the Kansas City
Royals in 1976. My first day in the big leagues I sat by
myself in the dugout for an hour, pinching my leg
every few minutes just to be sure I was really there. I
didn't play too much that season, but I didn't mind. If
they had told me to clean up the locker room, I'd have
said, fine, just let me stay. I didn't play too much my
second year either. I still didn't mind that much. If
they had asked me nicely to scrub the shower room, I
would have said okay, just let me stay. But by the
third season I wouldn't have cleaned a thing. I wanted
to play.

During my ten years in the major leagues I've
gone from being an obscure bench warmer to a platooned player to a regular catcher to a veteran who
needed to be rested once in a while to a part-time
journeyman to a bench player.

It was a lot more difficult sitting on the bench the
tenth year than the first one. That first year I wasn't
even sure I could play in the big leagues. I had a total
of forty-two at bats. Nobody except my immediate
family even knew I was in the major leagues. The
only time reporters spoke to me was when I was
standing between them and the player they wanted to
interview—until one of the last games of the season.
We were fighting the Oakland A's for the pennant and
were playing them in Oakland. I was playing my usual
position—the bullpen bench. Although it was a cold
night, for some reason I wasn't wearing my jacket. In
the middle of the game our pitcher, Dennis Leonard,
hit Oakland's Don Baylor and Baylor went out after
him. Both benches and bullpens emptied onto the
infield. It was a typical baseball fight, consisting mostly

of serious milling around. Finally the umpires broke it up and I went back to the bullpen.

The fans sitting next to the bullpen started screaming at us, then began throwing things. We were very brave out there—brave, not smart—and started screaming back at them. Then we started throwing punches. Once again our dugout emptied, but this time it emptied into the bullpen. It could have been a very nasty scene. Some fan tried to hit Hal Macrae with an umbrella, but Macrae grabbed the umbrella and, as he started to hit the fan, the umbrella popped open. So Macrae had no choice but to stand there bopping this fan with an open umbrella.

Reporters sitting in the press box really couldn't see what was going on in the bullpen, but because I wasn't wearing my jacket, I was the most identifiable player in the fight. So after the game they surrounded my locker. It was my first big league interview. Other players got interviewed about their hitting or pitching. I got interviewed about a fight in which a player was hitting a fan with an open umbrella. I wanted to be cooperative, but I didn't know what to say. "Don't ask me," I suggested helpfully, "why don't you speak to Mary Poppins?"

I was just happy they were talking to me. Until that time about the only person who ever talked to me, besides my teammates, was umpire Ron Luciano. And he wouldn't shut up. I had been warned by teammates that if I played first base or caught while he was umpiring, he was going to talk so much I would have a difficult time concentrating. I told them that probably wouldn't bother me, I never concentrate anyway. If I knew how to concentrate, it probably wouldn't have taken me six years to make the big leagues in the first place.

I never wanted to do anything else in my life except play major league baseball. In high school I had also played basketball and football. I never understood football. We would practice all week just to play one game, and then I got to play only half the game anyway. I hated practice, so I gave it up.

On the baseball team I played whatever position the team was weakest at. I played third base, first base, all the outfield positions. About the only thing I had trouble with in high school, besides high school, was chewing tobacco. I saw big leaguers chewing on television, so I wanted to do it. I couldn't take it straight without getting sick, so I tried mixing it with cherry Life Savers. That didn't work. I still got sick. I just got sick in a much brighter color.

By the time I started playing minor league ball, I could chew pretty good, particularly if I mixed in a little licorice. Once, though, I got hit in the ribs by a fastball. I couldn't breathe. I started gulping for air. I was turning white. Our trainer came running out to me, thinking that maybe the pitch had broken a rib which had punctured a lung. "The heck . . . with my . . . ribs," I managed to get out. "I . . . swallowed my chew." As it turned out, the pitch had cracked a rib, but that didn't bother me nearly as much as the embarrassment of spitting up the whole way down the first base line.

I still chew today. Usually I take it straight, but sometimes, toward the end of a long day, when my body is just craving something sweet, I'll mix the tobacco with a little bubble gum. I call it dessert. I don't think it's a marketable item.

With or without chew, I could always hit in high school. And at the end of my senior year, the scholarship offer came rolling in. One. It came from the University of San Diego, which I suppose is best known for not being San Diego State University. I was a history major there—I became a history major the day I was told that history majors didn't have to take any math. No math at all? I asked. No math at all, they told me. Then just call me a history major.

At the end of my junior year I was drafted by the Kansas City Royals. I had been born in Iowa, but had grown up in California and played in San Diego. I didn't know anything except what I saw on television about Kansas City: They had a lot of cows and Marshal Matt Dillon kept law and order. But I did know that the Royals were an expansion team and I felt signing with them would give me an excellent chance to get to the big leagues right away.

I did, too, if you consider six years right away. I had what is known as a down and down minor league career. About the only thing I seemed to be getting in the minors was older. In fact, in 1975 a Royals executive told me that I probably was not good enough to play in the major leagues and admitted that the only reason I was being promoted to the Triple A team in Omaha was that they didn't have any other catchers. Instead of being discouraged, I worked harder that season than I had ever worked before, trying to convince them that they were wrong. After hitting .250 for two years in Double A, I hit over .300 at Omaha.

I never earned very much money in the minor leagues. Nobody does. Each winter the Royals would send me a contract calling for something like five hundred dollars a month, and each winter I would send it back with a letter explaining: "I can no longer survive on five hundred dollars a month. The cost of living is going up, I'm married, and we have a child, and as soon as I get a fifty dollar a month raise, we're planning on having another child."

They would respond to that by writing: "Although we feel you are a credit to the organization, we simply cannot give you a fifty dollar a month raise. We will give you twenty-five dollars a month."

"As a credit to the organization," I would write back, "and the father of one lonely child, I cannot accept your offer of a twenty-five dollar a month raise." Eventually we would settle for something like $37.50.

When I reached the major leagues, I used the fact that I played so many different positions when negotiating my contract. I would figure out what back-up catchers, first basemen, and outfielders were making, and would then become whatever position was making the most.

After the great 1975 season I had at Omaha, I thought I was going to make the major league squad in 1976. But I was the last player cut by manager

Whitey Herzog in spring training. As the team left camp, Whitey told me that they intended to trade one of the two catchers they were taking north and, as soon as they did, I would be brought up. I was so full of enthusiasm that I went to Omaha and hit about .150. I didn't care that I wasn't hitting because I knew I was going to be called up any day, or any week, or any month. Finally catcher Fran Healy was traded to the New York Yankees for pitcher Larry Gura. I packed my bags. But the Royals decided to keep Gura. Things did not look good for me—the team had gotten rid of a catcher, I was still in Omaha, and I was hitting .150. I unpacked.

A week later catcher Buck Martinez slid into second base and spiked himself in the hand. Finally I was called up to the big leagues. A lot of players would be embarrassed to admit that it took another player spiking himself for him to get a chance to play in the big leagues. But not me. No way. I didn't care. I was absolutely thrilled to be there.

In my ten seasons with Kansas City I've been a catcher, first baseman, outfielder, and designated hitter. Some years I have even been the designated pitcher—that's the position player who pitches when a game is so completely out of control that the manager doesn't want to waste a real pitcher. In 1984 that player for the Royals was Leon Roberts, who got to pitch one night in Cleveland. I was catching, and when he came in, I went out to the mound to go over the signals. "What are we gonna use?" I asked.

"One finger is a fastball, two fingers are a strike," he said.

I waited. That was all he said. "Is that all you got?" I asked.

He nodded. "And I'm not even so confident about that."

I can honestly say I never really wanted to pitch. I've been back behind the plate and seen too many hard line drives go whizzing by the ears of real pitchers to have any strong desire to stand out there.

During my ten years with the Royals we've been

in the American League playoffs six times, in the 1981 mini-playoffs, and in the 1980 and 1985 World Series, so I've got to be doing something right. That something has nothing to do with hitting in the playoffs though. I'm oh-for-my-lifetime in the playoffs. I keep telling everybody that that sounds a lot worse than it really is, because it's no hits spread over a lot of years. "Try not to think of it as oh-for-15," I like to say. "Think of it more as an oh-for-three, an oh-for-four, an oh-for-five . . ."

My best full season was in 1980, when I hit .305 in 453 at bats, but I think the thing I'm most proud of is that I hold the major league record for stolen bases by a catcher. In 1982 I stole thirty-six bases, breaking the record of thirty set by Hall-of-Famer Ray Schalk in 1916. (I don't believe that is why he made the Hall of Fame, however.)

I broke the record in Texas. The Ranger's ground crew had planned to present me with the base when I broke the record, so they used an old base at second, assuming that that would be the base I'd steal. I guess they figured there was no use giving a new base to an old catcher. I fooled them; I stole third base. A new base. The game was stopped and the Ranger third baseman, Buddy Bell, tried to pull third base out of the ground. I stood there, the scoreboard announced the new record, the fans applauded. Bell couldn't get the base out of the ground. Our third base coach, Joe Nossak, tried to help Bell. I was still standing there, the fans were still applauding, they still couldn't get the base out of the ground. Third base umpire Bill Haller came over and tried to help Bell and Nossak. I was still standing there, the fans weren't applauding as loudly as before. "It's okay, Bill," I said to Haller, "I'll get it after the game."

"No way," Haller insisted as he started kicking the base. "It's a record, we're gonna get it now."

The fans stopped applauding and started mumbling. I was still standing there. "Honest, Bill, really, let's play."

Haller was getting angrier and angrier at that base.

"I'm ... gonna ... get ... that ... base ..." About five minutes later they finally got it up. So there I was, standing on third base, holding third base in total silence. I didn't know what to do. I hadn't set that many records that I knew how to act. Finally someone came and took my base away from me. It's now the top of a bar stool.

I think the thing that helped me most in breaking that record was not playing too much. Full-time catchers like Bob Boone or Jim Sundberg have been crouching behind the plate for ten years and more. I'm not surprised they don't steal bases, I'm just surprised they can still walk. I've caught more than one hundred games in a season only four times. Compared to players like Boone and Sundberg, I'm a sprinter.

Another thing I'm very proud of is that I've been ejected from only one major league game. There are some people who will say that if you don't play in too many games, it's hard to get thrown out, but I did play regularly for almost five seasons. My ejection took place in Minnesota. The game started at twilight and it was rough picking up the pitches. About the second inning the home plate umpire (no, it was not Ron Luciano) said to me, "It's really tough to see tonight, isn't it?"

I knew we were in trouble. I knew he couldn't see and he knew he couldn't see, but he wasn't supposed to *tell* me he couldn't see. "I know," I said, "but that's your job." He then proceeded to prove to me that he couldn't see. When I came up to bat, I knew I didn't have a chance. I'd been behind the plate, I knew he was having a bad night. I swung at two close pitches, then took a pitch way outside. He called it strike three. It was so far outside I screamed a few nasties at him and he ejected me.

Since it was the first time I'd been thrown out of a game, I really didn't know what to do. I went into the clubhouse and threw a few chairs. I figured that's what you do when you get ejected. Then I sat down and listened to the game. One inning after I'd been tossed out, the sprinkler system suddenly went on, soaking everyone on the field, including the plate umpire. As I later learned, at the end of the inning he came over to the Royals bench and said, "Ha, ha, I'll bet Wathan turned those sprinklers on, didn't he?"

I hadn't. I hadn't even thought of it. The next day that umpire asked me if I'd done it. "No, I didn't," I said. He looked really disappointed, so I added, "Tell you what though. If I had known where the switch was, I sure would've!"

"I knew it," he said. If that was good enough for him, it was good enough for me.

Probably the most difficult thing about being a utility player is keeping occupied during the game. When I'm not playing, I usually stay out in the bullpen in case pitchers have to be warmed up. Nothing much happens in the bullpen for the first few innings, so the crew out there usually starts the day by doing the *Kansas City Star*'s crossword puzzle and the Jumble puzzle. Our renowned groundskeeper, the great George Toma, has an office out there and there is a radio, a television, and a charcoal grill in that office. So we'd sit in the bullpen, watching the ball game, eating grilled hot dogs. Without question pitcher Marty Pattin is the best chef in baseball. Besides being a fine person, he would bring the bratwurst.

Before I had the chance to play regularly, sitting on the bench was frustrating. But going back to the bench after having been a regular was terribly difficult. I had a lousy year as a utility player in 1984 because I felt I should have been playing; I felt they were putting me out to pasture too soon. I couldn't accept the fact that a young player like Don Slaught was that much better than me. But during the winter of 1984–85 I spent a lot of time thinking about the situation. I had been a successful role player earlier in my career; with the experience I'd had since then, there was no reason I couldn't do it again. Besides, I realized, if I don't play too much, I can play in the big leagues until I'm fifty-five.

The fact that the Royals obtained Jim Sundberg, an outstanding catcher, in a trade also made the transition easier to accept. So I spent most of the 1985 season catching only on Sundays. For some reason manager Dick Howser used me just on Sundays. So it occurred to me that I had finally gone full circle—here I was again, practicing all week just to play one game.

FIELDER ON THE ROOF
by Mike Squires

I haven't set a lot of records in my career; I never led the American League in hitting and I never pitched a no-hitter. But I am in the record books—I can proudly claim that I am probably the greatest left-handed third baseman in baseball history, and I know for certain that I am the best left-handed catcher to play major league baseball in the last twenty-five years.

I don't think anyone has ever accomplished what I have in the major leagues. During my eight years with the Chicago White Sox I've played the infield and the outfield, I've been a pitcher and a catcher, I've been the judge in the team court, a scout, an announcer, a caterer, and, when they asked me to, I even raised the flag on the ballpark roof. Even Pete Rose can't make those claims.

I grew up in Kalamazoo, Michigan. My friends and I played every kind of baseball game, from Little League to taped-up wiffleball. We played the Yankees against the Tigers, and I was always the Tigers. When I was young, I was Charlie Maxwell, then I became Al Kaline, and I finally grew up to be Norm Cash. I was never allowed to pitch, though, because I threw too hard. But nowadays, one Saturday afternoon every fall we all get together for an annual game. The only difference is that now they let me pitch. I don't know what that says about my big league career.

It never occurred to me that I might have to do anything but be a ball player. I didn't know there was anything else but baseball. For example, after my first season in the minor leagues, my wife and I wanted to take out a loan to buy a car. The loan application asked: Employer. Naturally I put down "Chicago White Sox." The application asked: Present Position. And naturally I put down "First base."

The White Sox selected me in the eighteenth round of the 1973 draft. In September 1975 they brought me to the big leagues for a brief trial. I came up with a reputation as a great fielding first baseman, and I was determined to use this opportunity to impress the White Sox. In one of my very first games we were playing the Oakland A's and Reggie Jackson hit a slow bouncer to second baseman Bill Stein. Stein charged the ball and threw across his body in time to beat Jackson by at least half a step. I came off the base and started to throw the ball around the infield. But just as I was about to release the ball, I heard the umpire screaming, "Safe; he's safe."

I tried to hold up my throw. I threw the ball into left field. So much for impressing the White Sox with my fielding ability.

I wanted to argue with the umpire, but I also wanted to stay in the game. Manager Chuck Tanner came out and argued, but the call stuck.

Fortunately Jackson did not advance. When he came back to the base, he said to me, "Hey, rook, don't you know they don't call us superstars out on those plays?"

Uh, no, Reg, actually I didn't. He was kidding, of course. Of course.

The next batter hit a perfect double-play grounder to shortstop. When the throw came to me, I casually turned around, a·d slammed my foot down on the base as hard as I .ould.

But I didn't say a word to the umpire.

Three years later I was back in the big leagues to stay. But as I was to discover, staying there meant learning how to do a lot of unusual things. It started in spring training, 1980. My wife, Maureen, and I were sitting by our motel pool in Sarasota, Florida, talking with White Sox general manager Roland Hemond, when a young left-handed hitting catcher passed by. As he walked away, Roland said softly that the team could really use a left-handed hitting catcher.

I hit left-handed. And my father had been a catcher. The only problem was that I was also a left-handed thrower. The last left-hander to catch in the big leagues had been Dale Long, who had caught two games for the Chicago Cubs in 1958. "Uh, you know, Roland," I said finally, "I've always wanted to be a catcher."

He was very surprised. Maureen was also very surprised. "Really?" he asked. She looked at me as if she'd never heard me say that.

"Oh, sure," I said. "You know my father was a catcher." He was also a White Sox scout.

I could see Roland was interested. "You ever caught before?"

"Absolutely," I answered. I didn't think it was necessary to add "Twenty years ago in Little League."

So Hemond spoke to White Sox owner Bill Veeck— the same Bill Veeck who once hired a midget to pinch-hit and invented the exploding scoreboard—and Veeck thought the concept of a left-handed throwing catcher was a wonderful one. He even agreed to pay me all of my contract bonuses if I got hurt catching—which made me wonder if this was such a grand idea after all. But when manager Tony LaRussa agreed to try it, I had no choice.

So I got behind the plate in spring training batting practice to see if I could catch the ball without closing my eyes. I discovered I liked catching. And so I became the White Sox third-string catcher, although I figured it would be a long time before LaRussa dared to use me in a regular season game. I mean, how often does the third-string catcher get into a game?

In this case, about six weeks later. We were playing the Milwaukee Brewers and we were getting killed. Ed Farmer was pitching for us and in the top of the ninth inning LaRussa sent me out to catch. The home plate umpire was Larry Barnett, and he did some double-take when he looked through the steel bars of the catcher's mask and realized it was me looking back at him. "Spanky," he said. Spanky is my nickname, after Spanky from Our Gang. "Just what do you think you're doing?"

"Catching," I explained. I stopped myself from asking him, *What's the matter, Larry, haven't you ever seen a left-handed catcher before?*

Larry took a deep breath. The catcher is the only thing between the home plate umpire and a pitched baseball. I don't think Larry thought this was such a great idea.

The first batter went out easily. The second batter went out. Two out, one to go. I could almost hear Barnett beginning to breathe again. But Farmer hit the next batter, putting him on first base. Milwaukee had such a big lead, I knew the runner wasn't going to try to steal. Robin Yount came up to bat. The count on him went to three balls, two strikes.

I knew with a full count Yount would be expecting Farmer to throw him a fastball. That's what pitchers always do. I could see Robin grip his bat a little more tightly. I signaled for a curveball. Farmer threw a perfect curveball on the outside corner. Yount swung and missed, strike three, end of inning.

Before the game the next day Yount went over to Farmer. He was not happy. "Hey," he said, "I want to know one thing. How the heck can you throw me a three-two curveball with Squires catching for the first time in his life?"

Farmer shrugged. "Don't blame me," he said, "I wouldn't dare. Blame Squires, he called it!"

Even though that brief effort had been a success, I realized it had been almost twenty-five years since the

last left-handed catcher, Dale Long, had played, and I
didn't expect to catch again for a long, long time. I
caught for the second time three days later.

I didn't become a left-handed third baseman until
1984, however. Compared to left-handed third basemen, left-handed catchers practically grow on trees.
The last time a left-hander had started a game at third
base had been 1936—forty-eight years earlier.

The Great Third Base Experiment had started the
previous February. Tony LaRussa telephoned and said
enthusiastically, "I've got this great idea I want you to
listen to."

I had hit .222 in only 153 at bats in 1983. I was
willing to listen to any great ideas the manager had.
"What's that?"

"I want you to try to play third base," he said.

"You're kidding, right?"

"I'm serious. We need a left-handed hitting infielder, and there are none available."

"This is a joke, right?"

"The coaches all feel you can do as well defen-
sively as anyone we can get, and we know you'll hit
better."

What was I going to tell him, I was a catcher? At
worst, I figured, the experiment wouldn't work. That
was before I actually played there, of course. "All
right," I told him, "I'll give it a try." For a left-handed
thrower, playing third base is actually more difficult
than catching because in order to make the throw
from third to first, he has to either take a step backward with his left foot or spin around completely. If
the other team lays a bunt down the third base line,
well . . . On the other hand, wearing the glove on the
left hand makes it easier to stop balls hit down the
baseline. And, I figured, balls hit to third base are
usually hit so hard, the third baseman has plenty of
time to set himself and throw. That was the good
news, I decided.

I started taking ground balls at third base the first
day of spring training. After I'd been working out

there for a few days, I stopped LaRussa and asked, "Well, whattya think?"

"It's etched in stone," he said. "You can do it. You don't have a thing to worry about."

Easy for him to say.

And even if I could do it, I knew it would require a desperate situation before Tony would actually put me in a game.

Three weeks.

It was late in April, we were getting beaten by the Kansas City Royals, and he sent me out to play third base. And guess who was the third base umpire? "Spanky," Larry Barnett said when he saw me come out to take my position, "what do you think you're doing?"

Once again I resisted the urge to say, *What's the matter, Larry. Haven't you ever seen a left-hander playing third base before?* Instead, I said, "Just stick close to me, Larry. We're the answer to a great trivia question."

On May second that year I started a game at third, becoming the first left-handed fielder since Franklin Roosevelt was president to start a game at third base. I started four games there that season, and filled in during nine more. We shut out the other team in two of the four games I started, and I didn't have an error at third base all season.

I also didn't have an error as a pitcher that year, but I pitched in only one game. Just because my friends wouldn't let me pitch in taped-up wiffleball was no reason I couldn't pitch in the big leagues.

I made my first appearance on the hill, that's inside pitcher talk, in Detroit, against the team I grew up loving, the Tigers. I had started the game at first base and moved over to third in the seventh inning. In the ninth inning Britt Burns was pitching for us, and he was getting lit up worse than the Rockefeller Center Christmas tree. The only relief pitcher we had left in the bullpen was Ron Reed, and Tony didn't want to use him. Hey, the score was 10–0 in the ninth inning;

it didn't look real good for us. So Tony came walking slowly out of our dugout, and pointed to me.

Me? I was just standing there being a left-handed third baseman.

You, he nodded. "Come here." I trotted over to the pitcher's mound and he said, "I am now going to get the opportunity to see something I have always wanted to see. Mike Squires pitching in the big leagues. Go get 'em."

Now, why he wanted to see that, I am not exactly sure. I've never known him to be sadistic.

There were two outs in the inning. Catcher Carlton Fisk came out to the mound grinning. "So, Spank," he said, "whattya want to throw?"

"The usual. Fastball, curve, slider, and maybe the straight change-up." Fisk told me his signals and went back behind the plate. The Tiger Tom Brookens stepped into the batter's box. Fisk signaled for a fastball.

The first pitch of my major league baseball career was low and outside, ball one. Pitchers always remember their first big-league pitch.

Fisk signaled for another fastball. Again a little low and outside, ball two.

Fisk signaled for a slider. Brookens gripped his bat tightly. Nah, I thought, I don't want to throw him a slider. I wasn't sure I had a slider. I shook off Fisk's signal. Carlton signaled for another fastball.

Yeah, I thought. I threw a perfect pitch, fastball on the outside corner. Brookens uncoiled, trying to pull it into the left-field seats. He didn't quite get it, instead hitting an easy fly ball to left for the third out of the inning.

I led the American League in earned run average that season.

I've also played a number of games in the outfield, so the only positions I haven't played in the big leagues are shortstop and second base. I could play them; I know that. And I just might get the chance someday.

The position I play most often, and best, is first base. I play it well enough to have won the Gold

Glove as the best fielder at that position in the American League in 1981. I learned how to play first base on the frozen lakes of Kalamazoo, Michigan. We played a lot of ice hockey and because of my skating ability I usually ended up playing goalie. I used mostly baseball catcher's equipment as protection in the goal. Playing goal and first base require almost the same hand-eye coordination, I've learned, except, of course, that as a goalie you don't have to catch the puck, you can just knock it away. Can't do that in baseball.

I'm supposed to be one of the best cheating first basemen in baseball. In baseball cheating is legal as long as you're not obvious about it. Cheating means that I'm very good at taking my foot off the base just before the ball gets to me. If a player is quick enough, the umpires allow him to get away with it because they don't want to see anyone get his foot spiked on a routine play.

I particularly enjoy the social aspects of playing first base. The first baseman is the only player on the defensive team who really gets an opportunity to talk to the other team. When a runner gets on first, the first baseman keeps him close to the base by standing on it. Naturally a few words are going to be said. Conversations are usually about what pitch the runner hit or something as common. I've never had a serious political debate at first base, for example.

Some players don't want to talk when they're on base; others always have something to say. During my rookie year, for example, I was struggling at bat and Mickey Rivers singled. All I said to him was "Way to hit the ball, Mick."

"Hey, thanks, babe," he said. "All you gotta do is keep swinging, man, keep swinging and you're gonna be around here a long time because you can really pick it and I've seen you hit and you can hit and all you got to do is keep your head up and keep swinging the bat, that's all."

"You know, Mick . . ."

"I just keep swinging the bat and see what I mean, they're fallin' in, they're fallin' in, but if they don't,

I'm coming back the next time and keep swinging and that's what you gotta do."

That was between pitches.

One of the few people who didn't talk to me that first season was Yankee second baseman Willie Randolph. I had played with him in the 1974 Instructional League, so I didn't understand why he was so silent. Finally, before a game one day, I went over to him and said, perhaps a bit sarcastically, "Hey, Willie, sure is nice talking to you at first base."

Willie shook his head. "You gotta remember something, Mike," he said, "you didn't say nothing first either."

Probably the most polite base runner I've met is Ricky Henderson. We were in the middle of a conversation one evening as he took his lead off the base. Then suddenly he said, "Gotta go," and took off for second.

Although I've played almost everywhere, the only season I've had the chance to play every day was 1981, the year of the players' strike. I was hitting about .312 when we went on strike and hit about .212 after we came back. I supported the strike, it was the right thing to do at that time, but it killed me. I don't know why I didn't hit when we came back. I had worked out during the strike, I'd taken batting practice, but I'd lost that fine edge. I knew we had to strike, but there is no question in my mind that it hurt my career.

After that season I had to learn how to help the team when I wasn't in the starting lineup. When we won the Western Division pennant in 1983, for example, I played in 143 games, but I had only 153 at bats, so I wasn't in the starting lineup a lot. Although I led the league's first basemen in fielding that season, making only two errors in 557 chances, I probably made my most important contribution as a caterer.

As May started that season, the team was not doing well at all. Actually we were terrible. One Friday night before a game a group of players were sitting around talking about how hungry we were—for food as well as for victories. So we decided to order out for a pizza. We called Connie's Pizzeria, which is right down the street from the ballpark, and had them deliver a large pie. When the game started, some of the irregulars, like me and Marc Hill, and the starting pitchers not working that night—Jerry Koosman, Richard Dotson, Britt Burns—went inside and had a slice or two of pizza. We won the game that night.

We did not tell Tony LaRussa about this. You may have noticed, however, that LaRussa is an Italian name, and it is a proven fact that you cannot hide the existence of a pizza from an Italian. So I suspect LaRussa smelled a mushroom.

On Saturday night we decided, well, we ordered a pizza last night and we won. Who knows, pepperoni and anchovies might have had something to do with it. We weren't really hungry, just superstitious. Helloo Connie's! We won again.

Connie's doesn't deliver on Sunday. We lost. Then we went on a road trip and continued playing good baseball. The day we returned to Chicago we ordered a pizza and ordered every home game until the end of the season. We had pizza rules too. We ordered at 6:30, so it would get there near game time and still be warm in the first inning. We would not take a bite until the game had begun.

I knew I wasn't going to play until I went in for defense in late innings, so I'd eat my two slices early enough to have them digested by the sixth inning. I guess it would be accurate to say that during our pennant-winning season I wasn't so much a role player as a pizza player. Accurate, but in really poor taste.

I also served as judge in the team's kangaroo court, which was in session after every victory. We would fine people like Harold Baines, the most even-tempered player on the team, five dollars for showing emotion on the field. Or Juan Agusto, who got on an elevator and pressed every floor button, two dollars a floor The largest fine of the season was levied against team co-owner Jerry Reinsdorf. It cost him five hundred dollars for a nasty comment about my shorts. Hey, I was a tough judge.

That particular crime was committed after a home game one night. We were meeting our friends and relatives in the reception area and I was wearing some fashionable shorts. When I walked in, Jerry said, "Damn, Spank, what the @#$%¢& are you doing dressed like that?"

"You can't use that type of language when ladies are present, Jerry," I told him. "That'll cost you five bucks." Jerry agreed that that was unnecessary use of language and felt his crime was so heinous that he offered to match whatever was in the pot at the time. I'm sure he figured it was maybe seventy-five dollars. He just did not know how tough I was. We had $502 in fines collected when he made that offer.

At the end of that season I became the Fielder on the Roof. It was probably my most exciting moment in baseball. The day after we clinched the pennant we raised the championship flag. After the entire team had been introduced to the fans, the public address announcer said, "May we now direct your attention to the roof of the ballpark in right center field, where Mike Squires, who has been with the White Sox longer than any other player, will raise the flag."

I thought it was quite an honor when I was asked to do it. I still thought so as I started climbing the stairs to the roof. And climbed. And climbed. Have you ever been on the roof of a three-tiered baseball stadium when the wind is blowing about twenty-five miles per hour? I was terrified. Next time I want to be honored at home plate. Preferably in an indoor ballpark.

I was in the starting lineup that day, and when I finally got onto the field, the Sox fans gave me a standing ovation. I wasn't sure if it was because they liked me or were glad I had survived.

Even though I might not have accomplished everything I believe I was capable of doing in baseball, I have no regrets. If my career is over, I leave the game with numerous autographed balls and bats and hats, the first home run ball I ever hit in the big leagues, some wonderful memories, a Gold Glove, and a black glove.

The black glove is relatively new. I have a glove contract with Wilson, but one season I couldn't find a Wilson glove I really liked. So I took the glove I wanted to use, painted it black, like a Wilson, and drew the Wilson insignia on it. The picture on my 1985 baseball card shows me ready to field a hot grounder at third base wearing my black glove with the painted Wilson insignia on it. Otherwise it is entirely accurate.

Even then, my picture on that card is better than the one they show on the Comiskey Park scoreboard. Scoreboard photographs are always terrible. I know I'm not real photogenic, but the picture of me looks like somebody kissed me with an air hammer. It could be worse, I suppose; I could look like Cliff Johnson. His picture makes him look like a tire.

In spring training 1985 it became obvious I wasn't going to play too much for the Sox that season, so I went to Jerry Reinsdorf, and even though I had two years left on my contract asked for my release so I might hook on with another ball club.

As usual, Jerry was super about it. "If you want it," he said, "but if you want to stick around and fight to make the team, we'd like to have you try."

Oakland, the Yankees, and a few other teams had indicated they were interested in signing me, so I decided to take my release. While I was waiting until I cleared waivers and was free to sign anywhere, the A's Tony Phillips got hurt and they had to sign a middle infielder, and New York's Don Mattingly proved his leg injury wasn't serious enough to force the Yankees to sign another first baseman. I was without a job.

The White Sox offered me a job as scout, announcer, as anything else that might come up, adding that if another team offered me a playing job, I would be free to leave. So I spent the season staying in condition, learning how to scout and attempting to become a broadcaster.

Admittedly I did make a few mistakes. For example, before the Sox were to play Seattle, I watched the Mariners play five games. What you try to do as an advance scout is pick up weaknesses or tendencies—a team likes to hit and run on the second pitch, or they never bunt with one out—little aspects that might make a big difference. One of the things I noticed was that in five games the Mariners' Jim Pressley never swung at the first pitch. In twenty-two at bats, he took the first pitch every time. I got him nailed, I figured. I'll tell our pitchers he will not swing at the first pitch, they can throw a fastball strike, and they'll be ahead on the count. A small thing that could make a big difference.

Pressley's first time up against us he hit the first pitch for a single. His next time up he hit the first pitch for a home run. His third time at bat he hit the first pitch for a single.

Maybe the Mariners had an advance scout scouting the White Sox advance scout.

I was as good a broadcaster as a scout. One of my favorite names in baseball is Toronto Blue Jay pitcher Louis Leal. Not player, name. What a great name, Lee-al. So one night I was giving the Sox starting lineup. Our eighth batter was scheduled to be Luis Salazar. Not that night. "Playing center field for the Sox tonight," I said, "Luis Lee-al." That probably came as a surprise to everyone except me.

Other than the letters I received from my mother correcting my English, most Sox fans were supportive of my efforts.

The year was frustrating because I still believed I could play, but rewarding because I did not. The thing that surprised me most was that I didn't miss being on the field as much as I thought I would. I had believed baseball was a life and death situation. I didn't think I could live without it. I was wrong. I didn't play an entire season—and survived. Even enjoyed myself, in fact. I found out that there was life after baseball, that I could be happy, that I didn't need the game. It was an important and wonderful thing to learn.

Of course, if an offer to play came along . . .

RUN FOR YOUR LIFE
by Julio Cruz

I often tell people that my hometown, Endicott, New York, was so tough that in the town square we had a statue of Atlas holding up the bank. Actually Endicott is really a suburb of Johnson City, or "Sin City" as we used to refer to that big town. Johnson City was the shoe-repair capital of Upstate New York.

Major league baseball players come from every conceivable environment. Jim Palmer, for example, was an orphan adopted by millionaires. He grew up playing catch with the butler. Hey, he was very lucky, he could just as easily have been picked up by my parents. Dwight Gooden comes from a working-class neighborhood in Tampa, Florida. Earl Weaver . . . who knows where he comes from. And Julio Cruz grew up on the streets of New York. As people say, you get older younger there.

"The Cruiser" has quietly become one of the outstanding base runners and infielders in the major leagues. He is among the top five base stealers in baseball and shares the American League record for consecutive bases stolen without being thrown out,

thirty-two. I enjoy watching him play because he is so graceful in the field. To me, graceful is walking down a supermarket aisle without knocking over any displays, but few infielders are as smooth as Julio Cruz. And no one, absolutely no one, appreciates being in the big leagues more than he does.

During his rookie season with the Seattle Mariners I called him out on an attempted steal of second base. Maybe he was out, maybe he was safe; in a cosmic sense does it really matter? The play was very close. I felt bad about it. Here was this likable young player struggling to stay in the major leagues, and I gave him the short end of a long call. I expected him to jump up and start arguing. I squeezed my fists until my face turned red, figuring maybe he'd see I was so angry and he'd back off. I took a deep breath. Julio got up, dusted himself off, and trotted off the field. I liked the kid immediately.

When he came out to second base the following inning, I eased over next to him. I couldn't admit I was wrong. In my mind I wasn't wrong. I just wasn't as right as I might have been. "That was pretty close, you know," I said.

He knew. He just looked at me and smiled, then replied, "Hey, Ron, I'm just so happy to be here in the major leagues." My kind of player.

I was born in the Williamsburg section of Brooklyn, New York. I'm Hispanic, of Puerto Rican descent. It was a very tough neighborhood. I had two things to choose between in my life, hanging around on the streets getting into trouble, or playing baseball. A lot of kids thought I was chicken for playing baseball, but they changed their minds when they heard I was good at stealing bases.

I wasn't the best player in the neighborhood. I wasn't even the best player on my block. But some of the better players hung out with the wrong group, and I never heard about them again.

We had a Boys' Club in the area and every once in

a while we'd get tickets and go out to Shea Stadium to watch the Mets play. I don't remember who the Mets were playing the first game I went to, but I remember the great third baseman Ken Boyer was playing for the Mets. I know he was there because when we got to the game, I told all my friends I was going down to the field to get Ken Boyer's autograph. Nobody thought I could do it. So I went down to the railing next to the field, but just when I got close to Boyer, the guard said, "Hey, time out, you gotta get back." So what I did was I signed Ken Boyer's name on a piece of paper and told everyone it was his autograph. I was the hit of the town. In fact, sometimes I'll still do that today. When people ask me for my teammates' autographs, I'll just sign everybody's name on the ball.

One of the things that kept me out of real trouble was that my parents sent me to Catholic school from the first grade to the eighth grade. There is no such thing as having a good time in Catholic school. Besides, you had to receive good grades or they wouldn't let you play sports, so my grades were good or bad depending on the season. I was a baseball-season student.

The nuns wore their whole outfits then. Sister Bernard, God bless her, I know she's up in heaven now, she was the principal and she was the meanest sonofagun I ever met. She made us eat soap when we said a bad word, or sit under her desk when we were bad. I ate some soap under that desk, I'll tell you.

When I was sixteen my family moved to southern California. Boy, talk about a change, Brooklyn to California. For sixteen years I hadn't been off my block. Then suddenly I didn't have a block. At least not a New York kind of block. It took me some time to get going out there.

Baseball was the thing that brought me together with other people. In the old neighborhood we played a lot of stickball, that's where you try to hit a rubber ball with a broomstick, and stoopball, where you throw the ball against the point of a stoop, and running bases, where you run between two bases. We never played that much hardball. I didn't even have my own glove or spikes. But I was always a good athlete and I could play the game.

One of the friends I made in California had signed to play for the Angels. When he came home after playing his first year in rookie ball, he took me with him when he went to play in pick-up games at UCLA on Sunday afternoons.

After the third Sunday I played, a man came up to me and said, "Hey, Julio, how would you like to sign a contract?"

I said, "A contract? What's that?" I was nineteen years old but I didn't know anything about professional baseball. I never thought about playing baseball for a career; I just played because I loved to play.

"It's like this," he explained. "We give you five hundred dollars and you go with your friend to play baseball against other teams. We'll sign you for one year."

I shook my head. I couldn't do that, I couldn't leave home for a whole year. I'd never spent one night away from home in my life, no way could I go away for a year, for 365 days. But that five hundred dollars did sound pretty good to me. So I got in contact with my grandfather, who was in Puerto Rico, to talk to him about this contract. "No," he said, "you can't leave home for a year. What would we do without you?"

"That's what I said too," I told him. But the more we talked about it, the more money five hundred dollars seemed and the less time a year seemed like. Finally my family decided I would sign the contract to play baseball. Not only didn't I have an agent, I still didn't have a glove or spikes.

As I wrote my name on the piece of paper, I got up enough courage to ask the scout who signed me if I really had to be away from home for an entire year. I was hoping they might give me a little time off.

"Where'd you get that idea?" he asked. "It's just for three months." I didn't know that a baseball season was called a year, and in baseball a season in the minors can be as short as three or four months. When I heard that I was going to be away from home for only a few months and I would still get the whole five hundred dollars, I knew I wanted to be a professional baseball player.

As a bonus for signing the contract the scout gave me the first real glove and spikes I'd ever owned. I put that glove, the spikes, a pair of jeans, some underclothes, a couple of shirts, and my sneakers into a shopping bag and reported to Idaho Falls, Idaho, to play baseball. The glove busted the second week, the spikes got torn up the first month. But I was in baseball to stay.

I didn't know anything about the minor leagues. I thought it was just like the big leagues, but in different cities. I never thought twice about riding on old buses for ten or twelve hours, sleeping in crazy hotels that looked like they were used in scary movies, and eating nothing but cold hot dogs. Some of the other players were always complaining, but I thought everything was wonderful. Getting paid to play baseball? What could possibly be better? And if you had to take long bus rides and sleep on old mattresses? We still got to play games and people actually paid to see us play. That part I couldn't comprehend at first—why were people paying to watch me having fun?

The minor league fans were wonderful to me. Very often they would take us into their homes after games or on off days to give us a good meal. I didn't know why they did that. I figured, they must think we're very poor, or we're orphans. I appreciated it, but I never told anybody about the five hundred dollars I was getting paid.

I never played with the intention of making it to the big leagues. I didn't have any long-range goals—or short-range goals either. I just tried to play my best and have fun every day. Some of my teammates were always worrying because they knew if they didn't do well, they wouldn't go up. Since I didn't even know what "up" was, I never worried. So I never felt the pressure.

Since this was the first time I was away from home, I missed my family very much. I called home every day, absolutely every day. And when I got my paycheck every second week, I would take five dollars and send it home. My grandparents thought that was the greatest thing in the whole world. Julio, sending home money. Unfortunately I called home collect so often that the monthly phone bill was more than one hundred dollars a month, so even with the ten dollars I was sending them, it was costing my family money for me to play professional baseball.

My idols when I was in the minor leagues were the Cruz players. Any player named Cruz. I cut pictures out of the sports magazines of Hector Cruz and Tommy Cruz and Jose Cruz and taped them to my bedroom wall. I figured, I had a lot in common with them; we were baseball players with the same name.

The thing that got me a lot of attention in the minor leagues was my ability to steal bases. I had always been a fast runner; in my neighborhood in Brooklyn that was the best thing you could be. One year in the minors I stole eighty-three bases—in three different leagues. In six months I jumped from A-level ball to AA to AAA. The only time I had any trouble was in the Triple A. We were playing in Hawaii and Rick Sutcliffe was pitching against us. I was on second and as he went into his stretch motion, I took a long lead off the base. He lifted his leg into the air to pitch, but suddenly, instead of throwing home, he spun around on the pitcher's mound. He turned completely around—he looked just like a top—and threw to second base. I was caught at least ten feet off the base.

"Time!" I yelled, shaking my head. "No way, he can't do that."

The umpire told me it was a perfectly legal move.

I didn't know about that. "You sure?" I asked. " 'Cause that's definitely not legal in Brooklyn." The umpire was sure. I was out, and I walked off the field shaking my head. I never knew they could do anything like that.

But I got even with that Sutcliffe. After that, every time I got on second base against him I took a lead off the base like a Little Leaguer—I kept one foot on the base until the ball passed the batter. He used to turn around and look at me, and I'd stand there, tapping the base with one foot. He was just laughing so hard, there was no way he could concentrate on the batter.

I never believed I'd be playing in the big leagues, but one day when I was playing winter ball in Puerto Rico my manager, Jack McKeon, came over to me and told me congratulations. Well, I told him, thank you very much, I appreciated that. Then I asked him why he was congratulating me.

"The Seattle Mariners just selected you in the expansion draft," he explained.

"Ah, that's great," I said, and I was very happy. I didn't know that meant I was going to the big leagues. I was just happy to be noticed.

I was a good hitter in the minor leagues; twice I hit .300. I didn't have any theories about hitting or anything, I just got up to bat and hit the ball. But when I got to the big leagues with the Mariners, they had instructors for everything. They had an infield instructor, a base-running instructor, a hitting instructor, and they all wanted me to do things differently than I had been doing. What I had been doing had gotten me to the big leagues, but I figured since they were already in the big leagues, they must know what they're doing. I tried doing things their way.

If I had been smarter, I would have told them to let me hit my way instead of changing, but I was really intimidated. I tried to do everything everybody told me to. I got very confused. I had no consistent way of hitting. I would change stances for different pitchers. I even wanted to change bats for different pitchers. I figured, if the pitcher can change baseballs because one didn't feel good, I should change bats.

Every one of the coaches had a different idea about hitting. Some of them wanted me to hold my hands higher; others told me to keep them lower. One coach wanted me to move closer to the plate, another coach suggested I stand farther away from the plate. My problem became that I went up to the plate thinking instead of just hitting. But I tried to listen to everybody because they were nice people and we were all employees together.

The strangest theory came from a coach who decided I should use a heavier bat. He had me trying to hit with a thirty-six-inch thirty-six-ounce bat. My God, I couldn't even lift that thing. That bat was as big as I am. It was like trying to swing with a telephone pole. I used that bat for a month, and all I got out of it were sore wrists and a bad back. "I can't swing it, because every time I do I hurt my back," I told this coach, "so I'm just gonna hold it on the strike zone and let the pitcher try to hit it. Because with a bat that big, if the ball hits it, it's really gonna take off."

The first thing I realized about being in the big leagues is that there were no long bus rides. Just plane trips. I loved that. On the buses I used to climb up and sleep in the overhead racks. On the planes I could just stretch out.

My first year in the big leagues was like one long dream. I remember the first time the Mariners came to New York to play in Yankee Stadium. I walked out onto the field and thought, Mickey Mantle, Babe Ruth, Lou Gehrig, Joe DiMaggio, all of these great Hall of Famers had used the same batter's box, they had trotted across the same outfield, they'd sat in the same dugouts. I don't know if they showered in the same locker room, but there is an old weight scale in the visiting team locker room that they say was the one Babe Ruth used to weigh himself on. I was always weighing myself, or sitting on it, and thinking, this is where Babe Ruth found out how much he weighed.

The first time I came to New York I left about thirty tickets for my friends from the old neighborhood for each of the three games. About six people showed up for each game, so I had to pay for all those tickets myself. My God, I thought, it certainly does cost a lot of money to play baseball in New York.

Probably the thing that impressed me most about the big leagues was the Astroturf, or "carpet" covering the field in Seattle's indoor Astrodome. I remember walking on it for the first time and thinking, this is really something, I've never seen carpet like this in real people's homes, but they call it a carpet, and it looks like a carpet, so what are we doing playing baseball on it?

My first hit in the big leagues came off the late Francisco Barrios of the Chicago White Sox, may he rest in peace. It was my second at bat and I singled to center field. Oh, I thought, this is easy. I got on first base and the Seattle fans were all screaming at me to try to steal second because they had been reading in the newspapers that Julio Cruz, the Cruiser, was a real *phee*nom and had been stealing all kinds of bases in the minor leagues. Barrios barely looked at me, so I took off for second. As I was running, I figured, this is easy, I got it made. Then catcher Jim Essian made a perfect throw to second and I was tagged out. Uh-oh, Cruiser, I thought, this isn't going to be so easy after all.

My second season I managed to steal fifty-seven bases. The most important thing I had going for me was confidence. My first year I often found myself thinking, it's much harder to steal up here than in the minors. I was defeating myself. But I programmed myself to believe that I was going to beat them more than they were going to beat me, and that worked. I figured that a pitcher can get the good hitters out only seven of ten times at bat, so if I could be successful stealing eight out of ten times, I would be doing very well.

One of the things that helped was that in Seattle they let me steal anytime I wanted to, and I always wanted to. One of the things that hurt was that I just didn't get on base that much.

The most difficult pitcher for me to steal a base off was Luis Tiant. His pitching motion was so strange, I never saw anything like it ever. He would raise his arms above his head, and hold them there, and then, as he slowly brought the ball down to his waist, he would stop a number of times. He looked like a car with a bad transmission. Sometimes he would stop twice, sometimes six times. When I saw him pitch for the first time, I wondered, what is going on here? He can't do that. He started his pitching motion, then stopped, then started again. That's a balk, I thought. He stopped again, and started again. That's another balk. And another balk. In one pitch that man committed more balks than anyone I'd seen in my life. Combined.

I couldn't time him, or figure out his pitching rhythm, so I had trouble stealing on him. Then one day I just decided, I'm gonna run on this pitch. If he throws over here, he's got me; if he doesn't, I got him. I made it. So from then on that was the inside strategy I used to steal on Tiant. Guessing.

I hit my first big league home run in my fourth game. We were playing the Minnesota Twins. I was batting right-handed and I don't remember the pitcher's name. I do know that right after the game the Twins sent him back to the minor leagues.

After I hit the ball, I just put my head down and ran as fast as I could. A double, I thought. When I reached second, I slowed down and stood on the base. All the next batter has to do is hit a ground ball, I thought, and I'll get to third base. Then I looked at the umpire and he was making little circles with his finger above his head, the signal for a home run. I took off again. I was so excited that I circled the bases and was sitting in the dugout before he even put his hand down.

Once I hit a home run when Ron Luciano was the umpire at first base. I got to the base and he was clapping. I was thinking, what's Lucy clapping for? With him it could have been anything. Then I realized it was a home run and started trotting. But I still heard the clapping. As I got near second base, I looked over my shoulder and there was Luciano trotting beside me.

On another occasion I made a diving stop of a

hard ground ball behind second base in the Kingdome. Even before I got up to throw, Luciano was clapping again. After the play was over, I said to him, "Lucy, I wish you would wait until after I make a good throw before clapping. What would you do if I had made a bad throw, boo me?"

The biggest thrill I had when I was playing with the Mariners was being in the field when Gaylord Perry, the greatest spitball pitcher of all time, won his three hundredth game. Man, when there were two outs, I was really nervous. I kept reminding myself, Cruiser, if the batter hits the ball to you, make sure you grab it on the dry side.

I enjoyed playing in Seattle because the fans were very nice to the players. Sometimes there weren't too many fans, but the few who came to the games were very supportive.

It never occurred to me that I might be traded to another team. I was a Seattle Mariner. That's the way I thought of myself. But one morning when we were in Texas, someone knocked at my door. When I didn't answer it, a note was slipped under my door. Uh-oh, I thought, this can't be good. The note was from our manager, Rene Lachman. "Juice," it read, "you've been traded to the Chicago White Sox. I wanted to tell you in person, but you weren't in your room. Good luck and thank you for everything."

I just sat on the edge of the bed. I couldn't move. Just like that my whole life had changed. I couldn't decide if I was happy that the Chicago White Sox wanted me, or unhappy that the Mariners didn't.

I flew from Dallas to Chicago that afternoon and got to the ballpark in the third inning of a game that night. I was sort of in shock. For me the Mariners were the major leagues. It was like being traded by your parents. But it was very exciting going to a pennant contender.

At the end of the season the White Sox were playing the Mariners. We, Chicago, needed to win one game to clinch the American League Western Division pennant. I was on third base in the ninth inning of a tie game. Harold Baines hit a long fly ball to center field and, after the ball was caught, I tagged up and scored the winning run. As I scored, everyone broke out of the dugout and ran onto the field to celebrate. Before I joined that celebration, I looked into the Mariner dugout. Everybody was sitting on the top step watching the Chicago players jumping up and down. At that moment, when I was so happy, I was also sad for them. I had played with those guys for six years, and I wished very much that they could all experience the same feelings I had running through my body.

That feeling, that was another world. I don't know how to describe it, but something goes into your system and elevates you; it just puts you higher than anyone else for that time and that moment. It seems like you can walk on air.

The only other time when I've felt anything like that was when I went down to play winter league baseball in Puerto Rico. If you are Puerto Rican, when you play down there, the people believe that you are representing them. And you cannot mess up, because if you do, they think it means that they're messing up. They do not like to mess up.

They take their baseball seriously there, more than in the States. I've heard about the riots that have taken place in the Caribbean, but I've never seen a riot on the field. In the stands, that's something else. I saw a lot of riots in the stands. But on the field, never.

I did see a lot of beer bottles and rum bottles thrown, however, but I don't think they were really trying to hit anybody.

I don't play winter league baseball anymore because it just got to be too much. I was playing baseball all year round, and by the time it got to the middle of the season here, I was dragging. I just decided that if I played in Puerto Rico, I'd be cheating myself when it comes to here. And this is the show, right here.

After my first season with the White Sox, I signed a new contract. When we sat down to talk about money and years, I couldn't believe the numbers they were talking about. Hundreds of thousands of dollars just to play baseball. I had signed my first contract for a new glove and spikes. And if anyone had told me then how much money I would be earning, I would have laughed and told them they were crazy. Where's the money gonna come from, I would have asked. Is it legal, illegal, or what? They had to be talking about Monopoly money.

I learned then that money doesn't change me, I change it. The money allows me to take care of my family, but if I weren't healthy and happy, what good would it do? I really believe I'm the luckiest person I've ever known. There are approximately 650 players in the big leagues, and I'm one of them. It's an honor, a pleasure, to put on a uniform and go out and play a game that I had played just for satisfaction on the streets of New York City.

And they pay me to do it. What else could anyone ask for?

ROCKY'S ROAD
by Rocky Bridges

Rocky Bridges began playing professional baseball when men were men, grass was mowed, and players had nicknames. In those old days everybody was somebody else. George Ruth was "the Babe." Stan Musial was "the Man." Ted Williams was "the Kid," "the Splendid Splinter," and "the Thumper." Sal Maglie was "the Barber." And "Rocky" Bridges was "Rocky," as were "Rocky" Nelson and "Rocky" Colavito.

I've always enjoyed nicknames in sports. A great nickname creates a colorful image in my mind. I could always see Mickey Mantle, "the Commerce Comet," speeding around the bases. I knew Mike Garcia, "the Big Bear," was a strong, husky player. The closest I ever came to a nickname was "Loosh," as in "That guy must have a screw loosh to play like that." The art of nicknaming seems to have been lost. A nickname today usually consists of calling a player like Pedro Guerrero "Pete." Or Carl Yastrzemski "Yaz." Hasn't it occurred to anyone that Jim Rice doesn't have a great nickname? How can you not describe Ricky Henderson as "the Cyclone," or something hav-

ing to do with his speed. Doesn't Dale Murphy deserve to be known as something more colorful than "Murph"? In the old days Nolan Ryan would have been "the Texas Express" or "the Firing Flinger." And isn't there a better way to picture Dave Winfield than "Yankee right fielder"?

There are a few decent nicknames in baseball today. Dwight Gooden quickly became known as "Dr. K." I like calling Red Sox Dennis Boyd "Oil Can." Greg Minton is "Moonman." Bill Lee was "Spaceman." Tommy Lasorda, who really deserves one wonderful nickname, first called Tom Paciorek "Wimpy," but later Paciorek became, naturally, "Pac-Man." Free-swinging slugger Jeff Leonard is now "Hac Man." Ron Guidry will be known forever as "Louisiana Lightning." Tom Seaver became "the Franchise" in New York, Cincinnati, and Chicago. Most nicknames are still derived from nature: Ron Cey walked like "the Penguin." Mark Fidyrich thought like "the Bird." Jim Hunter was much better looking than any "Catfish." I don't know why Rich Gossage became a "Goose." "Moose" Haas looked like a Haas. I do know that the Cubs' Leon "Bull" Durham is named after chewing tobacco, not the animal. "The Baby Bull," Greg Luzinski, could be named anything he wanted to be.

And to me at least, six-seven, two-hundred-fifty-five-pound Frank Howard was always "Mister."

But where are "the Refrigerators" of baseball? As far as I'm concerned, the best nickname in baseball today is that of the San Francisco Giants catcher, Doug Gwosdz, known to his teammates and select fans as "Eye Chart." Great. Really.

Rocky Bridges had what can accurately be described as a rocky career as a player, coach, and manager. I first met Rocky when he was coaching. A baseball team has a pitching coach, a batting coach, some have "bench coaches" to help the manager make strategy decisions, and first and third base coaches. The thing I could never figure out is just exactly what the first base coach does. As far as I could determine, the first base coach's job is to pat every player that reaches first base on the rump and tell him "Nice going." "C" grown men do that for a living.

Coaching third base is a very different situation. Third base coaches have to direct base runners whether to hold up at third or continue home, whether to stand up or slide when coming into third base, and have to relay the manager's strategic decisions to the batter by using a complex series of signals.

Strategy is communicated to the batter by a series of signs. Signs consist of touching parts of the body and uniform in a specific order. For example, a third base coach might begin by touching the brim of his cap, which is the "indicator," meaning a play is on. If he doesn't begin by touching his cap, the batter simply ignores everything else he does. After giving the indicator, the coach may wipe his hand across his chest, tug his earlobe, clap twice, wipe his nose, grab his belt, and clap again. That might mean a hit-and-run play is on, or a bunt, or that he had too much for lunch.

Players do miss signs. Some players pay more attention than others. Mickey Rivers, "Mick the Quick," had a reputation of being very flaky. He just couldn't get the signs down straight, yet he never missed one. Part of the reason for that is that the teams he played for used to devise special signals for him. When they wanted him to bunt, for example, the third base coach would clap twice to get his attention, walk fifteen steps down the line toward home plate, cup both hands around his mouth, and shout, "Mickey. Bunt."

Rocky Bridges has been smart enough to stay in baseball for forty years. At the end of the 1985 season San Francisco Giants manager Jim Davenport and his coaching staff were fired, among them Rocky Bridges. When I asked him what he planned to do, he told me, "Probably go back to scouting. My dream is to go out there and find a player just like me and sign him. That way I can get even with everyone."

*   *   *

I signed with the Brooklyn Dodgers organization in 1946, although I couldn't start playing for them until 1947. Of course, the Dodgers hadn't seen me play too much, so they didn't appreciate how lucky they were. But there was another type of player draft at that time, being run by the United States Army. They wanted me. I was drafted in '46, but the rumor that I was going to be drafted was out a year earlier, and soon as the Japanese heard it, they surrendered. There are a lot of baseball managers who should have paid attention to that lesson.

My given name is Everett Lamar Bridges. That is no name for a tough baseball player. No name for much else good either. One day I was playing ball with the Dodger farm club in Greenville, South Carolina, and the public address announcer said, "Playing shortstop, Lamar Bridges." Well, that ballpark just about stopped dead. I thought they were upset that I was playing. I couldn't blame them, I'd seen me play before.

"What's a Lamar?" one of my teammates asked. A lot of people offered answers to that question, none of which can be repeated here, and it was finally decided that Lamar was no name for a baseball player. I could've told them that.

"Let's call him Rocky," someone else suggested. They weren't too creative in Greenville. I didn't mind though. I thought they were talking about my physique. Turned out they were talking about my face.

I came up to the big leagues for the first time in 1951 with the Dodgers. The Boys of Summer. I spent eleven years in the majors, playing for the Dodgers, Cincinnati Reds, Washington Senators, Detroit Tigers, Cleveland Indians, St. Louis Cardinals, and the expansion-born Los Angeles Angels. Eleven years. Imagine how long I would have lasted if I was any good. About the most important thing I learned in the major leagues was never send your shirts out to a two-day laundry.

My first roommate in the major leagues was Pee-wee Reese. He wore number one because that's what he was. 'Course, Peewee thought I was crazy. Like

he'd come into our hotel room and I'd be standing on
my head on the bed. He'd try not to notice too much,
but finally he'd ask, "What're you doing, Rocky?"

"I'm a modern lamp shade, Peewee," I'd tell him.

"Oh." Peewee took me under his wing and tried
to teach me how to act. I think he did the same thing
with Don Zimmer, Don Hoak, and the forty other
players who were going after his job. Didn't work
with me though.

Coming up with that team was a tremendous
opportunity for a young man who enjoyed watching
the game of baseball. Even though they called me
Rocky, I hoped I was wise enough to learn something
from that group. I knew I wasn't going to play. Where
could I? I played second base; Jackie Robinson was the
second baseman. I played shortstop; Peewee Reese
was the shortstop. One day the manager, Charlie
Dressen, took me aside and asked me if I could play
third base. "Hell, yes," I told him. "I can play it like I
was born there."

Never played there before in my life. The Dodgers
had Bill Cox at third, he was a great player, but at
least he wasn't going into the Hall of Fame like Jackie
and Peewee. So as we were coming up north on the
train to begin the '51 season, barnstorming against the
Yankees, Dressen put me in at third. That sort of
shook me. I expected to stay with the team, but there
was nothing in my contract that said I had to play.

I guess that series with the Yankees started my
major league batting slump. It lasted all the way
through 1961.

I was in the starting lineup at third base on opening day at Ebbets Field. I was shaking so much that
anybody who tried to read the number on my back
must've thought they had blurred vision. Robin Roberts was pitching for the Philadelphia Phillies against
us. He was a good guy to break in against because he
didn't necessarily try to strike you out; he tried to
make you hit the ball at his fielders. I went oh-for-3,
but I hit the ball every time.

My rookie season, 1951, ended with the famous

Dodgers–New York Giants playoff for the National League pennant. It was a best two out of three series. Each team won a game and the Dodgers went into the ninth inning of the final game leading by two runs. I was sitting on the bench, thoroughly enjoying the game. Hey, it was a great place to be so long as Dressen didn't think about making me play. In the bottom of the ninth inning the Giants' Bobby Thompson hit a three run homer to win the game and the pennant. I remember watching Thompson hit the ball, watching it sail into the first row of the left-field bleachers. The feeling . . . it was nothing like I'd ever felt before. I guess nowadays they'd call it a heart attack.

It took a long time for the shock of that home run to really hit me. Then suddenly *boom*! Season's over. No more games. No world series money. I cried.

Well, I thought, if this happened in my rookie season, I'm gonna have some interesting career.

It had been a good season for me personally, though, except maybe for the broken hand. One night we were playing the Giants in the Polo Grounds. By "we," I mean the Dodgers, not me. I was safe on the bench. Eddie Stanky was the Giants second baseman. Stanky was as tough a player as was in the league. Well, one night in the Polo Grounds Stanky slid into second base and kicked the ball out of Peewee's glove.

Naturally I was sympathetic, so I stayed up all night getting on Peewee. "I'll tell you what," I said firmly, "there is no way he would do that to me."

"You're right," Peewee agreed, "not unless he was sliding into the bench."

"Not even there," I insisted. As fate would have it, the very next evening Charlie Dressen made me play again. I don't know what I had done to deserve that. And in the sixth inning Stanky was on first base. Giants manager Leo Durocher decided to hit and run. Stanky took off and the batter missed the pitch. I covered second and our catcher, Roy Campanella, made a perfect throw to me. I had Stanky out a long way, and the intelligent thing would have been for me to just stick him with the tag and pull my glove up quick.

That would have been the intelligent thing.

I was going to prove I was as tough as Reese. I tried to slam that tag on him. Stanky kicked me in the back of the hand, just like he had kicked Reese. But I held on to the ball.

"You okay?" Stanky asked as he got up and dusted himself off.

"Fine." I said, and I was, except for the broken bone in the back of my hand. That was when I learned another truth—if you're not that great a player, after you get hurt, you don't have that far to come back all the way to where you were.

I spent most of the 1952 season with the Dodgers, and the more I played, the more it became obvious that no one there could take a joke. My batting average. But we did make it to the World Series and I certainly enjoyed watching that.

At the end of the season I was traded for the first time. It was a three-way deal between the Dodgers, Reds, and Boston Braves. In retrospect that figures to be one of the ten worst trades of all time: I was traded for Joe Adcock. Adcock went on to become a star for the Milwaukee Braves and one of the best power-hitting first basemen in the game. I just went on.

I spent four years in Cincinnati while the Reds tried to figure out why they had traded for me. They never did. The team was managed by Birdie Tebbets, an absolutely outstanding man and a fine manager. The thing we had on that ball club was great size. We had Big Ted Kluszewski, Gus Bell, Ed Bailey, Jim Greengrass—these were big people. The 1956 team tied a National League record by hitting 221 home runs. I didn't contribute to that record. I was a late-inning defensive replacement on that club, so by the time I got into the game, we were usually so far ahead; I couldn't do severe damage.

One good thing about being with that group was you didn't worry about getting into fights. Oh, we had our annual bouts. One night, I remember, we were having a brawl with the Milwaukee Braves. There was a big pile of people in the middle of the infield, and suddenly pitcher Joey Jay crawled out from underneath and just started walking away. "Hey!" Klu yelled at him. "Where you think you're going?"

Joey Jay shrugged. "I'm just going back to the dugout to sit down," he said. "Go ahead and finish this one without me."

Another night Birdie got real mad at Harry Walker, who was managing the St. Louis club. Harry always liked to argue. This time he was trying to make a protest. Now, he had nothing to protest about, which might have been what he was protesting. Finally Birdie went out to home plate and just took a big roundhouse swing at Walker. And missed. Walker just looked at him. "Well," Birdie told him, "that's the last time I'm going to do that."

Cincinnati traded me to the Washington Senators during the 1957 season. Before joining the Senators the most games I'd ever played in in one season had been 122 with the 1953 Reds. I hit .227, but I believed I could do better if I ever again had the chance to play regularly.

I played 120 games with the Senators that first year and I proved I was right. I hit .228.

About the best thing I could say about my hitting ability was that I was consistent. I really didn't hit anybody very well. There were some pitchers in those days that it just didn't even make sense for me to go to bat against. I mean, what was I going to do against Don Newcombe or Warren Spahn? But the one person I *really* hated to face was Sad Sam Jones of the St. Louis Cardinals. He had a vicious curveball, a good hard fastball, and poor control. I will guarantee you that it was a waste of time for me to even go up to bat against him.

I was such a poor hitter, I couldn't even get bats with my name on them from Louisville Slugger. I ordered them; they never showed up. It didn't matter. I probably wouldn't have used them anyway. Who'd want to hit with a bat used by a lifetime .247 hitter? When I went to bat, I always tried to use a bat signed by some great hitter. I figured maybe that had something to do with it. I can state right now that based on my experience it did not.

Playing for the Washington Senators was just like playing in the big leagues. We didn't draw very large crowds though. One time, I remember, I was arriving at our ballpark, old Griffith Stadium, and our fan stopped me and asked, "What time's the game start?"

"You name it," I said. "We'll play at your convenience." 'Course, that kind of humor used to get our hot dog vendor mad at me.

We lost a lot of games in 1957. We would have lost more, but the season ended. The amazing thing was that every player on that team went out there every day and gave it a full load. And against the better teams in the league, the Yankees, the White Sox, the Indians, we always seemed to play well. But we never played any good at all against the teams that were our equals. I suppose we were a team that was unequal to our equals.

I had one of the great thrills of my career in 1958. Yankee manager Casey Stengel selected me to represent the Washington Senators in the All-Star game. I was particularly pleased to have been selected by Casey, whom I always admired. He was a man who had fun and let his players go out and play. Of course, he had such good players, why was he going to mess with them?

The American League won that game. I had the same type of seating arrangement that I had enjoyed for the 1952 World Series. Casey never put me in the game, which did nothing but increase my admiration for the man.

The thing that hurt me most that year was a Frank Lary fastball. Lary was pitching for the Tigers one night and he had two strikes on me. I was trying to protect the plate and I fouled off a lot of pitches. Finally he came in close and I checked out his fastball with my jaw. I went down hard, but I didn't get knocked out. The stitches on the ball cut me up, and when they were sewing my chin together, they discovered my jaw was broken. I didn't mind; I was just worried it was going to ruin my career in the movies.

They had to wire my jaw shut. I went six weeks without sipping a beer, a personal record. The thing I minded most was that with my jaw wired shut, I couldn't tell when I was tired because I couldn't yawn.

I like to think that all the injuries I had during my career prevented me from being the ball player I could have been. The broken hand, broken jaw ... I broke my leg once ... I tore the ligaments in my ankle. So I like to think that even if it isn't true. Maybe I just didn't have as much ability as some other players. I'll tell you what, though, I played whenever they let me. And I wasn't afraid to get my uniform dirty. I am proud to say I was one of the elite four hundred—there were only four hundred major league baseball players during my career, and I lasted a long time.

How did I last eleven years in the big leagues? I'll tell you, I don't have the slightest idea.

I finished my playing career in 1961 with the Los Angeles Angels, an American League expansion club. We didn't have a bad team at all; we were in first place on July fourth and finished third. I hadn't really given any thought to retiring, but in August our general manager, Fred Haney, asked me, "So, Rocky, what are your plans for next year?"

I took that as a bad sign. "Well," I said, "long as they don't play me, I can probably play for a few more years."

Fred sighed. "Let me ask you, you ever give any thought to coaching?"

I hadn't until that very minute, but then again, I hadn't thought about playing third base on the Dodgers until Dressen asked. "Hey," I told Haney, "all the time. It's what I've always wanted to do." I'm Rocky, I'm not Stupid. I knew I was going to have to quit sometime, and I knew coaching jobs were difficult to get. So I retired at the end of that season and became a coach.

Two years later I was managing a minor league club in San Jose, California. I managed from 1964 to 1982, spending nine of those years managing the San Francisco Giants top farm club in Phoenix, Arizona. Phoenix is a nice place if you like to sweat. We used to say it was about three blocks from hell.

But it was enjoyable; all of it was enjoyable. This game can be a great deal of fun if you let it.

One year I had Johnnie LeMaster on the Phoenix club. Johnnie had lost the top half of his pinkie while growing up, but it did not affect his playing ability. One night he was at bat and an inside pitch just grazed him. Umpire Billy Lawson disagreed, claiming the ball had hit LeMaster's bat. He refused to award him first base. I came out to argue and Lawson and I went around in circles for a while, but he was pretty firm in his belief that the ball had hit the bat. Finally, in desperation, I turned to Johnnie and told him, "Go ahead, show him your finger."

LeMaster held up his pinkie with the top half missing.

I will say this for Billy Lawson, he didn't even blink. "Tell you what, Rocky," he said, "you find the rest of that finger, I'll give him first base."

I always tried to get along well with umpires. I figured they didn't make fun of my ability, I wasn't going to make fun of theirs.

I managed a lot of games in a lot of minor league seasons, but there is one that stands out. One year at Phoenix we had lost fifteen straight times to Salt Lake City. We played them only sixteen times the entire season, so we were close to being shut out. I was walking to the ballpark in Salt Lake before we were to play that last game with them, trying to figure out how to break that streak, when it started raining. I ducked under a canopy—it turned out to be the unemployment office, maybe that should have told me something. When the rain stopped, I took one step out and . . . a sea gull dived at me and *plop*. I looked down at my shirt and, well, let me put it this way, I was certainly glad that elephants can't fly.

That night we scored eight runs in the first two innings, and held on to win.

I've been a very fortunate man; I've experienced just about all the thrills that can be enjoyed in baseball. I've been a player, a manager, a coach, and a scout. I've played on one of the greatest teams in baseball history, and on one of the worst. I've been on a pennant winner and in a World Series. I've been selected for an All-Star team. I've even hit a grand slam home run, and I've been struck out by pitchers in the Hall of Fame. But there is one thing I've accomplished that very few other major leaguers can claim— I've started a triple play in both leagues.

Started, not hit into. One with Cincinnati, the other with the Senators. In both instances line drives were hit to me and we caught two runners off base. Both times, if I had thought quickly enough, I probably could have made them unassisted. But that was long before the days of calculators and I couldn't think that fast out there. When people hear about this feat, they ask me if I have a secret for starting triple plays. I tell them that the important thing is to be on a team bad enough to allow a lot of base runners.

Baseball has changed a great deal since I signed up. Not the competitive part—the players today play just as hard and want to win as much as we did—but other aspects. Certainly the salary structure has changed. I'm glad to see the players today making big money. More power to them. The only thing that bothers me about that is hearing them talking about the pressure put on them to produce because they are making so much money. Real pressure is when you have to go home at the end of the season and find a job to feed your kids. When I was playing, two days after the season was over you would have to start your plumbing job or your ditch-digging job or whatever seasonal work you could find. Sometimes it was hard to find a job too. Employers didn't want people who were going to leave the job every February.

I loved the game then and I love it today, but there are a few things I miss about those old days. Most of all, I guess, I miss the old ballparks. There never has been anything quite like Ebbets Field. I loved the Polo Grounds, the old Yankee Stadium, Boston Braves Park. Those old ballparks had a certain magic. The seats were so close to the field that the fans were really part of the game. The new ballparks are so much more spacious. At Dodger Stadium, for example, when I leave the dugout to go out to coach third base, I've got to pack a lunch. That's a road trip, and there are no 7 Elevens along the way.

I enjoyed being close to the fans because they have always been very kind to me. I think maybe they identified with me. They would see me out there and feel, hey, I'm as good as that guy.

I think the biggest change in me since I stopped playing was learning that baseball was not a life-and-death matter. Once a game is over, it's over. If you wake up in the morning and you can see the candles and smell the flowers, well, it's going to be a fine day.

When I was working with the young players in the minor leagues, I tried to teach them that there are many things in life far worse than a sharp breaking curveball or a bad hop.

The slider, for instance.

CONCLUSION

Becoming a fan has not been an easy job for me. Except for eating ballpark food, of course. But after years of thinking of players as !@#$%¢ and !@#@!*&, it was difficult for me to start rooting for them. As an umpire the only thing I rooted for was a fast game. But learning to be a fan has been a rewarding experience. I've sat with the Bleacher Bums in Chicago's Wrigley Field. I've watched people sitting in the cars in a gridlocked parking lot outside Baltimore's Memorial Stadium. I've sat in the Tipsy Bar in the Astrodome while remarking on the coincidence that the Astros used the same color scheme in the Astrodome as I used in my home—everything. I've talked baseball with the fans at Yankee Stadium and Fenway Park and seen my reflection in the waxed cement floors of Dodger Stadium. I've seen baseball played in ballparks all across the country, from seat to shining seat.

And there are two things that stand out in my memory. When I went to Minnesota to see the sponge field in the new Metrodome, I decided to stop by the old ballpark, the old Met. I had spent some of the most pleasant days of my career there, and just wanted to pay my respects to an old friend. When I got there, I discovered a huge hole in the ground. The ballpark had been knocked down; all that was left standing were a few steel supports. I pointed them out to a person standing nearby, explaining, "That's right behind home plate."

"Left field," he corrected me.

I used to think that there was nothing as sad as an empty ballpark. But that hole in the ground made me a lot sadder.

The second incident took place in Milwaukee's County Stadium. I've always loved Milwaukee fans. Wonderful people, knowledgeable baseball people, and they never yelled at me. People in the Midwest are the most polite people in the world. I was walking down an aisle in County Stadium when I came upon a fan in the middle of a heated discussion with a vendor. I had no idea what they were arguing about, but I saw the frustration on the face of the vendor. He obviously wanted to tell off this fan, but just couldn't do it. He just couldn't make himself say what he was thinking. This was in Milwaukee, not New York. Finally the vendor took a deep breath, scrunched up his face, shook his head, and delivered the ultimate midwestern insult, "Oh, I just *wish* you could read my mind."

Some people spend their lives trying to climb mountains; I do my best to avoid falling into potholes. I am one of those rare individuals born with the magic touch—everything I touch gets rusted. Football teams lose, entire leagues lose, stores go out of business, companies get bought; my real problem is that I am running out of things at which I can fail. Fortunately, I run very slowly.

Where do I go from here? Some people have suggested Cleveland. I have given some thought to trying a career in public speaking. I would say things like "Excuse me, sir, do you have any spare change?"

What I really need is a fail-proof job, something even I couldn't mess up. Something that takes advantage of my experience, an ability to make decisions while being screamed at, cursed, threatened, while having dirt kicked on you and people spitting at you. Which is why I am going into politics.

I am going to run for the New York State Assembly from the 123rd District. There are countless amusing things I could say about the profession of politics, but anything frivolous I write might well be used against me by my opponent. Since he already has my entire life to work with, I see no reason to give him any further material. Besides, let him make his own jokes. He's a politician, isn't he?

I've decided to run on my record. It's not exactly a record, it's more of a song. It was written for my television serie (the s is not missing, there was only one episode), by Sean Kelly and Steve Goodman and it is entitled, "It's Not Easy Being Perfect, But I Am." That is a title that works for politicians as well as umpires.

There are people who believe that I would change if I was elected to higher office. My friends, you people who have been so sympathetic to me in times of stress, let me simply say to you, my friends, you people that I cherish so dearly, that even when I sit in office, I shall not change at all. I shall remain the same decent, decisive individual, responsive to the needs of the rich as well as the poor, women as well as men, the tall as well as the short and, naturally, the overly chubby as well as the thin. I shall be even-handed in my administration of the laws of the State of New York to everyone, except Earl Weaver, and dedicate my term in office to improving the quality of life for every human being and umpire.

Will I win the election? There is one good omen—it's being held in the fall. This old Roman umpire's time of year.

THE AUTHORS
RON LUCIANO & DAVID FISHER

RON LUCIANO, author of the bestselling THE
UMPIRE STRIKES BACK and STRIKE TWO, was
an American League umpire from 1968 to 1979.
Upon retirement, he worked for a time as an
NBC sports commentator on the Saturday Game
of the Week.

DAVID FISHER, coauthor, once worked in the
baseball commissioner's office. He is the author
of more than twenty books, including the novel,
The War Magician, and the reference book, *What's
What*.